Wide-Awake in God's World

Australian College of Theology Monograph Series

SERIES EDITOR GRAEME R. CHATFIELD

The ACT Monograph Series, generously supported by the Board of Directors of the Australian College of Theology, provides a forum for publishing quality research theses and studies by its graduates and affiliated college staff in the broad fields of Biblical Studies, Christian Thought and History, and Practical Theology with Wipf and Stock Publishers of Eugene, Oregon. The ACT selects the best of its doctoral and research masters theses as well as monographs that offer the academic community, scholars, church leaders and the wider community uniquely Australian and New Zealand perspectives on significant research topics and topics of current debate. The ACT also provides opportunity for contributors beyond its graduates and affiliated college staff to publish monographs which support the mission and values of the ACT.

Rev. Dr. Graeme Chatfield
Series Editor and Associate Dean

Wide-Awake in God's World

Bible Engagement for Teenage Spiritual Formation
in a Culture of Expressive Individualism

GRAHAM D. STANTON

WIPF & STOCK · Eugene, Oregon

WIDE-AWAKE IN GOD'S WORLD
Bible Engagement for Teenage Spiritual Formation
in a Culture of Expressive Individualism

Australian College of Theology Monograph Series

Copyright © 2020 Graham D. Stanton. All rights reserved. Except for brief quotations in critical publications or reviews, no part of this book may be reproduced in any manner without prior written permission from the publisher. Write: Permissions, Wipf and Stock Publishers, 199 W. 8th Ave., Suite 3, Eugene, OR 97401.

Wipf & Stock
An Imprint of Wipf and Stock Publishers
199 W. 8th Ave., Suite 3
Eugene, OR 97401

www.wipfandstock.com

PAPERBACK ISBN: 978-1-7252-7456-3
HARDCOVER ISBN: 978-1-7252-7457-0
EBOOK ISBN: 978-1-7252-7458-7

Manufactured in the U.S.A.   09/09/20

The substance of this book was first submitted for the degree of Doctor of Philosophy at The University of Queensland, St. Lucia, Queensland, in 2017.

Unless otherwise noted, Scripture quotations are the author's own translation.

A large number of the original sources quoted use gender exclusive language, as was customary at the time of writing. This includes writings from Maxine Greene, who cannot be accused of being intentionally anti-feminist in her use of language. Gendered language in original sources has been preserved and will not be specified at each occurrence by the use of sic.

Chapters 3 and 7 contain material first published as:

Graham D. Stanton. "The Glory of Kings: Dialogical Practices of Bible Engagement with Teenagers in a Culture of Expressive Individualism." *St. Mark's Review* 240 (2017) 34–53.

Chapters 3, 6 and 9 contain material first published as:

Helen Blier and Graham D. Stanton. "Wide-Awakeness in the World: Exploring Pedagogical Dimensions of Youth Ministry in Conversation with Maxine Greene." *Journal of Youth and Theology*, 17.1 (2018) 3–20.

Chapter 9 contains material first published as:

Graham D. Stanton. "Making Sense of the World: Re-Imagining Bible Engagement in Christian Education with Teenagers in Light of Maxine Greene's Aesthetic Pedagogy." In *Reimagining Christian Education: Cultivating Transformative Approaches*, edited by Johannes M. Luetz, Tony Dowden and Beverley Norsworthy, 135–43. Singapore: Springer Nature, 2018.

For Juliet, Rosie, and Jono, my three favorite Australian young people: may you be wide-awake to all that God has prepared for you in his world as you continue to grow to understand this life in company with Jesus.

"The glory of God is to conceal a matter. The glory of kings is to search a matter out" Proverbs 25:2

Contents

List of Illustrations | viii
Preface | ix
Acknowledgements | xi
List of Abbreviations | xiv

1 Expressive Individualism, Bible Engagement, and Maxine Greene | 1
2 Practical Theology, Correlative Conversation, and Practice Frameworks | 16

Part I. Maxine Greene's Aesthetic Pedagogy

3 Education in and for Freedom | 31
4 Engaging the Arts | 58
5 Releasing the Imagination | 85

Part II: Dialogical Youth Ministry

6 Freedom, Authority, and the Martyr's Gift | 113
7 The Bible, Dialogue, and the Disciplined Imagination | 137
8 Imagination, Bible Engagement, and Being Known by God | 162
9 A Practice Framework for Dialogical Youth Ministry | 187

Bibliography | 213

Illustrations

Figure 1: Taxonomy of uses of the imagination in relation to the Bible | 164

Preface

THIS BOOK IS A reprint of my doctoral thesis completed at the University of Queensland in 2017. I am grateful to support from the Australian College of Theology to enable this publication and am privileged to join the list of researchers and scholars who are part of this monograph series. The text published here is largely unchanged from the thesis submission but for two significant differences. First, a reworked introduction attempts to express some of the origins of this project and demonstrate the core concern for how we might more effectively engage Australian young people with the Bible. Second, the name I have given to the approach to youth ministry proposed in this project is "dialogical youth ministry." The original thesis named this approach "Christian aesthetic pedagogy for youth ministry." So why the change?

Christian aesthetic pedagogy was so named to connect with Maxine Greene's educational philosophy that she named as aesthetic pedagogy. The problem with this formulation is that it suggests an approach to youth ministry that engages either with the creative arts or with a theology of beauty. Though both the arts and the beauty of the gospel find a comfortable home within this approach to youth ministry, neither are really the heart of the proposal. Dialogical youth ministry is not quite right either—there is more to the proposal than dialogue. Yet the philosophy, purpose, and practice of dialogue are all central to what I have to offer here, so dialogical youth ministry seems the better option.

The acknowledgements made at the conclusion of the thesis-writing marathon are re-printed in what follows. For this publication I am particularly grateful to Mike Southon for valuable help in writing clever computer code to save hours of time converting in-line referencing to footnotes, and to Gina Denholm for careful editing and gracious teaching of English grammar.

Acknowledgements

MUCH OF THE DOCTORAL journey is a solitary pursuit. Particularly as a full-time student, when the majority of my time was spent in the company of books and my computer screen, I often felt like I was pursuing a kind of monastic retreat from the world—albeit the kind of monasticism that included using various cafes, libraries, and airport lounges as temporary offices. However, despite the large amount of time spent on my own over the past three-and-a-half years, I have been very conscious of, and most grateful to God for, an extended support team in the wings.

For the genesis of the theological reflection on youth ministry pursued in these pages, I am indebted to my colleagues at Youthworks College, Sydney. Our conversations around the table in a crowded faculty office spurred one another on to think long and hard about ministry to children and young people that was theologically sound, gospel centered, missionally engaged, developmentally appropriate, and culturally relevant. Many preliminary thoughts about the Bible and the imagination arose out of conversations with Andy Stirrup, and I am confident that this thesis would have been much improved if I was still able to call upon him as a conversation partner. I am indebted to Tom Frame for generously sparing an afternoon in front of a whiteboard in Canberra in 2013 to bring some order to my inchoate thoughts and to Michael Jensen for helping to frame the project in its early stages.

As the project developed, I received invaluable feedback from various readers, particularly from Kaye Chalwell, whose enthusiasm for this work encouraged me to persevere through those times when I was convinced that I did not have anything very interesting to offer. I am grateful to colleagues in the International Association for the Study of Youth Ministry for the opportunity to present my emerging research at the international and Australasian conferences and to receive careful and considered responses. In particular I am grateful to Helen Blier and David White for the opportunity to share in a "dialogical space of mutual concern" in presenting at the 2017 IASYM conference in Sydney. Thanks go also to my research colleagues in the practical theology program at the University of Queensland, Dave Benson, Helen Dick, Jan-Albert van den Berg, Michelle Cook, Peter Lockhart, and Sarah Nicholl. Thanks for the robust discussion at each colloquium and for the lively conversation over burgers, pizza, and beers in the St. Lucia sun.

Among my academic colleagues, my thanks go chiefly to my companions Rowan Lewis and Chris Ryan. Whenever this Anglican, Baptist, and Catholic walked into a bar it was far from the start of a bad joke, but rather a time of intellectual challenge, emotional support, and spiritual encouragement. This thesis is stronger because of your input (thanks Rowan for the idea that led to imagining an aesthetic youth ministry; thanks Chris for making sure I understood Charles Taylor correctly). More significantly, my life is the richer for having met you both and having had the privilege of sharing the academic journey with you.

To my academic advisors, Aaron Ghiloni and Neil Pembroke, your advice and encouragement have been invaluable. I have heard many horror stories of PhD supervision gone bad but have no such stories of my own to share. Neil, your rapid response, detailed reading, and constant encouragement has shaped me as a researcher and practical theologian as much as shaping this thesis. It has been a privilege to work with you over these past years and I look forward to continuing to engage in theological reflection on Christian life and ministry with you in the future.

The freedom to complete this research full time was made possible through an Australian Government Research Training Program Scholarship, and the provision of consulting work with the Anglican Education Commission, Sydney, the Mathew Hale Public Library, Brisbane, and a new role at Ridley College, Melbourne. I have spent many hours traversing the south-east coast of this great continent and am grateful for the opportunity to share in such a variety of ministry settings while completing this research. In particular, I am grateful for the generous hospitality of Penny and Alex Crawford, who gave me a second home in the Ridley Room at Bennison Street on my frequent visits to Brisbane.

Alongside the intellectual challenge, greater still is the psychological/spiritual one. In such regard I am deeply grateful to God for the steadfast support of my prayer team: Reg and Dorothy Piper, Rob Stewart, Helen Elley, Jane Stanton-Gillan, Chris Trethewy, and Ron Webb. The knowledge of your prayers for me through the highs and lows of the past few years has been an enormous encouragement, the value of which I will only come to fully appreciate in the kingdom to come. To Chris Hudson and Ron Irving, I am grateful for Tuesday night beers, for the reminder that PhD or no PhD I'm just a regular boof-head, and for the fellowship of brothers. Thanks also to the church communities I've had the privilege of sharing in during this journey—to Steve Dinning and the people at Austinmer Anglican, you will always be our family's home, and thanks for the desk under the stairs; to James Hornby and the people at St. Jude's in Parkville, thanks for giving us a new home in Melbourne. To my wife Katy, thanks for allowing me to ditch work for a few years and become a student again, and for being my constant companion, most loyal supporter, and lead encourager.

Above my desk for the past few years has been a list of quotations with this from Paul Griffiths at the head: "To forget to pray before we study is to forget to acknowledge what it is that we are doing, and, very likely, thereby to tend toward the curious desire for mastery rather than the studious desire for intimacy."[1] I have been very conscious that the ideas contained in this thesis have come as a gracious gift of God, the Father, Son, and Holy Spirit—whether through a moment of inspiration, or providentially stumbling upon a crucial text, or rediscovering a forgotten thought. Through the discipline of this study, I have known the gracious gift of intimacy with God. This thesis is a reality by God's grace, and for God's glory.

---

1. Griffiths, *Religious Reading*, 116.

Abbreviations

AYM	Aesthetic Youth Ministry
BE	Bible Engagement
BG	Greene, Maxine. *Variations on a Blue Guitar: The Lincoln Center Institute lectures on Aesthetic Education*. New York, NY: Teachers College, 2001.
DF	Greene, Maxine. *The Dialectic of Freedom*. New York, NY: Teachers College, 1988.
DYM	Dialogical Youth Ministry
LL	Greene, Maxine. *Landscapes of Learning*. New York, NY: Teachers College, 1978.
RI	Greene, Maxine. *Releasing the Imagination: Essays on Education, the Arts, and Social Change*. San Francisco, CA: Jossey-Bass, 1995.
TS	Greene, Maxine. *Teacher as Stranger: Educational Philosophy for the Modern Age*. Belmont, CA: Wadsworth, 1973.

I

Expressive Individualism, Bible Engagement, and Maxine Greene

SUPPOSE YOU ARE LEADING a discussion with a group of young people about Jesus' parable of the two sons from Luke 15:11–31. While most of the group are not particularly engaged in the conversation, one young man is eagerly reporting how helpful this Bible passage has been in his own life. "My little brother and I fight a lot, mostly because I think he has got life easy and gets away with a whole lot more than I ever did. But this story is such a great reminder to me that older brothers should not be jealous of younger brothers."[1]

How will you respond? Will you rejoice that a young person has not only read the Bible, but has even chosen to use the Bible to shape the way he lives? Here is a young man who has chosen to position himself under the "authority" of the biblical story. In some way he has allowed Jesus' words to direct his experience. In a world of biblical illiteracy and wayward morality, surely this is a bright star in an otherwise darkened sky of teenage Bible engagement!

And yet, perhaps there is also the unsettling feeling (or maybe even the overwhelming conviction) that this young man's personal concerns have overshadowed the voice of the text? Read in the context of the whole chapter, to conclude that the parable of the lost son is about how older brothers should relate to their younger siblings is so far wide of the mark that it is quite shocking to experienced readers of the Gospels. The story of the two sons does not

---

1. This is my imagined extension of Hughes's account of a young adult's Bible engagement in Hughes, "Bible Engagement," 15.

stand alone but comes as the climax of one parable in three parts (the lost sheep, the lost coin, the lost son).[2] This three-fold story is addressed to those who are grumbling at Jesus' reception and dining with "sinners." While it could be argued that this young person has made a choice to position himself under the "authority" of the biblical story, at least in the sense that the story is used to direct his experience, one could also argue that his personal concerns have overshadowed the voice of the text.

Meanwhile, the other members of the group remain disengaged. Perhaps it is because they have already heard "the answer" to what this story is about. Or maybe they know from experience that you are about to tell them the answer before the study is done. Either way, reading the parable of the good Samaritan again is not offering them any sense of personal risk or adventure. As a result, Christian faith holds little appeal "because the great truths have already been revealed, and it is simply a matter of devoting oneself to what is already known."[3]

So, which will we choose? Must we give away commitment to objective authority and any sense of an orthodox reading of the biblical text in order to promote teenage engagement? Or do we sacrifice teenage engagement because of a commitment to theological truth?

The central concern of this book is to find a way to affirm both authority and freedom—to propose practices of Bible engagement in youth ministry that can effectively promote Christian spiritual formation in a culture of expressive individualism. In pursuit of that end, this study will correlate insights drawn from the aesthetic pedagogy of educational philosopher Maxine Greene with key themes of Christian theology in order to propose a practice framework for what I am calling a dialogical youth ministry (DYM). The chapters that follow will argue that DYM promotes the freedom of young people by inviting them to explore and construct meaning and to imagine how things could be otherwise for them and their world. DYM affirms the authority of Scripture by inviting Christian leaders to be present as people of conviction in dialogue with teenagers as together they think about the world, offering the gospel of Jesus as a possibility for meaning-making.

The journey towards DYM engages with three main areas of discourse. First, this study engages with literature that seeks to help the Christian church face the challenge of finding approaches to spiritual formation that engage appropriately with the contemporary culture of expressive

---

2. Luke 15:3 introduces the three stories as Jesus telling "this parable," singular.

3. David Tacey reports this as a commonly heard response from young adults who are interested in spirituality, but have no interest in pursuing those spiritual interests within the church. Tacey, *ReEnchantment*, 207.

individualism. Second, because of the specific focus on practices of transformative Bible engagement, the study engages with theological reflection on the relationship between the Bible and the imagination in light of a conservative evangelical theology of biblical authority. Third, the study engages with the critical analysis of the educational philosophy of Maxine Greene by educationalists and religious educators.

Spiritual Formation and Expressive Individualism

Expressive individualism is a highly significant—very likely *the* most significant—factor in the cultural milieu in which Australian young people engage with spirituality. First identified as the dominant culture of the United States of America in the twentieth century, expressive individualism has become a feature of modern secular culture across the Western world. Characterized by individual choice and the absence of external authorities,[4] in expressive individualism each individual must discover their true self by looking inward to their own thoughts and feelings. Then, having identified the authentic self, each individual must be free to choose how they will express who they really are. The only limits on which path you choose is that it causes no harm to others. Above all, discovering and expressing the "true self" must not be controlled or conformed to any form of external authority:

> each one of us has his/her own way of realizing our humanity, and . . . it is important to find and live out one's own, as against surrendering to conformity with a model imposed on us from outside, by society, or the previous generation, or religious or political authority.[5]

While expressivism of this kind is not entirely new, having seeds in eighteenth-century Romanticism, "what is new is that this kind of self-orientation seems to have become a mass phenomenon."[6] The notion of being "true to oneself" has become the highest calling of the modern identity.

The dominant form of religion in the age of authenticity therefore is one that is marked by a "spirituality of quest,"[7] where each individual has the right and responsibility to explore what might be their own path to wholeness and spiritual depth. "The focus is on the individual and on his/

---

4. Bellah et al., *Habits of the Heart*; Root, *Faith Formation*.
5. Taylor, *Secular Age*, 475.
6. Taylor, *Secular Age*, 473.
7. Taylor, *Secular Age*, 508.

her experience. Spirituality must speak to this experience."[8] The quest is not simply to make my own decision about religious beliefs, but to make a choice that best expresses my own spiritual path as I understand it. The only directive is to "let everyone follow his/her own path of spiritual inspiration. Don't be led off yours by the allegations that it doesn't fit with some orthodoxy."[9] Being true to oneself in the spiritual realm makes conforming to an external framework both unnecessary and incomprehensible.

Choice, rejection of external authority, and personal quest, key features of expressive individualism, are all evident in the spirituality of Australian young people.[10] The suggestion that young Australians "might like to pursue their spiritual interests in a church context" results in them becoming "defensive, even hostile."[11] From the perspective of expressive individualism, a major obstacle to young Australians' engagement with the church is that there seems to be no room in Christianity for personal quest. "Conventional forms of Christianity seem not to be interested in personal risk or adventure, because the great truths have already been revealed, and it is simply a matter of devoting oneself to what is already known."[12]

Conservative Christian commentators have been better at offering critiques of the quest for authenticity than at proposing productive avenues of collaboration. Certainly, there are serious deficiencies in the modern quest for individual freedom, especially as they relate to young people:

> A major problem with the current view of personal freedom is that it leaves people trapped in their own limited interior world of subjective feelings, impressions and limited perspectives . . . For adolescents and young adults in particular, they are left without any larger and more objective framework of meaning with which to make sense of their questions and to navigate a very confusing world. Coupled with prosperity and consumerism and the growth of a culture of entitlement and exaggerated individualism, they are set upon a journey that will lead them into a lifestyle of destructive self-interest.[13]

> The problem is that the appeal to authenticity can be just an excuse for questionable behavior. If I do something that is inconsiderate of others or even harmful to myself, I can just claim

---

8. Taylor, *Secular Age*, 507.
9. Taylor, *Secular Age*, 489.
10. Mason et al., *Spirit of Generation Y*; Sayers, *Road trip*; Tyson, "Spectral View."
11. Tacey, *ReEnchantment*, 189.
12. Tacey, *ReEnchantment*, 207.
13. Corney, "Assertive Self-Interest," 16.

I am being true to myself... What if my self is selfish? After all, the abusive spouse, the dishonest friend, the greedy workaholic, and the malicious gossip can all claim to be true to themselves when they behave in character. The problem with being true to yourself is that too often the self abuses the privilege.[14]

However, at the very least, Christian youth ministry in Australia needs to grapple with expressive individualism simply because this is the culture in which we find ourselves. As Taylor recognizes, "those who claim to possess some wisdom have an obligation to explain it persuasively, starting from where their interlocutor is, so here."[15]

Others call for the church to make radical changes to its beliefs and practices in order to engage more productively with the culture of expressivism. For the church to be "capable of dialoguing with the present social situation," it needs to "sacrifice its own claims to exclusive truth and begin to insist on the plurality and diversity of the living spirit."[16] Since the "keynote of contemporary spirituality is experience," if the church fails to "offer a pathway of experience, [it] can expect to decline or diminish."[17] Perhaps there is an opening for constructive dialogue with secular affirmations of the spiritual as a task of freedom and personal discovery.[18]

However, these proposals to embrace expressivism often require the church to loosen its grip on traditional doctrines of the church community and the authority of the Bible and Christian tradition. This emphasis on freedom in new approaches to spiritual formation is an oft-times "chaotic push toward an existential end, which by definition leads to less structure, more randomness, and a narrower focus on individuals."[19] Leading Christian Educator Robert Pazmiño argues that this over-emphasis on freedom stems from a focus in spiritual formation on individual persons, to the exclusion of the content of Christian faith and the context of Christian community.[20]

Reformed theology stands against the spirituality of quest in its understanding of spirituality in theocentric rather than anthropocentric terms. Christian spirituality is "not describing the activity or nurture of the human spirit" but is "the study of the work of the Holy Spirit in the life of the

---

14. Rosner, *Known by God*, 25.
15. Taylor, *Secular Age*, 494.
16. Tacey, *ReEnchantment*, 201.
17. Tacey, "Contemporary Spirituality," 476.
18. Fisher, "The Four Domains Model."
19. Yount, "The Role of Scripture," 34.
20. Pazmiño, "Christian Education."

believer."[21] "The gospel is not about an innate spirituality awaiting release, but about the divine Spirit acting upon a person from without."[22] Conservative evangelical youth ministries reflect this theocentric theology of spiritual formation in expressing the goal of spiritual maturity expressed as the formation of "mature disciples" equipped to participate in disciple-making ministries themselves.[23] The aim of Christian youth ministry is to see young people progress further along in a journey from no knowledge of the gospel through conversion to Christian maturity.[24]

The driving burden of this study is to articulate a way of pursuing Bible engagement in Christian youth ministry that is appropriate to the contemporary expressivist mindset evident among young people. But rather than facing a choice between engaging with the culture of expressive individualism or holding to conservative theology of the inspiration and authority of the Bible, my aim is to propose revised practices of Bible engagement that will enable the church to give young people freedom to choose their own spiritual path without relinquishing the church's commitment to biblical authority.

The tension between expressive individualism and the authoritative content of the Christian tradition is an expression of the freedom-authority dialectic in spirituality, biblical hermeneutics, and Christian identity. The relationship between freedom and authority has been a familiar theme in philosophy,[25] particularly in political philosophy,[26] theology,[27] education,[28] and religious education.[29] This study sets out to explore how the pedagogical valuing of freedom can be affirmed without undermining the theological commitment to authority; or, vice versa, how authority can be asserted (in an authoritative text, an authoritative interpretive paradigm, an authoritative meaning to life) without removing or diminishing personal freedom. While this discussion will engage to some extent with the philosophical, theological, and educational discourse, as a project in practical theology, my overriding concern is with the pedagogical practices that might be pursued

---

21. Raiter, *Stirrings of the Soul*, 343.

22. Dunn, *Paul*, 76.

23. Fields, *Purpose Driven Youth Ministry*; Fields, *Purpose Driven Youth Ministry One Step Beyond*; Moser, *Changing the World*; Hawkins, *Fruit That Will Last*.

24. Kageler, *Youth Ministry in a Multifaith Society*.

25. Gadamer, *Truth and Method*.

26. Cristi, *Hegel*.

27. Barth, *Church Dogmatics*, I. iii.19–20; Luther, *Freedom of a Christian*.

28. Cuypers, "Educating for authenticity"; Nash, *Authority and freedom*; Reich, "Educational authority."

29. Gates, *Freedom and authority*; Parker et al., *Religious Education*.

by adult mentors of young people that will promote the freedom of young people while preserving the authority of the Bible.

Bible Engagement and Imagination

"Bible Engagement" (BE) is a coverall term used by a number of Christian researchers and agencies across the world to refer to how people read and interact with the Bible.[30] Notwithstanding the variety of readings that different theological traditions bring to the Bible and the variety of beliefs and practices justified from appeal to it, engaging with the Bible remains a defining feature of Christian faith.[31] The normative authority of the Bible over all matters of Christian faith and practice is a particular feature of the evangelical movement,[32] and especially of the Reformed tradition.[33] In Australian Evangelical Anglicanism, the pietistic practice of personal Bible reading combined with the Reformed emphasis on exegetical preaching promotes BE as the central practice of Christian spiritual formation.[34]

However, emphasis on biblical authority and greater frequency of BE is not sufficient to promote personal transformation. Australian young people generally display low levels of Bible engagement and biblical literacy.[35] An exception to these trends are young people in Reformed evangelical youth ministries who display relatively frequent patterns of BE. Yet, researchers report that while these young people may know the biblical stories and make some connections between characters in the stories and their own situations, most are unable to draw that information together into a vision of what faith is all about and how that faith should be lived.[36] Biblical literacy seems present, but a biblically shaped imagination appears lacking. That practices of BE among teenagers are not necessarily producing deep transformation is also suggested by the oft-reported statistics on the drop-off of young adults from the church.[37] While many authors call for a change in the way churches

30. American Bible Society, *The State of the Bible*, 22.
31. Griffiths, *Religious Reading*; Volf, *Captive to the Word*; Root, *Unpacking Scripture*.
32. Bebbington, *Evangelicalism*.
33. Jensen, *The Revelation of God*.
34. Jensen, *Sydney Anglicanism*.
35. Hughes and Pickering, "Bible Engagement among Young Australians"; Hughes et al., "Bible Engagement among Young People"; Blenkinsopp, *The Bible According to Gen Z*. The same is true of young people in Canada, the United States of America, and the United Kingdom, Hiemstra, "Confidence, Conversation and Community"; Penner et al., *Hemorrhaging Faith*; Bible Society, *Pass It On*.
36. Hughes, personal communication, 26 March, 2014.
37. Kinnaman, *You Lost Me*; Powell and Clark, *Sticky Faith*.

conduct ministry to emerging adults, others point to inadequate discipleship in the teenage years as the root of the problem. Though there are many factors that influence the retention of young adults in Christian faith, developing and pursuing more effective practices of BE for spiritual formation of teenagers is a critical challenge for the church.[38]

On the other hand, transformative engagement with the Bible does not always recognize biblical authority. Recall the example given in the introduction: reading the parable of the prodigal son as "a reminder that older brothers should not be jealous of younger brothers!"[39] might suggest that there is a degree of imaginative BE at play, but to the detriment of the authority of the text.[40]

Imagination in BE, it seems, promotes freedom but at the expense of authority. Ricoeur suggests the combination of "Bible" and "imagination" to be "baffling" and even "paradoxical," since the imagination is regarded as "a faculty of free invention," and the Bible is considered to be "a closed book . . . whose meaning is fixed forever and therefore the enemy of any radically original creation of meaning."[41] Theologians who embrace imagination as the gateway to God, and see the task of theology as an exercise of imagining new ways to conceive and speak of the divine, often do so by diminishing the authority of the biblical text.[42] In contrast, Reformed evangelical hermeneutics rejects imagination in favor of "revealed truth": "Let the Scriptures cease to be heard and soon the remembered Christ becomes an imagined Christ, shaped by the religiosity and the unconscious desires of his worshipers."[43]

More recently however, various authors, including those from conservative evangelical traditions, have been arguing that the imagination ought be afforded a more prominent role in BE.[44] Such calls align with critiques of narrowly rational linguistic approaches to BE in Reformed evangelical spirituality as reflecting a truncated anthropology that affirms rationality and cognition to the exclusion of desire, emotion, and the body.[45]

---

38. Cosby, *Giving up Gimmicks*.

39. Hughes, "Bible Engagement," 15.

40. Whether there is *a* meaning *in* the text, or multiple meanings that can be read out of (or into) the text, is a significant point of debate that will be addressed in detail in chapter 7.

41. Ricoeur, "Bible and Imagination," 144.

42. Levy, *Imagination*; Kaufman, *Theological Imagination*; McFague, *Metaphorical Theology*.

43. Smart, *Strange Silence of the Bible*, 25.

44. Peterson, *Eat This Book*; Root, *Unpacking Scripture*; Veith and Ristuccia, *Imagination Redeemed*.

45. Smith, *Desiring*; Smith, *Imagining*.

Jason Lief calls for youth ministry to "help create space in which young people are able to imagine what it means to live as the new humanity in Jesus Christ."[46] This work of imagination affirms young people's freedom to construct spiritual meaning free from coercion or manipulation.[47] Lief's proposal affirms freedom only by diminishing authority. Drawing on the theology of John Caputo[48] and Gianni Vattimo,[49] Lief's approach is grounded in "weak theology" that "is opposed to every form of absolute Truth and every claim to certainty."[50] Poetic youth ministry invites young people to "renarrate" their lives "in the context of the revelation of Jesus Christ," and invites the Christian community to renarrate the Christian tradition in light of the cultural and social narratives of young people.[51] In contrast to Lief, my aim is to find a place for imagination and freedom without rejecting commitment to traditional notions of biblical and theological authority.

In this project I am interested in the theological and pedagogical assumptions that are needed to undergird new practices of imagination in BE. New practices are unlikely to take root, let alone flourish, if they are planted in soil that regards imagination as an exercise of human speculation inimical to submitting to God's word revealed in the Scripture. The challenge of correlating notions of freedom and authority in spiritual formation is particularly expressed in the challenge of finding a place for the free exercise of the imagination in such a way that does not undermine the normative authority of the Bible.

Maxine Greene

The major conversation partner in this book is teacher and educational philosopher, Maxine Greene. Hailed as "one of the leading educational philosophers of the past fifty years,"[52] the overriding concern in Greene's work is the reform of secondary education in the United States of America in response to what she called the dehumanizing effects of modernity,

---

46. Lief, *Poetic Youth Ministry*, 125.
47. Lief, *Poetic Youth Ministry*, 122.
48. Caputo, *The Weakness of God*.
49. Vattimo, *After Christianity*.
50. Lief, *Poetic Youth Ministry*, 25.
51. "The symbols and stories that make up the tradition must not become absolute principles or strong doctrines. Instead, the symbols and stories must be held loosely as they are interpreted and reinterpreted in relation to the experiences of young people" (Lief, *Poetic Youth Ministry*, 121).
52. Kohl, "Foreword," xi.

technicism, and rationalism.⁵³ Greene's pedagogy is an appropriate conversation partner in this project because of her embeddedness within the contemporary culture of expressive individualism and the central place given to the creative arts in her teaching methodology. Greene acknowledges the priority of personal quest yet critiques individualistic notions of freedom. Greene affirms personal freedom in human transformation and grants a sense of authority to the artistic voice in pursuit of such freedom. These relationships between freedom and authority, individualism and plurality are common themes in her work. In short, Greene's aesthetic pedagogy seeks to engage young people with the creative arts in order to release young people's imaginations and prompt the kind of "wide-awakeness" that will promote freedom and social transformation.

Greene spent the majority of her career in the philosophy of education department at Teachers College, Columbia University. After joining the faculty in 1965, Greene served as Associate Professor of English, Professor of English, and Professor of Philosophy and Education. In 1975 she was appointed as William F. Russell Professor in the Foundations of Education, and as professor emerita from 2000. Greene continued to teach up until three months before her death, aged 96, in June 2014. Greene is associated with the school of Progressive Education, and has been hailed as an intellectual successor to John Dewey, her predecessor at Teachers College (from 1904 to 1930).⁵⁴ Yet, like Dewey, Greene's interest and influence extends beyond the field of education, through her "interweaving of philosophy, literature, and social theory."⁵⁵ Greene's thought shares philosophical foundations common to other existential phenomenologists and contributes her signature use of literary sources⁵⁶ and emphasis on imagination.

Because Greene was an educational philosopher rather than a trainer in educational methods, her work prompts reflection on the theological foundations and implications of youth ministry practice rather than on teaching methodology alone. Yet, her thinking did not remain in the lofty preserve of academic abstraction. Greene's concern to serve the concrete challenges faced by classroom teachers is exemplified in her foundational role as philosopher-in-residence at Lincoln Center Education (LCE) in New York City,⁵⁷ and her regular involvement in the LCE Summer Sessions for

53. Kohl, "Foreword," xi.
54. Weber, "Maxine Greene."
55. Pinar, *Passionate Mind*, 1.
56. In Greene's time as the sole woman in the Teachers College Philosophy of Education department, she was criticized as being "too literary" (Kohli, "Philosopher of/for Freedom," 13).
57. Lincoln Center Education (formerly the Lincoln Center Institute for the Arts in

teachers and school administrators.⁵⁸ Greene's approach accords with broad definitions of pedagogy as "the act of teaching together with the ideas, values and beliefs by which that act is informed, sustained and justified."⁵⁹ Greene's philosophy, therefore, is not the abstract reflections of disembodied thought, but the situated thinking of phenomenology.⁶⁰

As a discussion of pedagogical methodology, Greene's work offers an often-frustrating lack of detailed instruction regarding concrete teaching practice. The intangibility of Greene's methodological proposals arises from her commitment to have teachers do the work of philosophy for themselves rather than to implement a set of pre-packaged teaching tips. Greene is insistent that making meaning of one's lived experience must be a personal quest. Meaningful existence cannot be achieved by simply adopting someone else's construction of meaning as one's own. Greene regarded her own writing to be a failure if, "after having read it, those with different backgrounds and orientations simply adopt or appropriate the selective vision they find presented here."⁶¹ Greene's aim was not to lay out an educational theory replete with recommended classroom practices. Her aim was to get teachers to "do philosophy" for themselves. This study heeds Greene's call to "do philosophy" by pursuing a correlational conversation between certain themes in Greene's pedagogy and key voices in Christian theology.

Alongside critical engagement from educationalists,⁶² Greene's philosophy has also generated some initial reflection from Christian theology.⁶³ O'Gorman describes Greene as "the religious educator's religious educator," despite Greene's secular Jewish background, which left her puzzled by the

---

Education) was established in 1975 to bring together the educational activities of the various arts companies connected with the renowned Lincoln Centre for the Performing Arts in New York. Founding director Mark Schubart insisted on having Maxine Greene serve as Philosopher-in-Residence so that her aesthetic pedagogy would shape the teaching and learning of the new center.

58. Noppe-Brandon and Holzer, "Maxine Greene." Greene, *Variations on a Blue Guitar*, collects various lectures given by Greene in the LCE Summer Sessions.

59. Cf. Smith, who seems to limit pedagogy to educational practices, yet nevertheless shares Alexander's affirmation of the importance of the philosophical assumptions that lie behind methodological proposals: "behind every pedagogy is a philosophical anthropology; that is, implicit in every constellation of educational practices there is a set of assumptions about the nature of human persons" (*Desiring*, 37).

60. Alexander, *Essays on Pedagogy*, 4.

61. Greene, TS, ii.

62. Ayers and Miller, *A Light in Dark Times*; Baldacchino, *Education beyond Education*; Pinar, *Passionate Mind*.

63. Douglass, "Aesthetic Learning Theory"; Foster, "Pedagogical Imagination."

way her ideas were adopted by religious educators.[64] My intention is to draw on Greene's established framework of aesthetic pedagogy as a launching point for constructing an approach to Bible engagement among teenagers for Christian spiritual formation.[65]

Overview

In essence, this study explores the implications of taking Greene's description of aesthetic education and replacing references to "the arts" with "the Bible" as a way of framing Christian youth ministry. I contend that adult mentors of young people can effectively navigate the freedom-authority dialectic in spiritual formation and Bible engagement by approaching youth ministry as

> an intentional undertaking designed to nurture appreciative, reflective, cultural, participatory engagements with the [Bible] by enabling learners to notice what is there to be noticed, and to lend [biblical texts] their lives in such a way that they can achieve them as variously meaningful. When this happens, new connections are made in experience: new patterns formed, new vistas are opened. Persons see differently, resonate differently.[66]

In making this substitution, the Bible is accorded a high value and a strong authoritative status. Therefore, the question is this: To what extent does Greene's aesthetic pedagogy offer an approach to youth ministry that is appropriate to a Reformed evangelical theological tradition? I will argue that aesthetic pedagogy affords young people the freedom to make their own authentic spiritual choices in ways that are appropriate to Christian theologies of humanity, creation, revelation, and Scripture. I will also argue that key themes in Christian theology are beneficial for providing a ground of security within which Maxine Greene's goals of dialogue, exploration, and imagination can flourish.

---

64. O'Gorman, "Maxine Greene."

65. McKoy's use of social constructionism as a tool for imagining new ways of doing youth ministry offers a rough parallel to my project (McKoy, *Youth Ministry*). I am using Maxine Greene's aesthetic pedagogy in a similar way, as a tool by which I might imagine new practices of BE for teenage spiritual formation.

66. Greene, *BG*, 6.

Chapter Outline

Still by way of introduction, chapter 2 grounds this study in the broad field of practical theology, outlines my particular approach to engaging in correlative conversation under the authority of Scripture, and introduces the concept of a practice framework.

The three chapters of Part I delve into Maxine Greene's aesthetic pedagogy. Each follows the same four-fold structure: I examine Greene's philosophical foundations, outline the educational principles that follow, explore how Green's theory would shape youth ministry if adopted without theological critique, and identify contributions and questions to be pursued in the correlative conversation in Part II.

The constructive work in Part I imagines what I am calling an Aesthetic Youth Ministry (AYM), meaning a youth ministry shaped according to Greene's pedagogy where the creative arts are replaced with the Bible. In essence I am asking, "What if Maxine were a youth pastor?" That is, how might Greene's educational philosophy shape the practice of Christian youth ministry if it were adopted without theological critique? Before engaging in theological dialogue with Greene's philosophy, chapters 2, 3, and 4 each explore the possibilities present in Greene's pedagogy "from the inside" by taking her philosophy and applying it as directly as possible to the practice of Bible engagement in Christian spiritual formation of teenagers. AYM is therefore my own construction, and necessarily provisional. At this stage of the argument, AYM is a way station on the journey, not the final destination. Rather than claiming this is how youth ministry must be constructed in light of Greene's pedagogy, I am merely experimenting with how youth ministry could be constructed. I am also not suggesting that this is how I think youth ministry ought to be conducted. AYM is an experimental step in the correlative conversation.

In broad terms, the three chapters of Part I explore freedom as the aim, creative arts as the means, and imagination as the method of Greene's pedagogy. Chapter 3 suggests that AYM would promote critical awareness by fostering dialogical community that emphasizes processes of meaning-making over specific outcomes of spiritual identity. In chapter 4, AYM invites young people to engage with the Bible as a classic text of human culture that proposes a possible construal of spiritual reality and provides cultural elements that young people could use as symbolic resources to make sense of their lived experience. From chapter 5, AYM looks for ways to equip young people with basic skills for biblical interpretation, to involve young people in creating their own works of meaning prompted by biblical forms, and to leave time and space for self-directed meditation and reflection.

The first three chapters in Part II respond to the questions raised at the conclusion of each chapter in Part I and pursue the performative task of practical theology by outlining key features of a dialogical youth ministry (DYM). If AYM is how I imagine Maxine Greene would do youth ministry, DYM is how I propose to do youth ministry in light of my conversation with Maxine Greene. In particular, my aim is to bring insights from Greene's aesthetic pedagogy to practices of Bible engagement in the specific context of church-based youth ministry.

Chapter 6 identifies the task of meaning-making as central to the contemporary quest for authenticity and acknowledges this as the necessary cultural starting point for contemporary youth ministry. Youth ministry leaders can welcome Greene's pedagogical aims of wide-awakeness and meaning-making and, by adopting the pedagogical stance of Christlike martyrdom, can pursue peaceful dialogue with young people without surrendering intentions to persuade. Chapter 7 argues that a commitment to Scripture as divine revelation focuses attention on the literary qualities and bodily dimensions of meaning in the text and requires interpreters to leave room for imaginative exploration. The Christian imagination is funded by the biblical text, and the exercise of the imagination invited in the Bible is one that needs to be disciplined by the text itself. Holding the Bible as an authoritative norm does not diminish, but rather magnifies, the importance of engaging young people in open dialogue to imagine how this text offers a way of making meaning in the world. Following a taxonomy of various roles ascribed to the imagination in theological discourse, chapter 8 argues that the imagination is the locus of divine revelation, and therefore that youth ministry will enable young people to recognize various paradigms for meaning as possible ways to imagine the world, and invite them to imagine an alternative by offering the image of Christ in the Bible as the paradigm of the Christian imagination. I argue that the offer of finding corporate identity in the gospel as a gift of divine grace enables imaginative exploration of meaning in an environment of security.

At various points it will be evident that the implications of DYM extend beyond the narrow focus of this study: There are other practices of spiritual formation relevant for youth ministry in addition to Bible engagement; there are other audiences for Bible engagement beside teenagers. While the study may suggest fruitful insights for these wider areas of interest, developing such is beyond the scope of the current project. Hence, the modest goal is to offer one piece of what a theologically faithful aesthetic pedagogy might look like.

The various threads of exploration are finally brought together in chapter 9, where I outline a practice framework for DYM. The practice framework is developed in three sections: the aims and purposes of youth ministry, the means by which those aims are pursued, and the values that undergird them.

Contributions of the Study

The study contributes to academic reflection on youth ministry by proposing an approach to Christian spiritual formation in an age of expressive individualism that can honor the freedom of young people while also affirming a theological commitment to the normative authority of the Bible. Youth ministries need to help young people become wide-awake in God's world, through an imaginative engagement with the Bible, in dialogue with adult mentors, whose trust in the Christian message of the beauty and goodness of Jesus Christ displaces any desire to control or manipulate a young person's spiritual choices.

The study also contributes to discussions applying educational theory to the practice of youth ministry.[67] Where other work has focused on pedagogical practices, this study explores the philosophical and theological framework within which teaching methodologies exist. In particular, the study contributes to calls for a greater engagement of the imagination in practices of Bible engagement in youth ministry by proposing a theological pedagogy by which such practices become meaningful, and within which such practices may flourish.

The study will also contribute to the work of reflection on the educational philosophy of Maxine Greene, following her recent death in May 2014.[68] Theological reflection on Greene's pedagogy will help guide ongoing use of Greene's approach by Christian religious educators.

---

67. Linhart, *Teaching*; Sedwick "Teaching."
68. Weber, "Maxine Greene."

2

Practical Theology, Correlative Conversation, and Practice Frameworks

THIS CHAPTER PROVIDES AN overview of Practical Theology as an academic discipline and outlines the correlative approach to theological reflection that I will pursue in the project. In particular, I outline how I understand the normative function of Scripture in the correlative conversation. The second section of the chapter outlines how the correlative conversation with Maxine Greene will be structured. The final section introduces the concept of the practice framework as the performative conclusion to the project.

Practical Theology

Practical theology is a "theology of practice" that focuses attention on the interaction between theological theory and human experience and action. This "theological discernment about human action" is particularly, though not exclusively, directed towards "those practices in which Christians wrestle with and express their faith through worship and witness, and in ordinary life."[1] Practical theology seeks to engage with the theories behind and within all human practice with a view to directing more faithful practice in the future.

Though different practical theologians employ a variety of methodological steps, practical theological inquiry broadly engages in four key movements. With its starting point in practice, practical theologians

---

1. Brown, "Hermeneutical Theory," 112–13.

engage in a descriptive task, asking what is going on in particular practices.[2] The analytic task draws on human and social sciences to develop "thick descriptions"[3] of human experience and Christian practice. Correlating insights from human and social sciences with the Christian theological tradition leads practical theologians to a normative task, asking what ought to be going on in a particular situation. The aim of determining faithful practice involves a performative task,[4] asking the question, how might Christian action be reformed or renewed in light of the theological reflection undertaken?

Practical theology as an academic discipline originated in the establishment of chairs in Practical Theology at the University of Vienna in 1774 and the University of Tübingen in 1794. Schleiermacher's *Brief Outline of Theology as a Field of Study*, first published in German in 1810, locates practical theology as part of the "cohesive whole" of theology as a science, necessarily interrelated with philosophical and historical theology.[5] Practical theology was not merely practical application, but "the theory of practice." To what extent Schleiermacher viewed practical theology as a constructive discipline, or whether it was merely the applicational arena for the constructions from historical and philosophical theology, is a moot point.[6] Gräb contrasts Schleiermacher's "theory of practice" with the applicational approach of his colleague Gottlieb Jakob Planck, who argued that practical theology was a subordinate field within theology proper, classifying it as "applied theology, *theologia applicata*."[7] Either way, as practical theology developed through the nineteenth and into the twentieth century, the constructive nature of practical theology was largely replaced by an applicational model of theory-to-practice. Theological knowledge constructed in biblical studies, systematic theology, and church history was applied to practical concerns of Christian life and ministry. It was not until the mid-twentieth century that practical theology regained its role in constructing theological knowledge, as the social sciences began to be taken as serious conversation partners.[8]

---

2. Osmer, *Practical Theology*.

3. Geertz, "Thick Description."

4. Osmer names this fourth task as the "pragmatic task." I prefer the language of performance over pragmatics as a way of emphasizing the necessary connection between normative direction for action rather than action based solely on practical concerns to the exclusion of theoretical insights.

5. Schleiermacher and Tice, *Brief Outline*, 1.

6. Schleiermacher, *Christian Caring*.

7. Gräb, "Practical Theology," 182.

8. Kim, "Hermeneutical-Praxis Paradigm," 420.

The practices at the center of practical theological enquiry can either be described empirically[9] or examined hermeneutically.[10] This project follows the latter course, pursuing the descriptive task through the exegesis and analysis of Maxine Greene's writings on aesthetic pedagogy. In terms of Gadamer's dialogical hermeneutics,[11] I am seeking a fusion of horizons between Greene's pedagogical vision and the theological vision of Christian faith. Fusion of horizons expresses the goal of interpretation; it does not outline a method. "The fusion of horizons that is understanding is not an achievement consequent on proper method, but an event that depends on a conversation-like, dialectical openness toward that which we hope to understand."[12] This project seeks to open a conversational space between Greene and Christian theologians through a methodology of mutual critical correlation.

Mutually Critical Correlation under the Authority of Scripture

Critical correlation finds its origins in Tillich's method of theological correlation, which "formulates the questions implied in human existence" and responds with "the answers implied in divine self-manifestation."[13] Tracy challenged Tillich's unidirectional method, arguing that theology can only be adequately carried out "by a method which develops critical criteria for correlating the questions and answers found in both the 'situation' and the 'message.'"[14] Tracy defines practical theology as "mutually critical correlation of the interpreted theory and praxis of the Christian faith with the interpreted theory and praxis of the contemporary situation."[15] Taking up Tracy's mutual critical correlation, Browning envisions a "fully critical practical theology" that is willing to risk, at least in principle, ending in "total discontinuity with the previous tradition and with the primordial revelation on which Christianity rests."[16]

In contrast to the correlationist approach, which seeks a philosophical exchange between theological and non-theological knowledge, the narrative approach to theological reflection emphasizes the biblical story as the

9. Heitink, *Practical Theology*; Ven, *Practical Theology*; Ward, *Participation*.
10. Browning, *Fundamental Practical Theology*.
11. Gadamer, *Truth and Method*.
12. Brown, "Hermeneutical Theory," 114.
13. Tillich, *Systematic Theology*, 69.
14. Tracy, *Blessed Rage*, 46.
15. Tracy, "Foundations," 76.
16. Browning, *Fundamental Practical Theology*, 220.

authoritative frame within which non-theological knowledge needs to be understood. Narrativists identify the theological task as discerning "how contemporary experience can be interpreted through the story that the Church tells about Jesus and to identify forms of practice that are coherent within this narrative."[17] Tillich names this approach "kerygmatic theology," which "emphasizes the unchangeable truth of the message (kerygma) over the changing demands of the situation."[18]

Reformed theology favors a narrative approach because of its emphasis on Scripture as setting the direction and boundaries of theological reflection. The narrative approach pursues forms of Christian practice that participate in the work of God in Christ rather than "languish[ing] in the pride of our own attempts to storm heaven."[19] The conservative evangelical tradition has largely held the correlational method of practical theology in low regard. Mutual critical correlation is seen to give greater authority to human culture and experience than to Scripture and tradition, resulting in emphasizing the sociopolitical dimensions of the Christian life in a way that marginalizes concern for personal and eternal salvation.[20] Barth's *Nein!* to natural theology applies equally to mutual critical correlation.[21] As Barth says in response to Schleiermacher's theological method, "One cannot speak of God simply by speaking of man in a loud voice."[22]

However, practical theology conducted as merely the application of "knowledge produced elsewhere, with no epistemological value of its own," neglects the significance of the meanings and values embodied in practice and overlooks the insights available in non-theological knowledge.[23] In this study, as I seek to identify Christian practices that are both theologically and culturally appropriate, I look to Maxine Greene's pedagogy to identify approaches to education and formation of teenagers that are at home in the culture of expressive individualism. A unidirectional narrative approach would be less likely to benefit from insights available from Greene's philosophy.

The conflict between correlational and narrative approaches to theological reflection is complicated by the frequent conflation of "Scripture and

---

17. Graham et al., *Methods*, 78.
18. Tillich, *Systematic Theology*, 4.
19. Purves, *Reconstructing Practical Theology*, ix.
20. Toren and Hoare, "Evangelicals and Contextual Theology."
21. Barth, *Nein!*
22. Barth, "The Word of God," 195–96.
23. Dean, "We will find answers," 29.

Tradition" as one pole of the theological conversation.[24] As a result, narrativists, such as Purves[25] and Torren,[26] construe the correlational method as a compromise of biblical authority and an assertion of human wisdom over divine revelation. Conversely, correlationists view the narrative approach as an arrogant claim to speak for God that fails to acknowledge their reading of Scripture as merely one of many possible readings, and as a denial of the freedom of the Spirit to be at work in the world beyond the confines of any one particular theological tradition. Further, by speaking in Christian jargon and dismissing the insights from human and social sciences, narrativists are charged with keeping theology and the church in a Christian ghetto.

In order to embrace the insights offered through mutual critical correlation at the same time as affirming the normative authority of the Bible, the approach to theological correlation pursued in this project maintains a distinction between Christian Scripture and Christian tradition. The biblical text is distinguished as primary revelation from the secondary work of human readings of, and reflection on, the biblical text. Even though there is seamless historical continuity between the writings that came to be recognized as canonical and those that form the earliest written deposit of the Christian tradition, "the church's recognition of the canon of Scripture created a real break, which gave the origin of the tradition, in this written form, a uniquely normative status in relation to the rest of the tradition."[27] Tradition, therefore, is distinguished as "essentially a hermeneutical process, in which the message of Scripture is interpreted and developed."[28] This is not a peculiarly evangelical Protestant conclusion. Pursuing a foundation for the critical-constructive integration of Orthodox, Catholic, and Protestant thought, Hans Küng affirms the Bible as "the permanent and unshakeable basis for any ecumenical, truly Christian theology . . . Scripture is *norma normans* (normative norm), tradition is *norma normata* (a norm that has itself been shaped by the Gospel)."[29]

With this distinction in place, non-theological knowledge (such as Greene's educational philosophy) and theological traditions are gathered in the same theological category as human reflection on divine revelation.

---

24. Bevans, *Models of Contextual Theology*, 32; Ward, *Participation*, 36–39. Bevans does distinguish the three sources of theology—scripture, tradition, and context—but groups scripture and tradition together as the "experience of the past" versus context as the "experience of the present" (*Models of Contextual Theology*, 7).

25. Purves, *Reconstructing Practical Theology*.

26. Toren and Hoare, "Evangelicals and Contextual Theology."

27. Bauckham, "Tradition," 127.

28. Bauckham, "Tradition," 128.

29. Küng, *Theology for the Third Millennium*, 59.

Thus, non-theological sources can correct aspects of Christian tradition, but neither non-theological sources nor Christian tradition can supplant the biblical text as norming norm. A fully mutual correlation is possible between "experience" and "tradition," where the insights from such a conversation are taken back to a re-interrogation of the biblical text. "A reformed practical theology therefore not only seeks a critical correlation between practice and theology but moves from that critical conversation to a re-reading of Scripture."[30]

Thus, the task of a Reformed critical correlation is to draw on expressions of human wisdom (whether in non-theological or theological sources) as resources to aid in listening to the divine voice speaking in Scripture. Approaching the Bible as the personal revelation of the living God requires an act of interpretation that can never be said to be complete. No theological tradition can ever lay claim to being final, and as such ought always welcome new perspectives that may be opened through dialogue with other human perspectives. The ultimate theological goal of Reformed critical correlation is to better listen to "the Holy Spirit speaking in the Scriptures."[31]

Critical Conversation

"Conversation" is an apt metaphor for this project because of its intended goal of using Greene's pedagogy as a creative and constructive partner for theological reflection on appropriate practices of engaging with the Bible in youth ministry. The language of conversation seems appropriate to this goal, having "an ease of use about it, denoting something friendly, mutual, flexible and evolutionary."[32] My aim is to engage in a dialogue with Greene's work, without suggesting a systematic or "correct" reading. I do not intend to offer a comprehensive critique and theological reconstruction of Greene's aesthetic pedagogy and make no claims to have conducted a definitive study.[33] On the contrary, my analysis betrays my focal interest in transformational pedagogy for practices of Bible Engagement for teenage spiritual formation in relation to the Christian faith.

Three features of conversation characterize this study. First, productive conversations require a willingness in all parties to listen and be attentive to others. There is an act of grace required from conversation partners to clarify assumptions and understandings. The effort is not without gain,

30. Stanton, "Reforming Practical Theology," 20.
31. Westminster Confession of Faith 1.10.
32. Graham et al., *Sources*, 277.
33. Baldacchino, *Education beyond Education*, 1.

and conversations graciously and rigorously pursued enable us to discover new things, seeing oneself and others from new angles and in a different light.[34] Milbank highlights the danger of theology naïvely entering into partnership with social theory, resulting in importing underlying assumptions that are either modifications or rejections of Christian orthodoxy.[35] In a bid to avoid this pitfall, I will begin by identifying the underlying philosophical foundations in Greene's approach. My reading of Greene will be at once critical and sympathetic.

Second, conversation invites questions and answers from each party, consistent with the methodology of mutual critical correlation. Because of my focal interest in theologically appropriate practices of BE for Christian spiritual formation, there will be times when the conversation with Greene prompts avenues of thought that I pursue through various theological partners. That is to say, the scope of the discussion in this study is not limited to the horizons of Greene's thought. The flexible and evolutionary nature of conversation is a way of capturing this idea.

Third, conversation will include moments of divergence, where the concerns of either party reach beyond that of the other. Pattison seems to refer to the same phenomenon, albeit in more negative tones of "silence, of disagreement, of lack of communication."[36] Nevertheless, I concur with Pattison that welcoming such "gaps" in theological reflection avoids forcing "dubious connections which tend to have a pious and unrealistic tenor" and instead understands theological refection as "active enquiry [that] is as much about exploring and living with gaps as well as with similarities."[37] Conversation does not require all parties to reach full agreement on all matters. Points of divergence are inevitable and can be acknowledged without supposing to undermine the ongoing value of the exchange. Thus, at points in the conversation with Greene my reading of the Christian tradition will push against certain aspects of her conclusions and proposals. My intention is that the grounds for such moments of divergence will be clear and cogent.

Theological Conversation with Maxine Greene

The conversation with Maxine Greene begins by paying attention to aspects of her philosophy that I recognize as relevant to the topic of BE for spiritual formation. I am drawing on arguments from Greene that present

34. Pattison, "Some Straw for the Bricks," 280.
35. Milbank, *Theology and Social Theory*.
36. Pattison, "Some Straw for the Bricks," 280.
37. Pattison, "Some Straw for the Bricks," 280.

an original way of looking at the educational/formational process in order to empower Christian educators to reposition Christian formation beyond customary approaches.

Chapters 3, 4, and 5 identify contributions from Greene's philosophy towards how Christian formation might be pursued in ways that connect with the culture of expressive individualism. These chapters will thus also identify questions to be addressed in the unfolding dialogue. Consistent with a mutual critical correlation, questions are posed from two directions—questions from Reformed theology to Greene, and questions from Greene to Reformed theology. These questions are taken up in Part II of the study.

The theological engagement with Greene in Part II engages with various interlocutors from conservative traditions of Christian theology. I have chosen a number of theological voices because each speaks to Greene in a unique and necessary way. Restricting the theological interaction with Greene to one or two conversation partners would limit the degree to which theological voices would interact with the key points of Greene's pedagogy and limit the extent to which productive themes relating to practices of BE could be pursued.[38] The danger inherent in engaging a variety of conversation partners is that the clarity of the conversation is lost as a result of conflicting theological perspectives. I have sought to ameliorate this danger by drawing on voices with shared convictions regarding biblical authority (this being the central theological concern of the dialectic of freedom and authority that this project is exploring).

The three major conversation partners are Roman Catholic social philosopher Charles Taylor, Reformed educational philosopher Nicholas Wolterstorff, and Reformed Evangelical theologian Garrett Green.[39] Taylor is particularly relevant to this project because of his engagement with expressive individualism in his account of the modern secular age.[40] Taylor's identification of an ethical core to the quest for authenticity provides a substantial point of contact between Greene's philosophy and Christian theology. Where Taylor engages with the philosophical

---

38. An alternative approach could have chosen one particular theological voice to adopt as a conversation partner with Greene. Apparent contenders for a correlational study of aesthetic pedagogy are the significant voices in theological aesthetics: Augustine, Jonathan Edwards, or Hans Urs von Balthasar. However, despite the similarity in terminology, theological aesthetics is concerned more with a theology of beauty and the place given to beauty in theological systems, whereas aesthetic pedagogy is particularly concerned with the role of the creative arts in promoting personal transformation.

39. In an attempt to avoid confusion in staging a conversation between Greene and Green, I will mostly refer to Maxine Greene by her surname only, but when referring to Garrett Green I will always use both his first and last names.

40. Taylor, *Authenticity*; Taylor, *Secular Age*.

foundations of Greene's pedagogy, Wolterstorff's reflection on Christian education engages with Greene's methodology.[41] Garrett Green's work in biblical hermeneutics connects with Greene's pedagogy via his theological engagement with the imagination.[42]

Given Greene's persistent advocacy for hearing the oft-silenced voices of women, it is appropriate that I acknowledge that the theological voices in this conversation all come from white males. This is not an unfamiliar position for Greene to be in. An account of the 1961 meeting of the Philosophy of Education Society notes, "there was a lone female listed on the program, though a formidable one—Maxine Greene."[43] Greene's voice is certainly strong enough to stand her ground in conversation with a group of men. Furthermore, Greene's concern for providing a voice for the voiceless is taken up in the project by calling for the church to pay attention to the contribution that young people have to make to the life of faith.

Practice Frameworks

The performative task of this project culminates in proposing a practice framework that embodies insights from Maxine Greene's aesthetic pedagogy in practices of BE in Christian youth ministry: A dialogical youth ministry. The "practice framework" is a frequently used concept in social work discourse, linking philosophical and theoretical underpinnings with particular interventions of social work practice. Most practice frameworks are personal constructions that articulate the professional identity of an individual, painting a picture of how they operate as a social worker.[44] Beyond the social work field, similar frameworks for practice have also been developed in fields as diverse as nursing,[45] midwifery,[46] aid and development,[47] cross-cultural business negotiations,[48] business control

---

41. Wolterstorff et al., *Educating for Shalom*; Wolterstorff et al., *Educating for Life*.

42. Green, *Theology*; Green, *Imagining God*. In addition to these three major contributors, I draw upon other theological voices at certain points in order to pursue areas of thought and practice prompted by the theological dialogue with Greene. Each theological contributor is introduced at the relevant point in the text.

43. Kohli, "Philosopher of/for Freedom," 14.

44. Connolly, "Practice Frameworks."

45. Moulster et al., "Implementation of a new Framework for Practice."

46. Piper, "Health Promotion."

47. Shrimpton et al., "Nutrition Capacity Development."

48. Prasad and Cao, "Improving Negotiation Outcomes."

practices,[49] and new product development.[50] Common to each of these fields of endeavor is the interaction of theory and values that drive practice. Rather than being presented as static blueprints, practice frameworks are intended to "develop over time, through practice, and become increasingly useful . . . for constructing unique responses in each practice encounter."[51] This dynamic interaction between theory and practice reflects the central concerns of practical theology.

A parallel to this project can be found in the "Seven Principles for Good Practice in Undergraduate Education" developed for colleges and universities in the United States of America.[52] The seven principles were grounded in an underlying view of education that sought to distil findings from research into the undergraduate experience. Because the seven-point framework is offered as a resource for university faculty members responsible for improving undergraduate education, the authors were concerned to avoid "the long list of recommendations" usually found in the appendix to official reports, as well as "general theories of student development and learning."[53] The principles needed to be "accessible, understandable, practical, and widely applicable."[54] In a similar way, this project is responding to research into the adolescent experience related to BE and is grounded in an underlying approach to spiritual formation in Christian theology. This project is aimed at enabling the adult mentors (parents, youth leaders, teachers) who are ultimately responsible for guiding young people in the church in their engagement with the Bible. Therefore, following Gamson, I intend for the practice framework developed to be accessible, understandable, practical, and widely applicable.[55]

The practice framework I am proposing is a step between philosophical foundations that give broad outlines for youth ministry practice and a detailed program and methodology to provide step-by-step direction for youth ministers. The latter is the antimony of Greene's desire that teachers exercise their own freedom to discover their personal philosophy of teaching.

49. Kinkela and Harris, "COSO Updates Practice Framework."
50. Kahn et al., "Perspective."
51. Healy, *Social Work Theories in Context*, 216.
52. Chickering and Gamson, "Seven Principles for Good Practice."
53. Gamson, "A Brief History," 6.
54. Gamson, "'A Brief History," 7.
55. Following the positive reception of the 'Seven Principles for Good Practice in Undergraduate Education' a self-assessment inventory was developed (Gamson and Poulsen, "Inventories of Good Practice"). Future research could refine and validate the usefulness of the framework proposed in this project with a view to developing a self-assessment inventory.

Conversely, the former is too abstract to provide practical benefit for youth ministers. Greene's commitment to leading teachers to "do philosophy" for themselves is demonstrated in her vehement opposition to the "capacities for imaginative thinking" developed by Lincoln Center Education (LCE). The LCE learning framework, ostensibly developed as an expression of Greene's pedagogy, offers ten questions to help focus conversations about a work of art.[56] Greene rejected the suggestion that her philosophy of teaching could be reduced to a ten-point learning framework. After the publication of LCE's learning framework, Greene cut ties with the center, demanded her name not be associated with the learning framework, and no longer allowed the center to describe her as philosopher-in-residence, but only as founding philosopher or philosopher emeritus.[57]

An argument in support of developing a detailed methodological framework is that for educational philosophy to make a difference in the concrete reality of students' lives, pedagogical theory must be implemented by classroom teachers. A teaching framework such as LCE's capacities, it could be argued, is a form of instructional scaffolding[58] that enables teachers to develop their own methodology of aesthetic pedagogy. However, there is the real possibility that teachers would simply adopt a ten-point plan without doing the hard work of personally reflecting on their own philosophy of teaching. My

---

56. The ten capacities and guiding questions are:

Notice Deeply: How many layers of detail can you identify if you take the time? Can you go deeper?

Embody: Use your body to explore your ideas. Try it out.

Pose Questions: What do you wonder?

Identify Patterns: How might different details relate? Analyze them.

Make Connections: How is this like something else? Make personal, textual, and wider connections.

Empathize: Can you understand how others think and feel? What are their perspectives?

Live with Ambiguity: What if there is not just one answer? Be patient with complexity.

Create Meaning: Bring together what you've thought so far. What new interpretations can you make?

Take Action: What will you choose to do with your ideas? Put them into practice.

Reflect/Assess: Look back on what you've experienced. What have you learned? What's next?

(Lincoln Center Institute, "Lincoln Center Institute Capacities for Imaginative Learning").

57. Janet Miller, personal communication, 19 February, 2015.

58. Coyne et al., *Effective Teaching Strategies*, 89.

intention is to provide a scaffold to prompt others who are involved in pedagogical and theological reflection on youth ministry and Christian education to develop their own philosophy of formation. As such, the practice framework offered in this project is intended as a voice in an unfolding dialogue in service of young people from within the Christian faith.

The practice framework offered here serves two further purposes. First, it draws together the various thoughts raised in the preceding discussion and begins the pragmatic/performative task of practical theology of directing concrete action. This ambition is entirely consistent with Greene's philosophy that constructions of meaning need to be expressed in intentional action.[59] The proposed framework merely begins this task, since it is beyond the scope of the current project to develop a detailed proposal for an actual youth ministry intervention. Thus, the second purpose of the practice framework is to lay out the contours of how DYM could be applied to youth ministry in order to guide a future project to investigate the validation of the conclusions drawn here.

Greene believes that the academy (at least the educational research academy) has learned the need to move "beyond relativism, beyond narrative for its own sake" and urged researchers to "discover how to take positions that are comprehensible, honest, fair; we have to learn more than we have about what it means to persuade."[60] This project seeks to persuade, as much as it seeks to be comprehensible, honest, and fair.

Summary

The overall aim of this study is captured succinctly by Greene herself:

> I am interested in studies that tap many voices and open many perspectives on education and other situations. It should not be "soft"; it should not equalize and tranquilize all points of view. It should penetrate and expose the silences and discover what lies behind the silences. It should have a normative dimension, identifying the deficiencies of the voids I have mentioned, going beyond the merely technological "fix."[61]

This project has a strong normative dimension and seeks to establish the case for that vision through tapping into many voices and, using those perspectives, to cast light on silences and build a case for an alternate vision. While

---

59. Greene, *LL*, 153.
60. Ayers, "Social Imagination," 328.
61. Ayers, "Social Imagination," 327.

the ultimate goal is to provide practical direction to church-based youth ministers, the vision for renewed practice is not merely a novel technique, but a holistic vision for the aims, means, and methods of youth ministry.

Thus, this project is both apologetic and dialectical.[62] On the one hand, I am intending to indicate how the Christian tradition fulfils and completes Maxine Greene's desire for an education that promotes human freedom in pursuit of a vision of intersubjective community. On the other hand, I want to glimpse some new theological understanding through Greene's "secular" thought forms and hope to demonstrate how her philosophy makes a vital contribution to the practice of Christian ministry among young people. By learning from Greene's philosophy and reimagining aspects of the practice of spiritual formation among young people, this project will also offer a defense of Christian spiritual formation as an activity that can be pursued in ways that are free of domination and control without abandoning intentionality or belief in biblical authority.

---

62. Graham et al., *Methods*, 139.

Part I

Maxine Greene's Aesthetic Pedagogy

THE FIRST TASK OF this project is to detail elements of Maxine Greene's aesthetic pedagogy that address key dimensions of the freedom-authority dialectic in secondary school education. Each of the following three chapters begin with my reading of Greene, offering an analysis of her thought under the headings of aims, means, and method. Across three chapters I will outline and analyze freedom as the aim, engagement with the creative arts as the means, and releasing imagination as the method of aesthetic pedagogy.

The second section of each chapter seeks to lean into Greene's pedagogy and imagine Christian youth ministry in line with her philosophy. The subjunctive mood comes to the fore in these sections as I explore the question, "what if" Greene's pedagogy were to be applied to Christian youth ministry without significant theological adaptation? As far as possible, I am transferring what Greene says about "teachers" to "youth ministers," about "teaching" to "youth ministry," and about "students" to "members of youth groups." Theological critique will be held in abeyance for the sake of developing a sympathetic and appreciative reading of Greene's pedagogy and its possible implications for Christian work with teenagers. The concluding section of each chapter moves into the correlative conversation by posing questions of Greene's pedagogy arising from Christian theology, and questions of Christian theology (and practice) arising from Greene's pedagogy. Theological dialogue in response to these questions will be taken up in detail in Part II.

3

Education in and for Freedom

MAXINE GREENE DESCRIBES HER pedagogical project as "education in and for freedom."[1] Since freedom is a ubiquitous value in contemporary Western culture, exploring this aim will require analyzing the philosophical commitments that shape Greene's understanding. I suggest that Greene's commitment to existential phenomenology is expressed in a constructivist ontology, in a dialogical epistemology, and in a volitional anthropology. These commitments build towards Greene's vision of inclusive democracy that embodies and promotes freedom. Arising from her philosophical commitments, Greene's educational agenda seeks to move young people to wide-awakeness through developing dialogical spaces of mutual concern that enable young people to take up their responsibility and capacity for meaning-making in their lived experience.

Greene's vision suggests that youth ministers would need to focus on the processes of meaning-making over the accomplishment of specific outcomes of spiritual formation. Youth ministers would curate dialogical community, where young people are able to explore spirituality from various perspectives. Applying Greene's thought to youth ministry highlights the value of process over outcome in spiritual formation, the personal agency of young people to make their own spiritual choices, the imperative to preserve young people from coercion in relation to their spiritual formation, and the reminder that young peoples' spiritual experience can be a blessing to the whole church. Two questions are raised which will be taken up in the correlative conversation in Part II: First, how does Greene's concept of freedom relate to Christian

1. Greene, *DF*, 133.

understandings of sin? Second, how can human freedom be preserved in company with commitments to divine authority?

Philosophical Foundations: Existential Phenomenology

Greene's pedagogy is embedded in her philosophical commitments as an existential phenomenologist. Greene connects with the way students experience the world from their own unique locations and perspectives. Greene writes, "we are grounded in experience, in an ineluctably human reality . . . there can be no such phenomenon as an objectless consciousness."[2] Human consciousness, Greene argues, "is always situated" such that the situated person "reaches out and grasps the phenomena surrounding him/her from a particular vantage point and against a particular background consciousness."[3] As a phenomenologist, Greene affirms that reality is not an objective given but is rather the result of our subjective interpretations from our particular vantage point. What we hold as "real" are not things in themselves, but our interpretations of our experiences of things. "To talk of meaning," Greene writes, "is to talk of interpretation, not immediate awareness."[4]

Beyond borrowing from other philosophers, Greene's "phenomenology of imagination" is a unique contribution that establishes her as an existential phenomenologist in her own right.[5] With the other existential-phenomenologists Greene affirms that consciousness is intentional (involving moving out into the world rather than retreating into a privatized interiority), and perceptual, and therefore open to multiple interpretations.[6] Greene argues that the only way any one individual is able to engage with this multiplicity of meaning is through the imagination.[7] Greene speaks of the imagination as a mode of awareness necessary for careful noticing of the world around us. There is a rational and cognitive dimension to perception that is necessary but not sufficient for full awareness of our context. Imaginative awareness is required to "search for openings" amidst the narrowing spaces of life;[8] awakening us by disclosing what is "ordinarily unseen, unheard and unexpected" in contrast to "the

---

2. Greene, *LL*, 16.
3. Greene, *DF*, 21.
4. Greene, *LL*, 16.
5. Morris, "Existential and Phenomenological Influences," 133.
6. Greene, *LL*, 14–15.
7. Greene, *RI*, 26.
8. Greene, *RI*, 17.

conformist, the respectable, the moralistic, and the constrained."⁹ In order to become more fully aware of what is available to us, we need to imagine how things are from multiple perspectives.

This work of imagination enables empathetic awareness. Greene says of empathy and the imagination:

> Imagination is what, above all, makes empathy possible. It is what enables us to cross the empty spaces between ourselves and those we teachers have called "other" over the years. If those others are willing to give us clues, we can look in some manner through strangers' eyes and hear through their ears. That is because, of all our cognitive capacities, imagination is the one that permits us to give credence to alternative realities. It allows us to break with the taken for granted, to set aside familiar distinctions and definitions.¹⁰

In this description of the role of imagination, Greene touches on three key aspects of her philosophical foundations: her constructivist ontology that permits alternative realities, her dialogical epistemology that acquires knowledge through empathetic engagement with others, and her volitional anthropology that calls individuals to make choices to break with the taken-for-granted.

Constructivist Ontology

Crucial for understanding Greene's approach to freedom and transformation is the recognition that all reality is open to change because what is taken as "real" is only an interpretation. Greene says of our everyday reality, "taking it for granted, we do not realize that that reality, like all others, is an interpreted one. It presents itself to us as it does because we have learned to understand it in standard ways."¹¹ Greene is looking therefore for a freedom "that will permit [men and women] to choose what they will become in whatever they decide will be their common world."¹² Persons exercise their freedom when they take on the responsibility of constructing the self through the way they make meaning of the contexts in which they exist.

Though Greene affirms the social and personal constructions that constitute "reality," her position is not that of radical constructivism. Greene

---

9. Greene, *RI*, 28.
10. Greene, *RI*, 3.
11. Greene, *LL*, 44.
12. Greene, *DF*, 63.

acknowledges the concrete realities in which we exist and around which we pursue free choice and a democratic future. Echoing Heidegger's notion of *Geworfenheit*, thrownness, Greene recognizes that though we exist in a world we did not choose, we continue to bear a responsibility to choose what we will make from and in the landscapes of our learning:

> We are conditioned, entangled, thrust into a world not of our choosing, but also free to understand what is happening to us, to interpret, to envision possibilities, to act against all the "determinisms," to repair the deficiencies we find. We cannot choose to live in a non-nuclear world, for example, but we can, indeed, we must choose who to be in the light of the threat of nuclear annihilation.[13]

The freedom to choose the world we inhabit requires us to break free from what is "taken-for-granted." We will do so only by recognizing our everyday worlds as something constructed, since if they are constructed, then they are also open to change.

The pursuit of freedom requires us to identify and reject the "mystifications" that dictate what the world is like and how we ought to act within it. Greene adopts Marx's language of mystification for the invisible and unnamed powers that exert control over individuals.[14] A mystification is a form of "illusion" that leaves people feeling "completely at home" even while they are alienated and repressed. To be held in a mystification refers to "the sense of ineffectuality and powerlessness that comes when persons feel themselves to be the victims of forces wholly beyond their control, in fact beyond any human control."[15]

Mystifications arise when social constructs are allowed to ossify into objective truth. Mystifications are difficult to resist because the experience of living within a confined story diminishes our ability to see and evaluate the story itself. Cultural stories or myths are no longer taken as offering possibilities for how we will choose our world. Instead they hold demands that oppose freedom. Stories such as "woman as love goddess" or "woman as mother and homemaker"[16] are carried in a culture, and when they are accepted as just-the-way-things-are-around-here they constrain the ability

---

13. Ayers, "Doing Philosophy," 6.

14. Marx named as "mystifications" the social constructs that maintain the power of one social class over another (Marx and Engels, *Capital*, 599).

15. Greene, *LL*, 64.

16. Greene quotes Carol Gould's assessment of the childbearing/housewife story as a mystification that "seeks to keep woman in her place by making it her lot; it seeks to make her role acceptable by making it inevitable" (Greene, *DF*, 62).

of individuals living within that story to make free choices. Even though women living within such stories may choose how they will live out that story as an individual, the mystification has "narrow[ed] the spaces in which they could choose."[17]

The reason that hegemonic stories need to be challenged is not because living within a particular "mystification" is necessarily a bondage—a woman may choose to dwell within the "woman as mother" story—but because one's life story must be chosen freely. Though she did not regard the family to necessarily be an obstacle to freedom in and of itself, Greene says that

> the kind of social reality that demands such mystifications must be interrogated; the illusions must be exposed if women (and men as well) are to achieve the kind of freedom that will permit them to choose what they will become in whatever they decide will be their common world.[18]

Greene's "focal interest" therefore is on human freedom understood as "the capacity to surpass the given and look at things as if they could be otherwise."[19] It is this ability to choose how we will construct our world and our place in it that is the essence of being human.

Volitional Anthropology

Greene holds that human beings are "condemned to make meaning."[20] To be fully human is to exercise the critical understanding required to interpret our experience, to make meaning[21] grounded in our unique landscapes of

---

17. Greene, *DF*, 60.
18. Greene, *DF*, 63.
19. Greene, *DF*, 3.
20. Miller, "Condemned to Make Meaning," 32.
21. Affirming the task of meaning-making as the task of human life connects Greene's educational philosophy with hermeneutic approaches to identity formation stemming from Frankl's *Man's Search for Meaning*. Robert Kegan, for example, explores the development of identity as the activity of making sense of experience through discovering and resolving problems, concluding "it is not that a person makes meaning, as much as that activity of being a person is the activity of meaning-making" (Kegan, *The Evolving Self*, 11). Meaning-making is, however, only one way of theorizing human identity formation. Côté ("Identity Studies") offers a taxonomy of approaches to identity studies built upon contrasting assumptions regarding the nature of social reality, social order, and psychosocial focus. In terms of Côté's paradigm, Greene takes both an individual and a social focus, within a subjectivist epistemology, and a critical/contextual approach to social order. While Greene's recognition of mystification sits alongside

learning. Choice expresses the inescapable connection between thought and situation. In contrast, grounding identity in rationality abstracts humanity from our situation. The human quest for transcendence can only emerge when we are grounded in our personal histories and lived live.[22]

In Greene's anthropology, to be human is to be a decision-making subject. In contrast to the Cartesian approach that establishes human identity in rational thought, Greene grounds identity in choice: I choose, therefore I am.[23] With Kierkegaard and Sartre, Greene pursues the existentialist commitment to constructing the self through free choice. As conscious beings, Greene argues, we "constitute the world we inhabit through the interpretations we adopt or make for ourselves. To take that world for granted as predefined or objectively *there* is to be uncritical, submissive, and submerged."[24] Ayers summarizes this theme in Greene's philosophy: "to be human is to be involved in a quest, a fundamental life project that is situated and undertaken as a refusal to accede to the given."[25]

Freedom therefore is a process of "personal becoming."[26] Greene speaks of freedom as something that must be "achieved."[27] Freedom is not an inherent quality of human experience. Freedom for Greene is not just the ability to choose, but the ability of individuals to make choices that

those identity theorists who accept existing social order as is, and therefore inevitable, Greene's proposal for breaking free of the taken-for-granted recognizes social order as one of many potential contexts for different types of identity formation. See also Schwartz et al., *Handbook of Identity Theory*, for an overview of the field of identity studies, proposing a unifying approach to the various streams of identity theory and research.

22. Greene, *LL*, 2.

23. Greene's emphasis on choice here appears to be in conflict with Hauerwas's argument for "vision" rather than choice as the more appropriate metaphor: "The moral life is not first a life of choice—decision is not king—but is rather woven from the notions that we use to see and from the situations we confront. Moral life involves learning to see the world through an imaginative ordering of our basic symbols and notions" (Hauerwas, *Vision and Virtue*, 2). Greene's emphasis on imagination (discussed further in chapter 5) is more in line with Hauerwas's conclusion. Yet, despite Greene's focal interest in creative arts, her emphasis on choice, arising from her existentialist roots, is an indication that her thinking remains influenced by an intellectualist paradigm of transformation. Chapter 8 explores in more detail the way the Bible provides us with a vision of life shaped by the kingdom of God. By contemplating this vision, we are transformed into the likeness of what we behold. "What we are grasping for here is a total way of viewing self, others, life, and God that informs and molds all our words and actions" (Pembroke, *Moving Toward Spiritual Maturity*, 141).

24. Greene, *LL*, 17.

25. Ayers, "Doing Philosophy," 7.

26. Greene, *DF*, 80.

27. Greene, *DF*, 101.

are "fully their own."[28] By choosing certain actions over others, persons construct the self. "No one's self is ready-made; each of us has to create a self by choice of action, action in the world."[29] To be moral, Greene writes, "involves taking a principled position of one's own (*choosing* certain principles by which to live) and speaking clearly about it, so as to set oneself on the right track."[30] Greene's anthropology expresses the familiar postmodern concept of "persons in process."[31]

Greene therefore considers the challenge of being authors of our own worlds and lives to be the enduring human occupation:

> [Authorship] carries with it the feeling of temporality, the sense of being in communication, the awareness of perspective in a constructed world. Human beings, of course, devise their life projects in time—against their own life histories and the wider human history into which those histories feed... To be aware of authorship is to be aware of situationality and of the relation between possibilities of action and of choice. This means that one's "reality," rather than being fixed and predefined, is a perpetual emergent, becoming increasingly multiplex, as more perspectives are taken, more texts are opened, more friendships are made.[32]

Greene is arguing that the challenge in self-authorship involves coming to terms with the inherent uncertainty and complexity in our experience. Yet this ought not inhibit the pursuit of meaning and action. On the contrary, such recognition opens the door for exploration and underlines the need for interpersonal relationship.

Dialogical Epistemology

The free choices to be made are not those of a libertarian freedom of personal rights free from any external consideration or constraint. The "space" within which freedom is to be pursued is unavoidably social. Greene insists therefore that freedom must be, and can only be, pursued in community with others. In this, Greene stands against the "negative freedom" of radical individualism with its emphasis on self-dependence, self-regulation, and self-expression but with little concern for connectedness or

28. Greene, *DF*, 101.
29. Greene, *LL*, 18.
30. Greene, *LL*, 49. Emphasis original.
31. Greene, *RI*, 41.
32. Greene, *DF*, 23.

community. Negative freedom is characterized by "self-dependence rather than relationship; self-regarding and self-regulated behavior rather than involvement with others. Above all it means an absence of interference or . . . a deregulation."[33] This concept of freedom fails from a phenomenological perspective to take account of the context in which freedom might be pursued. Greene's account of freedom is not an abstract concept, but one that is situated in human nature and in human society.

Greene argues that negative freedom undermines human nature and diminishes human society. Human nature is undermined, since the quest for autonomy masks an enslavement that results from a thoughtless acquiescence to what is taken for granted. While "most Americans are convinced they are free," Greene observes, "many are likely to share a feeling of subservience to a system, or to a faith, or to an Establishment they can scarcely name."[34] While mere autonomy may have the appearance of freedom, it is nothing more than the residue of freedom left when persons fail to resist the mystification of individualistic consumerism that has grown out of the *laissez-faire* economics of nineteenth-century American industrialization.[35] Such an individualized concept of freedom diminishes human society, since it is not able to produce a common world, a community of compassion and solidarity, or a civic order where shared problems are solved through solutions grounded in shared values and norms.[36]

Greene regards the social space as the unavoidable context in which we pursue freedom, noting that we are "inextricably involved with other people."[37] Not only am I pursuing my freedom through acting on my choices resulting from my subjective interpretation of reality, but I do so in the presence of other human beings pursuing their freedom through acting on their choices resulting from their subjective interpretations of reality. Greene writes,

> It is clear enough that choice and action both occur within and by means of ongoing transactions with objective conditions and with other human beings. They occur as well within the matrix of a culture, its prejudgments, and its symbol systems. Whatever

33. Greene, *DF,* 7.

34. Greene, *DF*, 19.

35. Greene quotes Henry David Thoreau writing in 1863, "even if we grant that the American has freed himself from a political tyrant he is still the slave of an economical and moral tyrant . . . what is it to be born free and not to live free?" (Greene, *DF*, 35).

36. "Greene encourages individuals to re-enter public life through recovering their collective voices and experiencing the agency that results from participation with others to produce changes" (Davies, "The Dialectic of Freedom," 43).

37. Greene, *LL,* 49.

is chosen and acted upon must be grounded, at least to a degree, in an awareness of a world lived in common with others.[38]

Greene concludes, therefore, that freedom calls individuals to act "to make a space for themselves in the presence of others."[39] Because individual freedom can only be pursued in the given landscape of the social domain, we need to recognize that individual subjectivity is exercised in an intersubjective realm. True freedom for Greene is "to be continually empowered to choose ourselves, to create our identities within a plurality."[40] Since choosing our world and who we will be in that world necessarily involves making promises and pursuing action, no one is able to create a meaningful identity on their own.

As we exercise our individual subjectivity in intersubjective space, we become aware that our perspective on the world is simply one among many. And since every viewpoint can only ever be partial, there is always more to be discovered in the human conversation. "Multiple interpretations constitute multiple realities; the "common" itself becomes multiplex and endlessly challenging."[41] Greene is partaking in "the post-modern rejection of inclusive rational frameworks in which all problems, all uncertainties can be resolved."[42]

In this world of multiple meanings with no final resolution, the human quest for meaning becomes a never-ending endeavor. Arguing from postmodern perspectivism, Greene argues that

> to recognize the role of perspective and vantage point, to recognize at the same time that there are always multiple perspectives and multiple vantage points, is to recognize that no accounting, disciplinary or otherwise, can ever be finished or complete. There is always more. There is always possibility. And this is where the space opens for the pursuit of freedom.[43]

It is not simply making meaning that is the essence of human life, but the ongoing pursuit of making meaning. There is no utopian end beyond the pursuit of meaning; the pursuit itself is its own end. Human life is continually offering new experiences requiring new interpretations from multiple perspectives.

38. Greene, *DF*, 4.
39. Greene, *DF*, 56.
40. Greene, *DF*, 51.
41. Greene, *DF*, 21.
42. Greene, *RI*, 16.
43. Greene, *DF*, 128.

This unending quest is part of what it means to be conscious. Greene suggests that consciousness is defined in part "by the way it always reaches beyond itself toward a fullness and a completeness that can never be attained. If it were attained, there would be a stoppage, a petrification. There would be no need for a quest."[44] Thus, claims to "know the truth" in a decisive or settled manner is not only an illusion, but constitutes a withdrawal from the social space and an abandonment of what is essentially human.

A Vision of Freedom

In Greene's vision, the human endeavor is a never-ending quest for meaning undertaken by individual persons who, through free choice of action, are constructing the world and their place in it, in company with other persons on the same journey. This is what it means to be free. "Dialogical freedom . . . arises out of particular situations in which individuals band together to participate in a process that affirm [sic] their identities and fulfils their promises through naming and overcoming obstacles."[45]

This ongoing pursuit of freedom in the context of community promotes Greene's ultimate vision of democracy. While the pathway to this vision begins in local communities and classrooms where people know each other's names, ultimately the vision is a universal one. Greene's hope is for a democracy where individuals are free "to understand the ways in which each of them reaches out from his or her location to constitute a common continent, a common world."[46] Greene writes of her hope to "remind people of what it means to live among others, to achieve freedom in dialogue with others for the sake of personal fulfilment and the emergence of a democracy dedicated to life and decency."[47]

Educational Principles

In light of these philosophical commitments, Greene's question as a teacher educator is "how can we educate for freedom?"[48] Though Greene is primarily a philosopher of education, her philosophy remains grounded in the concrete demands faced by teachers in the specific contexts of American

---

44. Greene, *RI*, 26.
45. Davies, "The Dialectic of Freedom," 43.
46. Greene, *LL*, 70.
47. Greene, *DF*, xii.
48. Greene, *DF*, 116.

schools.[49] However, despite this involvement in teaching practice, there is a two-fold challenge in attempting to delineate practical themes in Greene's pedagogy. First, the form of Greene's writing is reflective and recursive rather than being analytical and structured.[50] Greene has not set out a guide to aesthetic pedagogy that works sequentially through philosophical foundations, implications for teaching, and examples of classroom practice. Instead, as different issues are explored from various perspectives and viewpoints, themes arise and recur which, over time, build into a web of ideas that are intended to prompt teachers to make their own search toward what it means for them to be teachers. In this, Greene's form matches her philosophical commitments and is an instance of her approach to teaching. The teacher's task is not to provide meaning for her students but to goad them into their own search for meaning. Teachers aim to enable students to take on the burden of their existential condition, to recognize themselves as being "condemned to make meaning," not to condemn them to carry the burden of someone else's conclusions.

What I am proposing in this analysis of Greene's pedagogy, therefore, is not a teaching strategy or a sequence of instructions for "best practice" in the classroom. Rather, the discussion that follows describes three pedagogical themes that resonate with my particular concern for the practices of Bible engagement in Christian youth ministry: moving young people to wide-awakeness through enabling critical judgment, encouraging imaginative projection by opening dialogical spaces of mutual concern, and prompting decisive action in light of personally constructed meaning.

Wide-Awakeness

A fundamental task of education is to move young people to an "awareness of what it is to be in the world."[51] Drawing on Austrian phenomenologist, Alfred Schütz, Greene describes this sense of awareness as "wide-awakeness." Schütz defined wide-awakeness as "a plane of consciousness of highest tension, originating in an attitude of full attention to life and its requirements."[52] To

---

49. Greene's interactions with teachers are exemplified in her involvement in the Summer Sessions for teachers and school administrators at the Lincoln Center Institute for the Arts in Education (Noppe-Brandon and Holzer, "Maxine Greene").

50. Janet Miller described Greene's teaching as "stream of consciousness lecturing" which often came alive through responding to students' questions (personal conversation, 19 February, 2015).

51. Greene, *RI*, 35.

52. Schütz, *The Problem of Social Reality*, 213.

be wide awake is to take an interest in things, to replace conventionality and indifference with exploration and wonder; it requires thinking about what we are doing and taking responsibility for our choices.

Teachers need to enable students to exercise critical judgment to recognize the world they experience as constructed and therefore open to change. In place of accepting their experience as "taken-for-granted" and "so much part of the accustomed and the everyday that it escape[s] notice entirely," Greene argues for intentional actions to be undertaken to "bring things within the scope of students' attention, to make situations more palpable and visible."[53] Students need to be given "a heightened sense of agency" in order that they might be empowered "to pursue their freedom and, perhaps, transform to some degree their lived worlds."[54] Teachers are able to help students overcome feelings of being dominated and powerless through "conscious endeavor . . . to keep themselves awake, to think about their condition in the world, to inquire into the forces that appear to dominate them, to interpret the experiences they are having day by day."[55] In this conscious act of interpretation, teachers help students lay bare life's "givens," and to "tell the truth," in Heidegger's sense of "unconcealment."[56]

Once the world is rendered open to change, students need to recognize impediments to their freedom before they will be willing to investigate possibilities, let alone pursue action. Educators set out to "problematize" the world,"[57] pointing out the tensions that need resolving, the boundaries beckoning to be traversed. Part of the task of uncovering what has been "obscured by the familiar" is to "defamiliarize things, to make them strange."[58] Not until we come to recognize deficiencies will we act to bring change. Greene writes, "a rock is an obstacle only to the one who wants to climb the hill. Not caring, the traveler merely takes another path."[59] The absence of such a search explains why young people appear to have so little motivation or interest in school, since "without being 'onto something,' young people feel little

---

53. Greene, *DF*, 122. Young peoples' experiences often leave them feeling "conditioned, determined, even fated by the prevailing circumstances," and this as much so for "advantaged children" who feel locked in by a "sense of entitlement and privilege" as for members of minority groups or the poor. Even though "young people may not chafe under the inequities" they experience at school, "they are likely to treat them as wholly 'normal,' as predictable as natural laws" (Greene, *DF*, 125).

54. Greene, *RI*, 48.

55. Greene, *LL*, 44.

56. Greene, *DF*, 58.

57. Greene, *DF*, 124.

58. Greene, *DF*, 122.

59. Greene, *DF*, 5.

pressure, little challenge. There are no mountains they particularly want to climb, so there are few obstacles with which they feel they need to engage."[60] But once students begin to search, it becomes a case of "seeing more, feeling more, one reaches out for more to do."[61]

The challenge for educators lies in the fact that, according to Greene, many, even most, people do not take up this task. Rather than live in the wide-awakeness that pursues free action, most persons simply acquiesce to the way things are. Greene writes, "Even given conditions of liberty, many people do not act on their freedom; they do not risk becoming different; they accede; often, they submit."[62] Instead of taking up the task of constructing meaning from their experiences, most people regard their circumstances as being "objectively there" rather than critically examining what is taken for granted. In light of Greene's anthropology, to acquiesce is to abandon our humanity. Education for freedom is nothing short of restoring young people to their essential humanity.

Wide-awakeness is therefore not a stage through which one passes on the way to deeper learning experiences. To be wide awake is to be in a state of awareness, a state of wonder, as the necessary space within which learning and transformation can take place. In a state of wide-awakeness, students are able to exercise a "social imagination" that draws from the multiplicity of viewpoints that others bring to our experience of the world. Recognizing multiple viewpoints and interpretations of reality brings us to realize the vast range of possibilities that lie open before us as responsible agents in the world. Given the unavoidable social context in which we pursue freedom, our task is to discover, in company with others, how we might create a better world.

Dialogical Spaces of Mutual Concern

Encouraging the social imagination calls for the creation of social spaces open to dialogue and possibility. The point of "the human conversation" is not just to let everyone have a turn to speak, but to bring multiple voices together as valuable lenses on our shared world.[63] Greene's idea of the common good is

---

60. Greene, *DF,* 124.
61. Greene, *DF,* 123.
62. Greene, *DF,* 116.

63. It is in this context that Greene speaks of the central role to be given to works of art in the conversation. Greene's understanding of the nature and purpose of art is explored in chapter 4.

a deeply relational social vision, "a context of solidarity, a context of shared human stories within a changing human community."[64]

In pursuit of this social vision, education needs to involve teachers and students in a particular kind of conversation. Showing influences from Freire's liberative pedagogy,[65] Greene identifies teaching as "a summons on the part of one incomplete person to other incomplete persons to reach for wholeness."[66] Of particular significance here is Greene's emphasis on mutual conversation,

> the kind of conversation that allows a truly human way of speaking, a being together in a world susceptible to questioning. Each one, including the one who is the teacher, might articulate his or her particular themes of relevance, might speak truthfully and simply about backgrounds and foregrounds, and what it means to be present, what it means to reach out and to question and to learn. It is indeed the case—or it ought to be the case—that formal inquiry, scientific thinking, and the rest are significant to the degree they nourish the human conversation.[67]

Consonant with the emphasis on freedom, and recognizing teachers as themselves in pursuit of wholeness, Greene urges teachers to empower students to make their own choices rather than supposing to choose on their students' behalf:

> Teaching is a question of trying to empower persons to change their own worlds in the light of their desires and their reflections, not to change it for them. The point of it all is for individuals to make sense of their own situations. Their social situations, their root situations have to feed back into their own sense making and their own actions.[68]

Making choices of meaningful action for which a student is personally responsible is, in Greene's understanding, the defining feature of the moral life. Greene does not equate morality with law-keeping or the exercise of virtue. The opposite of moral is not, according to Greene, to be immoral, but amoral, being "totally indifferent, irresponsible, uninvolved," or "nonmoral . . . the kind of behavior that demands no conscious choosing, that

---

64. Greene, *RI*, 62.

65. Freire, *Pedagogy of the Oppressed*; cf Moore, "Conscientization and Christian Education."

66. Greene, *RI*, 26.

67. Greene, *LL*, 69.

68. Ayers & Miller, *A Light in Dark Times*, 2.

is wholly automatic, determined, coerced, or routine."[69] By creating dialogical spaces, teachers challenge students to a more aware, and therefore more moral, kind of life.

In order to sustain this kind of conversation, Greene argues that the plurality that characterizes social spaces needs to acknowledge both equality and distinction. Students and teachers need to have equal regard for one other so that the space between them is truly public, open to equal participation by all. Students and teachers also need to be recognized as having distinct or unique voices to contribute, or else "people would have no need for speech or action to make themselves understood."[70]

The purpose of education is therefore "to discover how to open spaces for persons in their plurality, spaces where they can become different, where they can grow."[71] These spaces are such that persons are free to "appear before one another as who they are and what they can do."[72] Education cannot therefore be reduced to a set of cognitive or practical outcomes. Those kinds of goals will only serve to shut down the sense of personal discovery essential to human identity. Greene urges teachers to explore a wide range of possibilities and be attentive to the many possible "modes of being" open to young people.

Greene wants teachers to ask questions and encourage students to do the same. However, questions are not merely an entree to providing the "correct answers." On the contrary, the very concept of "the answer" is inimical to students constructing their own meaning. Somewhat hyperbolically, Greene argues that "teachers, like their students, have to learn to love the questions, as they come to realize that there can be no final agreements or answers, no final commensurability."[73] Rather than denying an ability to ever make definitive statements, Greene's point is that the process of teaching can never be thought to have reached an "end" when the students have supplied the teacher with "the right answer." Any such "answer" will always prompt a new question, and hence teaching and learning will continually be engaged in ongoing dialogue.

In keeping with Greene's anthropology that regards human consciousness as a never-ending quest, teachers will seek to establish a dialogue that enables students to make imaginative projections as to how they might act in their freedom.

69. Greene, *TS*, 214.
70. Greene, *DF*, 116.
71. Greene, *DF*, 56.
72. Greene, *DF*, 115.
73. Greene, *DF*, 134.

> I hope we can ponder the opening of wider and wider spaces of dialogue, in which diverse students and teachers, empowered to speak in their own voices, reflect together as they try to bring into being an in-between … They may through their coming together constitute a newly human world, one worthy enough and responsive enough to be both durable and open to continual renewal.[74]

Meaningful Action

Wide awake to their agency and responsibility to make sense of their experience, and with their visions enlarged through empathetic dialogue, young people's education in and for freedom is incomplete without the empowerment to act in accord with the choices of meaning they are making. "It seems eminently clear that the freedom of wide-awakeness has to be expressed in intentional action of some kind."[75] The challenge educators face is to teach students to examine what would otherwise be taken for granted, in order that they might begin to name the obstacles to their choices. Having identified obstacles, they can begin to imagine possibilities. From those possibilities they can make choices and act on the basis of those choices to pursue a better world.

Greene's educational philosophy is anchored in the demand for action in the actual locations in which students exist. According to Greene, understanding human freedom requires acknowledging the human capacity for choice as well as the responsibility each person bears for those choices. Human beings are not only condemned to make meaning, but "condemned to action," since the human problem, Greene writes, "is not simply to interpret the world in various ways. The point, as Marx wrote long ago, is to change it."[76] Upon "the existential educator" therefore, Greene impresses the "inescapability of responsibility," affirming that "each person is 'the author' of the situation in which he lives; he gives meaning to his world, but through action, through his project, not by well-meaning thought."[77] Freedom is an ever-present possibility but needs to be continually achieved through the pursuit of concrete action.

With Sartre, Greene describes an "anguish" in pursuing free action:

---

74. Greene, *RI*, 59.
75. Greene, *LL*, 153.
76. Greene, *LL*, 109.
77. Greene, *TS*, 280.

> The person who chooses himself/herself in his/her freedom cannot place the onus on outside forces, on the cause and effect nexus. It is his/her interpretation or reading of the situation that discloses possibility; and yet there is no guarantee that the interpretation is correct. If there is proof to be found, it is only in the action undertaken; and the action itself closes off alternatives.[78]

That is, there is a risk involved in choosing decisive action. Teachers work to enable students to pursue decisive action in the world despite the burden involved. The burden is a personal one: not a general burden of pursuing any kind of action, but the personal burden of pursuing this particular action that I as an individual have chosen to pursue.

No Guarantees

One of the major implications of Greene's pedagogy is that neither educational systems nor individual teachers are able to determine the outcomes of learning. When a person "tries to tell the truth and act on it, there is no predicting what will happen."[79] Thus, even though Greene is optimistic regarding the power of education for promoting social freedom, she recognizes in a number of places that there are no guarantees:

> Given the complexity of our technetronic society, given its hierarchies and its distinctions, we cannot invest all our hopes in education, certainly not in what happens in the schools. But we can try—in whatever educational roles we find ourselves.[80]

> There can be no guarantees, but wide-awakeness can play a part in the process of liberating and arousing, in helping people pose questions with regard to what is oppressive, mindless, and wrong. Surely, it can help people—all kinds of people—make the conscious endeavors needed to elevate their lives . . . "The first thing is not to despair."[81]

> Neither the teachers' colleges nor the schools can change the social order. Neither colleges nor schools can legislate democracy . . . We can at least try to surpass what is insufficient and create conditions where persons of all ages can come together in

78. Greene, *DF*, 5.
79. Greene, *DF*, 58.
80. Greene, *LL*, 19.
81. Greene, *LL*, 51. The final quote is from Albert Camus's essay, "The Almond Trees," 135.

conversation—to choose themselves as outraged and destructive, when they have to, as authentic, passionate, and free.[82]

Greene instructs teachers to create classrooms marked by care and concern so that they might set a table where freedom is invited to sit down. "It remains a matter, for men and women both, to establish a place for freedom in the world of the given—and to do so in concern and with care, so that what is indecent can be transformed and what is unendurable may be overcome."[83] There is no guarantee that students will take up the freedom offered to them, but teachers create the space in the hope that someday someone will.

Implications for Youth Ministry

Holding theological critique to one side for the time being, the following section considers how a church-based youth ministry might be shaped in line with the philosophical foundations and educational principles of Greene's aesthetic pedagogy. As outlined earlier, I am constructing an imagined aesthetic youth ministry as an aid to exploring possible new contributions from Greene's thought for the practice of Christian youth ministry.

In broad terms, AYM could be conceived of as the task of supporting and encouraging young people to make sense of their experience of life in the company of adults who are themselves continuing to construct their understanding of the world and their place in it. Central to this task would be to create social spaces that allow young people to be present to one another in their differences so that they might support one another in the work of meaning-making and performing meaningful action. If youth ministers were to pursue this approach to spiritual formation, they would need to give up both the aim and the desire to control the outcome of young peoples' searches. Youth ministers would instead need to be willing to embrace the unexpected and be open to finding resources for their own ongoing spiritual journey in the emerging spiritual identities of young people.

Process over Outcome

AYM would confront young people with the need, opportunity, and skills for interrogating their experience so that they might be able to make personal commitments of spiritual identity. Mason's research identified most Australian young people as having

82. Greene, *LL*, 71.
83. Greene, *DF,* 86.

no overarching vision, whether religious or secular, inspiring them and shaping their lives, but seemed content to pursue short-term goals like passing exams, getting a job, finding a relationship . . . their view of the world seemed to consist of a collection of fragmentary ideas and values from a wide variety of sources, tentatively held, not necessarily consistent with each other nor put into practice in any planned or regular way.[84]

In such a context, using Greene's language, adult mentors need to move young people to be "wide-awake" to the mystifications that keep them bound in the "taken-for-granted" in both the physical and the spiritual dimensions of life. There is little point presenting young people with dogmatic conclusions and ethical imperatives when they remain asleep to the need for change, let alone the possibility of such.

AYM would concentrate its efforts on helping young people make sense of their own spiritual experience. This is in contrast to statements about the aims of youth ministry that focus on establishing young people as disciples of Christ. Approaching spiritual formation of young people consistent with Greene's pedagogy therefore involves leading them in an act of interpretation in line with Gerkin's model of pastor as "interpretive guide."[85]

Youth leaders therefore could help young people make sense of the "limit experiences" of human life, of "finitude, contingency, mortality, alienation or oppression."[86] Specific to youth ministry, AYM would focus on interpreting the "limit experiences" of identity (who am I?), agency (what do I have to contribute?), and affinity (to whom do I belong?).[87] In Greene's language, each of these concerns is an expression of becoming wide-awake to one's social location.

Instead of naming specific outcomes, therefore, AYM would concentrate on the *process* of spiritual formation over its *content*. In this regard, AYM affirms Andy Root's negative assessment of providing young people with religious knowledge:

> In youth ministry we too often try to provide young people with religious knowledge, asking young people to choose this knowledge over the assertions of the surrounding culture. Then

84. Mason, "Spirituality of Young Australians," 57.

85. Gerkin, *The Living Human Document*. This emphasis on interpretation and meaning-making connects with David Tracy's affirmation that interpretation is central to human life: "To be human is to act reflectively, to decide deliberately, to understand intelligently, to experience fully. Whether we know it or not, to be human is to be a skilled interpreter" (Tracy, *Plurality and Ambiguity*, 9).

86. Tracy, *Analogical Imagination*, 160.

87. Hall, *Adolescence*; Oestreicher, *Youth Ministry 3.0*.

> we judge our ministries by how well our young people are growing, advancing, and preparing to commit themselves to this knowledge. But up against the struggle between possibility and nothingness, such knowledge is of little help, because the cultural assertions have often wrapped themselves around the young person's ontological state. And when our young people give in to the pull of the dominant culture, we find ourselves saying things like, "If only they knew more about the faith or believed it enough!"[88]

AYM would recognize that arming young people with religious knowledge is not sufficient to equip them to face the existential challenge of the "struggle between possibility and nothingness."[89]

Youth leaders in AYM would therefore seek to lead, equip, and accompany young people in developing a critical awareness of their lived experience. Whatever content adult mentors hope to share with young people, whether biblical, theological, and/or ethical, needs to wait until young people are aware of the purpose for which this content is to be used. The simple act of providing religious knowledge will provide only limited help at best to young people immersed in a taken-for-granted cultural story that denies a place to spiritual and/or religious concerns. Equally so, the "taken-for-granted" applies to the all-encompassing Christian piety that prescribes an entire way of life for those young people raised in the church. AYM would regard both versions of inherited spirituality as mystifications requiring critical interrogation before young people are able to make a personal spiritual choice. According to Greene's vision, young people need to be given the skills to interpret their experience in whatever way they decide will make most sense of their world.[90]

Concentrating on process over outcome would require youth leaders to surrender the "illusion of control" that often accompanies teaching.[91] Giving up control does not mean simply recognizing the theological reality that youth leaders are not omnipotent. Rather, AYM requires youth leaders to make a firm commitment of intention to not seek to control the

---

88. Root, *Taking the Cross to Youth Ministry*, 54.

89. Root's phrase comes from Jüngel, (Webster, *Eberhard Jüngel*, 70).

90. Root's "hermeneutic" approach to youth ministry has a narrower focus than what Greene's philosophy would propose. Root's model of ministry as discerning God's continued ministry in the world through Christ, "discerning Christopraxis" (see also Anderson, *The Shape of Practical Theology*), focuses the work of "interpretation" on the task of helping young people discern God's continued ministry in the world so that they might join God's action in the midst of the crisis of possibility and nothingness.

91. Pautz, "Views across the Expanse," 33.

outcome of any teenager's spiritual formation. It is essential, Greene argues, that educators refuse to "control what is discovered as meaningful."[92] Seeking to control what choices a young person makes in their spiritual formation, whether in terms of the convictions they hold, or the actions their convictions lead them to pursue, amounts to a desire to leave young people trapped in someone else's construction of meaning. This is the opposite of the foundational commitments of aesthetic pedagogy. Acknowledging one's lack of control is no bad thing for a youth leader who is either prone to pride at how well she has engineered spiritual outcomes or one prone to despair at how little her efforts seem to have made a difference.

Eschewing control means that AYM would hold a place for young people who are not Christians to be actively involved in Christian youth ministries. There is nothing new in suggesting that not all the members of a Christian youth group will claim personal faith in Christ. The more challenging implication of AYM is that young people who have chosen to not make a commitment to Christian faith would still be regarded as "successful products of" a Christian youth ministry. That is to say, the ministry may result in young people who are critically aware of their social context, who actively pursue personal construction of spiritual convictions, but who choose to pursue a spirituality constructed in ways that are in conflict with traditional Christian belief and practice.

The key observation in AYM is that young people need to be recognized as responsible agents of their own "authoring" of their life story, not seen merely as the recipients of youth ministry. But neither are young people abandoned to bear the sole responsibility for their spiritual formation. Youth ministry needs to be a social space that invites young people together with adult mentors to make meaning of the world.

Dialogical Community

If AYM is to intentionally create space for the freedom of young people to explore and commit to their own constructions of spiritual meaning and purpose, they would need to be places of dialogical community. Critical, therefore, for AYM would be to create social spaces that make room for different perspectives to be openly shared. Moreover, the social spaces of AYM need to be ones that harness different perspectives as necessary resources for constructing meaning. In this light, the individual perspectives that young people bring to the questions of spiritual life become part of the teaching content of the youth ministry. If young people are given more

92. Greene, *RI,* 125.

opportunities to contribute their point of view, the group as a whole will have more options presented to them, options that group members can draw on as they construct meaning for themselves. The common practice of "discussion" in youth ministry becomes retooled for a new purpose. Discussion groups could be more than simply opportunities for young people to interact with predetermined content while a leader gently steers the conversation around to the intended outcome. Rather, a youth ministry discussion could aim for Greene's vision of open-ended dialogue, which opens up more and more possibilities.

AYM could therefore embrace the multi-faith environment as a great asset for spiritual formation rather than an obstacle. Through interfaith dialogue, "Christian students may ask questions of their faith they may not have been inclined to ask before."[93] The social space of AYM would be such that even those young people choosing what the leaders may consider to be "unorthodox" spiritual choices would not only have freedom to express their views but would also be encouraged to voice them in such a way as to contribute to the ongoing dialogue around spiritual things at the center of the ministry. Creating a space where young people are able to share in the religious expressions of other faiths as resources for their own task of identity formation would appear to be particularly relevant for youth ministry conducted in the secular landscape of contemporary Australia. AYM would not be afraid of having non-Christian young people contribute to the ongoing dialogue in the group, since the offering of various perspectives would be regarded as a valuable stimulus for other young people to reflect critically on their own spiritual commitments.

Clearly, therefore, the character of those who teach and lead young people will be critical in constructing the kind of environment required for AYM. As school teachers aim to help children make choices about their own action in the world, Greene notes the kind of teachers needed to shepherd such a task: "teachers as persons able to present themselves as critical thinkers willing to disclose their own principles and their own reasons as well as authentic persons living in the world, persons who are concerned—who care."[94] The same qualities are required of adult mentors of young people in AYM: disciples who are critical thinkers, ready to take responsibility for their own faith choices, pursuing plans of action toward a better future and willing to act in concern and care for the young people entrusted to them by God.

---

93. Kageler, *Youth Ministry in a Multifaith Society*, 153.
94. Greene, *LL*, 48.

Furthermore, if adult mentors are able to embrace the individuality of young people and be open to the variety of ways each will make sense of their world and their place in it, youth leaders would be in a position to recognize the spiritual explorations of young people as gifts from God for the sake of the church. The variety of spiritual commitments and proposals for action generated by the dialogue at the center of an aesthetic youth ministry could become a rich source of inspiration and challenge for adult believers across the church.

Contributions and Questions

In light of Maxine Greene's foundations and aims for aesthetic education, education in and for freedom, I have imagined how a Christian youth ministry might be constructed in line with that vision, that is, an aesthetic youth ministry. AYM would focus on the processes of spiritual formation, seeking to bring young people to critical awareness of their inherited spirituality and creating a social space in which young people would be free to share their emerging spiritual journeys with each other as together they imagine how things might be otherwise both for themselves and for the church. Youth ministry leaders would therefore be willing to recognize their lack of control over what choices a young person might make in relation to their spirituality and would be ready to find in young people partners for their own journey of spiritual exploration and discovery.

What, then, has been gained from this imaginative exercise? The concluding section of this chapter identifies key contributions made by AYM and raises questions that will need to be addressed in the correlative work to come in Part II.

Contributions

AYM offers a valuable reminder of the importance of process in spiritual formation. While questions remain concerning what kind of outcomes might be appropriate to aim for, following Greene's pedagogy highlights the importance of giving teenagers a clear purpose for what the teaching ministry of the youth group is designed to achieve. Youth ministry leaders need to have a clear sense of what they suppose teenagers will do with the resources of the Christian tradition they seek to share. By drawing attention to the importance of process in spiritual formation, reflection on Greene's pedagogy highlights that there is an element of "spiritual skill" involved in religious belief. As Griffiths observes, religious faith is principally and paradigmatically, a skill. It consists essentially in knowing how to do certain sorts of things. Only secondarily, and quite inessentially, does it involve the possession of occurrent or dispositional information.[95]

With Griffiths, youth ministry that is seeking to build young peoples' personal agency in relation to their spiritual lives will benefit from helping them with "know how" rather than simply "knowledge of." That is not to say that theological content can be regarded as inessential to Christian formation,[96] but simply that without the skills of critical awareness and meaning-making, young people will be ill-equipped to engage reflectively with spiritual content.

A second key contribution of aesthetic pedagogy to reflection on youth ministry is the recognition of personal agency in young people as decision makers and meaning makers. Greene's pedagogy foreshadows the affirmations of the Positive Youth Development (PYD) movement that "emphasizes the manifest potentialities rather than the supposed incapacities of young people."[97] Taking a theological perspective on PYD, Wright concludes that youth ministers need to affirm adolescents as made in the image of God *as adolescents*. Young people therefore need to be embraced as full partners in the life of the church, including, Wright argues, "full partnership in the construction of and reflection on theology and theological truths within communities."[98] Greene's optimism for the creativity that young people can bring to a community committed to hearing from voices

---

95. Griffiths, *Religious Reading*, 15. The "certain sorts of things" religious faith involves are specifically those required for giving a "religious account" of life. Three phenomenal properties characterize religious faith: comprehensiveness (that the account "takes account of everything, and that nothing is left unaccounted for by it"), unsurpassability ("the account is not capable of being replaced by or subsumed in a better account of what it accounts for . . . the essential features of the account I offer will not, in my judgment, be changed, surpassed, or superseded"), and centrality ("it must seem to be directly relevant to what you take to be the central questions of your life, the questions around which your life is oriented" (*Religious Reading*, 6–10).

96. Griffiths himself is not suggesting this, since his argument about religious information being inessential concerns the broadly human activity of religious belief rather than the specifics of any particular faith system.

97. Damon, "What is Positive Youth Development," 15. Damon traces the development of PYD through three bodies of research: the first in the 1980s identified "resilience" in children in hostile environments. The second body of research in the 1990s looked beyond children living in hostile environments and identified developmental assets that contribute to positive youth development. The third body of research in the late twentieth century identified positive social behavior in infants, positing that positive social capacities are hardwired in human beings.

98. Wright, "The Kids are Alright," 109.

previously overlooked is a reminder that the teenage spiritual experience could be regarded as a gift to the whole church. This is a corollary of recognizing young people as created in the image of God. They, like any other human person or group of persons, can be a source of God's blessing to other members of the human community. The teenage experience will not always be pleasant or comfortable for older members of the church. So one of a youth minister's responsibilities would be to advocate for teenagers as they seek to bring their experience, in its uniqueness as much as its commonality, to help bring the church more fully under the reign of God.

Finally, AYM also gives a welcome reminder that youth ministry leaders ought not expect to control the outcomes of teenage spiritual formation. This does not mean teenagers should be given liberty to decide and act in any way they see fit. Youth ministry may not need to reject any notion of "outcome" for spiritual formation (a theological concern that I will raise in the questions below), but adult mentors of teenagers will certainly need to enable young people to explore spirituality and to make spiritual choices free from coercion and manipulation.

Questions

Beyond these points of contribution, the correlational dialogue that I am pursuing in this study seeks to respond to the questions raised against Greene's pedagogy from Christian theology, with particular attention to the concerns of the Reformed evangelical tradition of the church. As a dialogue, the correlational work will also engage with questions raised against Christian theology from the perspective of Greene's pedagogy.

Christian theology will be concerned to consider how Greene's concept of freedom (freedom from mystification, freedom to construct meaning, freedom to pursue meaningful action) relates to the theological notion of sin as willful choice of action contrary to the divine will. Christian commentators often critique the kind of personal construction of meaning that Greene advocates as the source of social ills rather than their solution.[99] If God is only made known to human beings through God's own self-revelation, and if the fall has left human beings unable to know God through unaided human capacity, then what place could there be for leaving young people to construct their own meaning in relation to the spiritual world? Theological dialogue on this point picks up on the relationship between traditional and constructivist pedagogy. Christian educators have tended to side-step constructivism because of its roots in

99. Corney, "Assertive Self-Interest."

postmodernism and epistemological relativism.[100] The same concerns appear to be relevant for engaging with Greene's pedagogy.

It might seem therefore that the fundamental assumption of Greene's pedagogy is at odds with the fundamental assumptions of Christian faith. Using Paul's language from Romans 1:22–23, human beings reject the created order given to them by God and, claiming to be wise, presume to take on the task of interpreting life on their own terms. Giving young people freedom to make their own choices and construct their own meaning can sound like just another manifestation of a life turned in upon itself characteristic of human fallenness.[101] Chapter 6 will consider how the invitation to meaning-making relates to the cultural value placed on authenticity, and how both might be reconciled within a Christian theological vision.

Where Christian theology asks what place there is for divine authority in the face of human freedom, Greene's pedagogy responds by asking how human freedom could be preserved in the face of commitments to divine authority? In particular, chapter 6 will grapple with the extent to which Christian youth ministry could legitimately pursue intentional outcomes of spiritual formation. Is the imposition of authoritative norms inimical to the quest for personal construction of meaning, or is there a place for authority in Greene's vision? Must it be the case that pursuing an intended outcome of spiritual formation would be a violation of a young person's freedom? Can a Christian youth ministry aiming for young people to be conformed to the image of Christ truly honor the personal agency of young people to make sense of their own experience? Greene is willing for teachers to engage in dialogue with their students as people of conviction as teachers and learners together "appear before one another and show, in speech and action, who they are and what they can do."[102] Yet what happens when "what Christians are" includes holding to a conversionist piety that regards persuading others to come to faith in Christ not only as an act of obedience to God but as an act of neighborly love?

Summary

In this chapter I have identified the philosophical foundations of Maxine Greene's aesthetic pedagogy in terms of a constructivist ontology, a

---

100. Mitchell, "Truth, Traditional Teaching, and Constructivism."

101. From Luther: "'Scripture' describes man as so curved in upon himself [*incurvatus in se*] that he uses not only physical but even spiritual goods for his own purposes and in all things seeks only himself" (*Works*, vol. 25, 345, see also 291–92).

102. Greene, *RI*, 44.

volitional anthropology, and a dialogical epistemology, each geared toward achieving a social vision of democratic harmony and freedom. Teachers take up these philosophical commitments by moving students to wide-awakeness, to exercise critical judgment to recognize that the world they experience is socially constructed and is therefore open to reconstruction, to being changed. Teachers seek to construct dialogical spaces of mutual concern in which individuals are free to be who they are in the presence of others. Teachers enable young people to draw on the multiple voices and perspectives available to them in the social space in order to make sense of their experience and to pursue meaningful action in their lives.

Shaped by Greene's pedagogical perspective, I proposed an aesthetic youth ministry focusing on the processes of spiritual formation within a dialogical community. This imaginative exercise helped identify the contributions of Greene's pedagogy to how we might shape Christian youth ministry. Aesthetic pedagogy contributes to the practice of youth ministry by highlighting the importance of process in spiritual formation and by emphasizing the agency of young people as decision makers and meaning makers in matters of the spirit. Though adult mentors of young people would have to surrender control over the intended outcomes of these explorations, the variety of approaches to spiritual life by young people could be a rich resource for the spiritual growth of the whole church.

Finally, the need for further theological conversation was identified in relation to two key questions: How can Greene's emphasis on freedom be compatible with divine authority? And how does an assertion of divine authority leave room for human freedom and authenticity? I will return to these critical questions in Part II.

4

Engaging the Arts

THE CENTERPIECE OF GREENE'S pedagogy is close engagement with works of creative art as the primary means by which young people might be moved to wide-awakeness and to take hold of their freedom. Placing interaction with works of art at the heart of all teaching and learning is the outworking of Greene's understanding of aesthetic experience and the nature and function of art. The first section of this chapter outlines key elements of Greene's aesthetic theory upon which the centrality of the arts for teaching and learning is built. The second section identifies how engagement with works of art stimulates critical awareness, supplies symbolic capital for meaning-making, and promotes concrete ways of being in the world. Applying these insights from Greene's educational philosophy to Christian spiritual formation of teenagers in an imagined aesthetic youth ministry focuses in particular on the implications of approaching the Bible in a manner akin to how Greene approaches the arts. If we were to conceive of the Bible as a work of art, how would adult mentors engage young people with the biblical text in order to encourage an "aesthetic moment" that would promote personal transformation? As previously, the chapter concludes by noting contributions and questions to be taken up further in the correlational conversation in Part II.

Art and the Aesthetic Experience

Greene's aesthetic theory begins with the notion of "aesthetic experience," drawn in particular from John Dewey's seminal work, *Art as Experience*.

Aesthetic experience is another way of expressing Greene's goal of wide-awakeness. The connection is amplified in Greene's frequent reference to Dewey's view that the opposite of "esthetic"[1] is "anesthetic."[2] For Greene, "anesthesia implies numbness, an emotional incapacity" that leaves people immobilized and prevented "from questioning, from meeting the challenges of being in and naming and (perhaps) transforming the world."[3] Anesthesia is the opposite of wide-awakeness.

Greene looks to close engagement with the creative arts to wake young people from their anesthetized slumber. The reasoning behind this lies in Greene's understanding of the nature of works of art, and the relationship between the artist, the artwork, and the audience. Greene speaks in two ways of the "human achievement" of works of art.[4] There is the achievement of the artist, and there is the achievement of the audience in conversation with the artist. The artist's intention and the concrete work they produce only comprises part of the nature of "art." The artist's creation remains a privileged object, not yet a "work of art," until that object is engaged with by a human being on their own quest of meaning-making. It is only when privileged objects are brought into transactions with a human consciousness that they take on aesthetic existence:[5]

> Works of art ... must be directly addressed by existing and situated persons, equipped to attend to the qualities of what presents itself to them, to make sense of it in the light of their own lived worlds ... all art forms must be encountered as achievements that can only be brought to significant life when human beings engage with them imaginatively.[6]

---

1. Dewey's spelling.
2. Dewey, *Art as Experience*, 41.
3. Greene, *BG*, x.
4. Greene, *LL*, 163.
5. Greene finds a paradigm for many works of art in Georges Poulet's reflection on the act of reading: "Books are objects. On a table, on bookshelves, in store windows, they wait for someone to come and deliver them from their materiality, from their immobility. When I see them on display, I look at them as I would at animals for sale, kept in little cages, and so obviously hoping for a buyer. For—there is no doubting it—animals do know that their fate depends on a human intervention ... Isn't the same true of books? Made of paper and ink, they lie where they are put, until the moment some one [sic] shows an interest in them. They wait. Are they aware that an act of man might suddenly transform their existence? They appear to be lit up with that hope. Read me, they seem to say. I find it hard to resist their appeal" (Greene, *BG*, 14).
6. Greene, *LL*, 163.

A work of art might "exist" as a physical object, but its "aesthetic existence" is dependent on whether and how that object is used. Artists construct meaning resulting from their own interaction with lived reality. The work produced remains dormant until it is taken up by a human audience who will attend to what is being offered and interact with it in their own task of making meaning up against the concrete demands of their own world.

This view of art reflects Greene's existential philosophy, that knowledge (or meaning) does not exist independently of a knower, or meaning-maker. As a phenomenologist, Greene accepts the existence of artworks as objects of perception, but there is no independent "meaning" of a work of art that resides either in the work itself or in a Platonic world of forms. Rather, knowing and meaning are constructed through the interaction between a human observer and the artwork. The significance of a work of art emerges from the interaction between the form the work takes and the person who interacts with it:

> Significance in art, however found, must be seen as emergent. It is not something buried in a work; it is not something inherent in the subject, distinct from its form. We know that whatever affective meanings we enjoy must be apprehended through and by means of form, as we know that the form must express some effective meanings.[7]

In what follows, I outline three key dimensions of Greene's aesthetic theory arising from this foundational understanding of art. First, "aesthetic experience" expresses the awareness of meaningfulness that characterizes wide-awakeness. Second, works of art arise out of an artist's own aesthetic experience, becoming "privileged objects" particularly intended to spark aesthetic experience in others. Third, by exercising "aesthetic perception," those who engage with a work of art develop the same imaginative capacities needed for meaning-making.

Aesthetic Experience

"Aesthetic experience" (also referred to as "the aesthetic moment") drives the explorations of meaning-making that are at the heart of Greene's aesthetic pedagogy. Greene describes aesthetic experience as an experience of becoming aware of aspects of one's life and existence. The moment of awareness

---

7. Greene, *BG*, 236. Greene's approach to art reflects that of the Romantic Movement, particularly in the way art offers an alternative to traditional religious accounts of transcendence. See Taylor's discussion of the shift in the understanding of art as mimesis to art as creation (*Secular Age*, 352–61).

includes making connections between previously disparate aspects of one's existence; accounting for what had previously been unexplained.

Central to aesthetic experience is drawing the parts of one's life into a more and more meaningful whole. Greene's emphasis on bringing disparate aspects of experience into a unified whole comes from Dewey's account of experience. For Dewey, "an experience" has a unity about it, a bringing together of various elements into something complete, coherent, and whole. The various elements of inchoate experience become meaningful as they are brought together into a meaningful whole where one perceives all the relationships between action and consequences. Dewey names this sense of coherence and wholeness the "aesthetic quality" of an experience. An experience has an aesthetic quality when "its varied parts are linked to one another, and do not merely succeed one another . . . the parts through their experienced linkage move toward a consummation and a close, not merely to cessation in time."[8]

Greene regards a work of art as a "privileged reality" that results from an artist's aesthetic experience which has been embodied in the physical artefact produced. It is this interaction between the real (that which is experienced), the imagined (the meaning constructed) and a return to the real (that which is produced) that gives art potency for promoting new ways of being in the concrete world of lived experience.

Art and the Artist

Rather than being merely mimetic, works of art, in Greene's understanding, are a re-presentation of reality; reality reorganized and reinterpreted. Works of art are neither "the worlds of ordinary reality, of the commonplace" nor "the world of total gossamer or fantasy."[9] Artists, specifically poets, propose a new take on reality when their imagination "transmutes the particulars, changes them, gives them symbolic form."[10] In works of art, the familiar particulars of human experience are invested with new meaning as a result of being located within an imaginative whole. Though it is possible for interaction with the natural world to produce the same aesthetic experience that Greene hopes to engender through interaction with artworks, ordinarily, Greene suggests, we grow so accustomed to what is around us that we need to be jolted out of the familiar and taken for granted. Works of art are created for this very purpose. The potency of

8. Dewey, *Art as Experience*, 57.
9. Greene, *BG*, 35.
10. Greene, "Real Toads," 420.

art lies, therefore, not as representation (simply re-presenting the natural world in durable and portable form) but in transformation, changing the natural form into a newly meaningful whole.

It is this interaction between the world of concrete experience and the realm of imaginative construction that make works of art particularly relevant for achieving Greene's pedagogical aims of wide-awakeness and meaning-making. Drawing on Marianne Moore's poem, "Poetry,"[11] Greene speaks of the way that artists transfigure the familiar by placing "real toads" in "imaginary gardens."[12] Moore shows that poems can be "useful," not as a result of putting "high sounding interpretation" upon them, but because poets are "literalists of / the imagination."[13] Poets "present / for inspection, 'imaginary gardens with real toads in them.'"[14] Moore is asserting that poetry is not simply imaginary with no connection with our lived reality—these are real toads being presented for our inspection. Yet neither is poetry just presenting factual information as in "business documents and / school-books"[15]—the toads are placed in imaginary gardens. The garden is a created environment that brings everyday things into clearer focus and places them in a meaningful whole. Greene says that "the poet's garden may suggest some aesthetic ordering" when particular aspects of the world are "selected by emotions that pulled at them, separated them from the density of things, and made them part of a new order."[16] By so doing, an

---

11. Moore, "Poetry." In the quotations that follow, virgules indicate line breaks.

12. Greene, "Real Toads."

13. Moore, "Poetry." Moore is quoting Yeats who was commenting on Williams Blake and his illustrations to *The Divine Comedy*: "The limitation of his view was from the very intensity of his vision; he was a too literal realist of imagination, as others are of nature; and because he believed that the figures seen by the mind's eye, when exalted by inspiration were 'eternal existences,' symbols of divine essences, he hated every grace of style that might obscure their lineaments" (Moore, "Moore's Notes to *Observations*," 662). Where Yeats sees Blake's literalism as a limitation (resulting from his belief that what he was depicting were eternal and divine), Moore (and with her, Greene) seems to be celebrating the way poets combine the literal with the imaginary.

14. Moore, "Poetry."

15. Moore, "Poetry." Moore is quoting Tolstoy, "Poetry is verse: prose is not verse. Or else poetry is everything with the exception of business documents and school books" (Moore, "Moore's Notes to *Observations*," 662).

16. Greene, "Real Toads," 420. Elsewhere Greene says of poetry, "Each work . . . is a selection from the appearing world . . . The poet is moved to make metaphors when, after exploring and paying imaginative attention to aspects of the phenomenal field (the world as it impinges on his/her consciousness, as it presents itself, as it appears), he/she selects out that which seems to call out to him/her, to hold potential meaning, to give off a kind of light" (Greene, *BG*, 12).

artwork challenges and enables those who engage with it to look at their own experience in a new light.

Interacting with works of art is significant for meaning-making essentially because such interactions are interpersonal connections. "Coming into contact with a work [of art] is like meeting another human being."[17] Works of art therefore provide another voice in the human conversation. This is not just another voice repeating what can be heard elsewhere. A work of art brings an expert voice, a voice of one who is specially tuned to the meaning-making task, who has herself had an experience, and who has been able to express that experience in a concrete artefact. The artist's voice, mediated through a work of art, can then be offered for others' contemplation and interaction.

It is evident, therefore, that Greene recognizes at least some form of artistic intention as being relevant for engagement with works of art. Greene does not presume to say precisely what an author or artist intended, especially for those works where the author is no longer alive to be asked.[18] Nevertheless, Greene does not favor radical postmodern theories of art appreciation that focus exclusively on audience reception and ignore the question of what the artist may have been trying to express. Drawing on Abrams's schema of critical theories of art,[19] Greene recognizes the need for attending to an artwork from all four poles of analysis: universe, artist, work of art, and audience.[20] Such an analysis of art and artists parallels Wolterstorff's distinction between interpreting for "authorial intent" and interpreting for "authorial discourse."[21] In Wolterstorff's terms, a work of art is an intentional action, an act of "discourse," and while audience members may not presume to come to know the artist herself, they can, and ought, aim to understand what the artist said, or is saying, through the work she has constructed.

Audience and Aesthetic Perception

Aesthetic perception is the work undertaken by an audience as they bring the various parts of an artwork together in order to perceive the various elements as a coherent and meaningful whole. An artist has an aesthetic experience that they seek to embody in a creative work. The artist constructs

17. Greene, *BG*, 16.
18. Greene, "Qualitative Research," 71.
19. Abrams, "Orientation of Critical Theories."
20. Greene, *LL*, 175.
21. Wolterstorff, *Divine Discourse*; Wolterstorff, "A Response to Trevor Hart," 340.

the work to have its own unity of meaning. The work of art is offered to others so that, through their interaction with the work, through aesthetic perception, they might come to their own aesthetic experience.

This kind of close engagement with works of art will, Greene argues, exercise the imaginative capacities of noticing and connecting that are necessary for meaning-making:

> Those who can attend to and absorb themselves in particular works of art are more likely to effect connections in their own experience than those who cannot. They are more likely to perceive the shapes of things as they are conscious of them, to pay heed to qualities and appearances ordinarily obscured by the conventional and routine. I believe that teachers can release people for this kind of seeing if we ourselves are able to recover—and help our students to discover—the imaginative mode of awareness that makes paintings available, and poetry, and sculpture, and theatre, and film.[22]

Greene's point here is that it is a deep engagement with art that is required. Teachers need to help students "attend to" and "absorb" art. Art can be "made available" to students, not through cognitive study alone, but through "an imaginative mode of awareness." In so doing students develop their ability to be aware of, and give attention to, those aspects of life that are otherwise hidden from sight, those things which have been taken for granted.[23]

It is important to note that Greene's focus in aesthetic perception is not on interpretation per se, but on meaning-making. "The point is not to prescribe; it is not conclusively to explain. It is to increase the likelihood of people actively engaging with works of art, moving inside them through acts of imagination, achieving them (against their own personal histories) as meaningful."[24] Greene therefore invites students to consider the multiple perspectives through which a work might be viewed in order that "new vantage points, may bring the unseen into visibility, may make the taken-for-granted palpable and strange."[25] The final purpose for interacting with works of art is not to understand art, but to *use* works of art as tools for the personal task of making sense of one's own experience.

---

22. Greene, *LL*, 186.

23. The aesthetic moment does not arise just from observing an artwork as a finished product. Aesthetic cognition, according to Greene, is enhanced by interacting with the artist's processes of construction. I will discuss this further in chapter 5.

24. Greene, "Spaces," 59.

25. Greene, "Qualitative Research," 71–72.

Thus, the way audiences construct their own meaning is connected to, but not limited by, the meaning constructed and proposed by the artist. By engaging with works of art we are given access to various symbol-systems that are made available for our own work of meaning-making. "We learn to make sense, all kinds of sense, but we make the culture's symbol systems our own, including those associated with the arts."[26] The point is not to adopt the meanings constructed by others, but to construct one's own meaning, making use of the artist's construction wherever it is fitting to one's own purposes.

Greene speaks of a "resonance" in literary material that invites audiences into a personal exploration of meaning. Explaining why she makes frequent reference to images drawn from imaginative literature, Greene observes that "literature, unlike documentary material, resonates. That is, the words mean more than they denote, evoking in those willing to pay heed other images, memories, things desired, things lost, things never entirely grasped or understood."[27]

The "resonance" is not merely an echo, but produces new significance when the meaning proposed in the concrete artefact of the work of art comes into conversation with the concrete reality of the audience. The meaning-making that results from interaction with works of art is an experience of engaging in the "intersubjective world," this social space where freedom is promoted and pursued.

Greene provides numerous examples such as this of how meaning arises through experiencing literary art. In this she is not attempting to be a literary critic or an exegete; Greene is a reader, a person engaging in conversation with these authors as she searches for her own interpretation of her world. The principle that arises for how we approach the power of literature is that "ultimately it is the action, exploratory and productive, of the reader which must be emphasized."[28] "Works of art" therefore "function as experiences only when they are viewed as presentations, not representations or revelations or commentaries. They are realizations of certain possibilities in the particulars that compose them."[29]

Because artists take the everyday and refashion it in extraordinary ways, engaging with a work of art offers a new perspective on one's lived experience. "What we have discovered in [works of art] is qualitatively other than the everyday. Being other, offering us new vantage points, it has made

26. Greene, *BG*, 6.
27. Greene, *RI*, 44.
28. Barone, "Maxine Greene," 139.
29. Greene, "Real Toads," 420.

us hear as never before; it has enabled us to see."[30] By offering a new vision of the everyday, artists demonstrate the malleable nature of existence: what we experience is open for interpretation. Here in a work of art is one interpretation of human experience. By interacting with the artwork our senses are awakened such that we might recognize our own experience as open to the same construction of meaning. For example, Greene describes Nathanael Hawthorne's novels as works of art that "consistently mirrored what simple daylight had screened."[31] Though the same sense experience is open to everyone, "simple daylight" has the ability to screen experience from those not accustomed to paying attention. Not so for artists.

Aesthetic perception therefore promotes "thoughtfulness, attentiveness, imaginativeness;" the same values required for social spaces that connect individuals together in their plurality. Nurturing these skills of "aesthetic literacy" will, Greene argues, "liberate students to look through alternative perspectives and take new vantage points on the world," creating the kind of public spaces needed to achieve the social freedom that is at the heart of her educational vision.[32] Greene's desire for "people to choose to appear before one another as the best they know how to be" requires us to engage with one another as persons, as "active, growing beings in mind, centers . . . of valuation, decision and choice."[33] Thoughtfulness, attentiveness, and imaginativeness enable us to recognize others as persons, rather than reducing them to "human resources."

The Means of Aesthetic Pedagogy

Given Greene's assessment of the power of the creative arts for wide-awakeness and meaning-making, it is no surprise that Greene insists on making engagement with the arts central to the school curriculum. Such potency in the creative arts lifts their significance beyond the merely ornamental or decorative. The arts ought not be "easily disposed of as 'frills.'"[34] Neither should the aesthetic experience that interaction with the arts can produce be marginalized as optional. As a moment of recognizing meaningfulness and as a prompt toward personal construction of meaning, aesthetic experiences lie, according to Greene's philosophy, at the heart of what it means to be human. The arts are therefore not merely decorative, an optional

30. Greene, *BG*, 35.
31. *PP*, 71.
32. Greene, "Aesthetic Literacy," 124.
33. Greene, "Spaces," 56–57.
34. Greene, "Aesthetic Literacy," 118.

illustrative addition, or a frivolous hiatus from more serious learning. "They ought to be, if transformative teaching is our concern, a central part of curriculum, wherever it is devised."[35]

Beyond describing works of art as "privileged objects" constructed by artists to give expression to their own aesthetic experience, Greene resists giving a "definition" of art. Given the growing variety of art forms, Greene concludes that it is not possible to establish a definition of art that could give an adequate account of this ever-changing field of human activity.[36] Thus, consonant with Greene's phenomenological philosophy, the apposite question is not what is art, but what does art "do," or, more accurately, what do humans do with art?

Flowing out of the aesthetic theory outlined above, Greene urges teachers to pursue three functions of the arts. First, teachers expose young people to works of art in order to stimulate critical awareness and meaning-making. Second, teachers use works of art as sources of symbolic capital with which students can learn to construct their own meaning of their lived experience. Third, by emphasizing the concrete nature of artworks, teachers urge learners to fulfil imaginative visions through embodied action in the world.

Art Stimulates Critical Awareness

With Dewey, Greene recognizes that the function of art "has always been to break through the crust of conventionalized and routine consciousness."[37] Teachers therefore should expose students to those art objects, whether literary texts, music, painting, or dance, which have particular capacity to move them to wide-awakeness,

> to hear and to see what they would not ordinarily hear and see, to offer visions of consonance and dissonance that are unfamiliar and indeed abnormal, to disclose the incomplete profiles of the world . . . to defamiliarize experience: to begin with the overly familiar and transfigure it into something different enough to make those who are awakened hear and see.[38]

This work of defamiliarization leads teachers to include in their classrooms those works of art that may be unpleasant. Art can often be grim and ugly,

---

35. Greene, *DF*, 131.
36. Greene, "Spaces," 60.
37. Dewey, *The Public and its Problems*, 183.
38. Greene, *DF*, 129. This capacity is not magic, but is open only "when authentically attended to." How one attends authentically to a work of art is the topic of chapter 5.

"images and figures that speak directly to our indignation."[39] The value of art lies not in being pleasant, but in presenting alternate ways of being in the world, constructed by artists and offered for contemplation to those who would pay attention long enough, that their eyes might be opened and their wills moved to pursue change. Wide-awakeness will not come from making life easier for people. Greene illustrates this idea from Kierkegaard's decision to become an author: after witnessing people spending all their time working out how to make life easier, Kierkegaard decided, "with the same humanitarian enthusiasm as the others . . . to create difficulties everywhere."[40] Engaging with works of art creates difficulties that provoke students to face up to existential challenges.

As examples of constructed meaning that are able to break through the taken-for-granted, works of art are therefore able to challenge students to pursue their own work of making sense of their experience. Thinking particularly of motion pictures, Greene speaks of the way works of art move those who engage with them to ask questions of their own lives:

> Engaging with them, the individual gains no factual information. If he is fortunate and knows the stance to take and how to look, he may well see facets of his own experience afresh; he may even reevaluate some of his knowledge. He may be moved to ask the kinds of questions about his condition basic to self-consciousness.[41]

Greene is emphasizing that the power of the creative arts lies not in providing content knowledge ("factual information") but in encouraging and enabling new perspectives that may lead to re-evaluating the meaning or significance of what we have come to know. The kinds of questions that are "basic to self-consciousness" are raised by the disruption and defamiliarization that comes through engaging with the arts.[42] Art functions, Greene argues, "to confront the individual with himself; to stimulate a personal search for patterning and meaning; to open perspectives beyond the everyday."[43] Close interaction with art encourages individuals to do their own work of making meaning of their world. As Barone summarizes, "good literature prompts new imaginings of the ideal and the possible. It can even stir action against the conventional,

39. Greene, *RI*, 143.
40. Greene, *LL*, 161.
41. Greene, *TS*, 16.
42. This is particularly evident in contemporary art, which, "by tampering with inherited conventions" questions "the very idea of art" and thereby forces us "to examine our own preconceptions and expectations" (Greene, *TS*, 12).
43. Greene, *TS*, ii.

the seemingly unquestionable, the tired and 'true.'"[44] Developing abilities of aesthetic perception "liberates students to look through alternative perspectives and take new vantage points on the world."[45]

Art Supplies Symbolic Capital for Meaning-Making

Not only does Greene use creative arts as the stimulus for personal quests of meaning-making, the creative arts also provide the building blocks out of which meaning might be constructed. Greene gives frequent examples of how she herself uses art, particularly literary art, to shape and influence her scholarly work. This incorporation of imaginative writing within educational discourse is regarded as the greatest achievement of Greene's scholarship.[46] Parallel to Greene's practice, via an ever-broadening engagement with the various arts, teachers give their students an expansive and expanding pool of resources from which students will be able to construct their own interpretations and proposals for their lives. Making and attending to artworks offers students "new symbolic languages through which to express themselves."[47]

Greene's frequent use of imaginative literature exemplifies Tania Zittoun's theory of symbolic resources for the task of meaning-making.[48] A symbolic resource is a cultural element being used by someone in a situation beyond the element's immediate cultural use to create an imagined sphere of existence. For example, when Greene takes the image of the noxious cloud in DeLillo's novel, *White Noise,* and uses it to picture the challenge presented to school education by a social world polluted by a cloud of givenness,[49] she is using this element of the novel as a symbolic resource. Teachers enable young people to build their own library of cultural elements that they could use as symbolic resources by exposing them to a variety of works of art.

---

44. Barone, "Maxine Greene," 137.
45. Greene, "Aesthetic Literacy," 124.
46. Barone, "Maxine Greene."
47. Greene, *BG*, 20.
48. Zittoun, *Transitions*; Zittoun, "The Role of Symbolic Resources." Zittoun identifies three independent processes of developmental transition, each with relevant resources to enable successful progress through the transition: The process of identity repositioning relies on social resources; the process of skill and learning acquisition relies on cognitive processes; and the process of meaning-making and the elaboration of emotions relies on symbolic resources (*Transitions*, 65).
49. Greene, *RI*, 45.

Art Promotes Concrete Ways of Being in the World

The physical nature of works of art is critical to Greene's understanding of the value of engaging with art for promoting transformation. Because of Greene's commitment to existential phenomenology, she so emphasizes the concrete reality of lived experience that learning cannot be reduced to trading in abstract concepts. Greene is emphatic that "wide-awakeness has a concreteness, it is related . . . to being in the world."[50] Works of art are particularly beneficial in this regard precisely because of the way they take intangible experiences and convey them in tangible forms. Painters, Greene notes, "make their perceptions real by embodying them in images."[51] Authors in a similar way, having experienced "the shocks of awareness" that come in the midst of life, "put the severed parts together" and "make [the experience] real by putting it into words."[52] Particularly significant for Greene is literary language that works by "embodying (rather than simply conveying) that which is not conceptual" and which is therefore "able to evoke in readers an image that is directly sensed."[53]

Greene therefore argues that "the beholder who knows how to absorb [art] . . . is bound to discover something new about his encounters with reality."[54] "Aesthetic experiences" Greene argues, "provide a ground for the questioning that launches sense-making and the understanding of what

---

50. Greene, *LL*, 163.

51. Greene, *LL*, 185.

52. Greene, *LL*, 185, quoting Virginia Woolf.

53. Barone, "Maxine Greene," 142. For example, the particular contribution of the artistic vision in *Public School and Private Vision* arises from interaction with the concrete reality of schooling in America in contrast to abstract generalizations of policymakers. Greene contrasts the often-competing visions of the "schoolmen" and the "artists" as the "high view" versus the "below view" (*PP*, 4–5). The high view is abstract, reasonable, and pragmatic. From their lofty vantage point, politicians and social reformers look out over the American landscape and construct an education system that will accommodate the needs of the many and serve the nation as a whole. In contrast, the artistic vision arises from below; the below view is individual and concrete. Rubbing shoulders with the personal concerns of individual men and women, these literary artists connect with the actual challenges of American life. Greene insists that both views are necessary in order to gain a full account of experience and adequately discern what she calls "the meaning" of the history of public schools in America. However, despite recognizing the value of both perspectives, Greene chooses to give the position of prominence to the literary viewpoint as a "foil" to the high view. Too much in education has been settled as a result of generalizations without regard for the real concerns of individuals. Greene argues that interaction with the physical artefacts produced by artists will help avoid repeating that mistake.

54. Greene, *TS*, 12.

it is to exist in a world."⁵⁵ Once a person has been grounded in reality through engagement with the arts, they are then able to engage in aspects of analysis or generalization without thinking that such abstractions are accurate pictures of reality.

Granting the Arts their Mystery

The power of the arts to awaken aesthetic experience is all the more effective in Greene's thinking because of their marginal status in contemporary life. Quoting Irish literary critic Denis Donoghue, Greene notes that

> the main text of life [is] the text of need, of food and shelter, of daily preoccupations and jobs, keeping things going. This text is negotiated mostly by convention, routine, habit, duty, we have very little choice in it. So long as we are in this text, we merely coincide with our ordinary selves.⁵⁶

In contrast, the arts operate on the margins of life, in those spaces in our lives that are free from constraints. The "view from the margins" as it were, provides a perspective from which we are better able to recognize and reject the dominating mystifications that make up the taken-for-granted world.

Greene urges teachers, therefore, to "grant the arts their mystery."⁵⁷ Again quoting Donoghue, Greene affirms the Romantic notion that even in a world that has rejected transcendent reality, the arts provide a refuge for our intuition of mystery. That there is something more to life, formerly the preserve of religion, is evident in the creative spaces opened by the arts. Entering those spaces, or allowing those spaces to impinge on the main text of life, usher us into a place of freedom:

> Even in a world most secular, the arts can make a space for our intuition of mystery, which isn't at all the same as saying the arts are a substitute for religion . . . It's enough that the arts have a special care for those feelings and intuitions which otherwise are crowded out in our works and days. With the arts, people can make a space for themselves, and fit it with intimations of freedom and presence.⁵⁸

---

55. Greene, *LL*, 166.
56. Donoghue, *Arts without Mystery*, 129.
57. Greene, "Spaces," 61.
58. Donoghue, *Arts without Mystery*, 129.

Bible Engagement in Aesthetic Youth Ministry

As in chapter 3, the following section imagines the features of a church-based youth ministry constructed according to Greene's educational philosophy. What I am calling aesthetic youth ministry is an exploratory exercise seeking a deeper understanding and appreciation of Greene's pedagogy as worked out in the concrete context of Christian spiritual formation. As previously indicated, theological critique will be suspended for the moment; my sole focus at this stage is on using Greene's perspective to identify fresh ideas and approaches.

At the very least, AYM will bring young people into contact with various forms of creative art in order to move them to wide-awakeness. Engagements with creative art would be acknowledged as an effective way to lead young people to engage fully with life and to thereby open the way for people to engage with spirituality—and with God. The arts function as "means of grace" and "sacramental presence," not in a formal sense of mediating the presence of God, but in

> the capacity to hint at an underlying reality that transcends and grounds our normal, everyday experience . . . by transfiguring and re-ordering the elements of everyday experience in new ways, revealing the depth and profundity that lies beneath the surface.[59]

As engaging with certain works of art develops skills in aesthetic perception anchored in concrete existence, this "aesthetic imagination" can "become means by which we are addressed and engaged fully as spiritually embodied creatures."[60] AYM would guide young people in developing skills in reading various forms of art, not solely for technical insight, but as a stimulus for personal meaning.[61] Given that the history of Western art is dominated by the presentation and exploration of biblical stories and theological themes,[62] AYM would particularly be able to draw on visual art as an avenue into exploring biblical stories and themes with young people.[63]

However, while there is potential for identifying new practices of engagement with the creative arts in Christian youth ministry, this project is primarily concerned with the dynamics of Bible engagement for spiritual formation. The more pertinent question for AYM in this regard is to ask

---

59. Bauer, *Arts Ministry*, 101.
60. Brown, "Ascension," 167.
61. Botton and Armstrong, *Art as Therapy*.
62. Toman et al., *Ars Sacra*.
63. Debray, *New Testament through 100 Masterpieces*; Debray, *Old Testament through 100 Masterpieces*; Rynck, *Understanding Paintings*.

how young people might be led in interaction with the Bible if the Bible were approached in a manner parallel to Greene's conception of creative art. That is to say, if the collection of literature gathered in the Bible were received as the imaginative constructions of literary artists, produced in response to their own spiritual-aesthetic experience, proposing new ways of understanding and being in the world, focused on the concrete demands of lived experience, and intended to spark spiritual-aesthetic experience in those who will attend to these texts, what would the task of Bible engagement for spiritual formation of teenagers look like?

Pursuing Dialogue

Approaching the Bible as a work of art connects with David Tracy's concept of the "religious classic."[64] Tracy posits an analogy between the experience of being "caught up" in a work of art and the recognition of "truth" in those cultural elements named as "classics." Tracy says of the authentic experience of art, "we find ourselves 'caught up' in its world, we are shocked, surprised, challenged by its startling beauty and its recognizable truth, its instinct for the essential."[65] This aesthetic experience (to use Maxine Greene's language) is analogous to the experience of encountering a classic (to use Tracy's language):

> We all find ourselves compelled both to recognize and on occasion to articulate reasons for the recognition that certain expressions of the human spirit so disclose a compelling truth about our lives that we cannot deny them some kind of normative status . . . What we mean by naming certain texts, events, images, rituals, symbols and persons "classics" is that here we recognize nothing less than the disclosure of a reality we cannot but name truth.[66]

With Tracy, AYM could conceive of "the event and person of Jesus Christ" as the Christian classic.[67] The New Testament, being the original response to the Christ event by the early church, becomes, together with the Hebrew Scriptures, the normative expression of how the Christian community experiences that event in the present. Consequently, AYM would not locate the authority of the Bible in extrinsic claims to univocal truth. Rather, as a

64. Tracy, *Analogical Imagination*.
65. Tracy, *Analogical Imagination*, 110.
66. Tracy, *Analogical Imagination*, 108.
67. Tracy, *Analogical Imagination*, 233.

classic, the Bible confronts us with "the force of recognition," that here lies something important, something that makes a difference.[68] On this conception, the Bible would be offered to young people with "a non-authoritarian notion of authority and norm."[69]

AYM would lead young people to interact with the Bible in such a way that would spur them on to ask significant questions of spiritual life and to enter into an open dialogue with others to propose various ways of answering those questions. In this regard, the Bible prompts young people toward personal explorations of meaning. The biblical texts contain examples of how various human beings have sought to make sense of their own experience, and the texts propose concrete ways of responding that are consistent with their interpretation of reality. The various texts of Scripture expose young people to a vast range of human questions and experiences and offer a plurality of ways of making meaning within those contexts. The performative challenge for AYM is to lead young people in dialogue that invites them to an alternative way of seeing and being in the world.

Tracy posits an "excess of meaning" in a classic that "both demands constant interpretation and bears a certain kind of timelessness—namely the timelessness of a classic expression radically rooted in its own historical time and calling to my own historicity."[70] Like every classic, the Bible, so conceived, "contains its own plurality and encourages a pluralism of meanings."[71] Such a pluralism of meanings promotes the kind of dialogue for which Greene advocates. AYM would recognize a plurality of questions to be asked, as well as a plurality of possible interpretations to be made. This does not require youth leaders to give in to relativism, but rather to recognize the possibility of more than one legitimate reading, acknowledging their own thinking as radically finite and situated in their own history.

The kind of dialogue prompted by engaging with the Bible as a "Christian classic" is reflected in the so-called "New Homiletics"[72] which shifts the locus of authority in preaching away from the preacher's interpretation to the way listeners appropriate the text.[73] Because the expectations regarding the structures of youth ministry are largely free from requiring a traditional monological sermon, AYM could focus on actual dialogue with young people in relation to the biblical text. The dialogue in youth ministry

68. Tracy, *Analogical Imagination*, 115–16.
69. Tracy, *Analogical Imagination*, 100.
70. Tracy, *Analogical Imagination*, 102.
71. Tracy, *Analogical Imagination*, 113.
72. Buttrick, *Homiletic*; Craddock, *As One without Authority*.
73. Ringgaard Lorensen, *Dialogical Preaching*, 68.

could lead young people into an "encounter with the text" that is "not simply the content of the tradition, nor an application of that content to present issues," but is rather "the address of God to the hearer who sits before the text open to its becoming the Word of God."[74] In the same way that Greene invites engagement with works of art because of the promise of engaging with the artist and her construal of reality, AYM would invite young people into an engagement with the text of the Bible as a place of possibility; a place where they might confront life's deep existential questions and experience personal encounter with God.

Affirming History

The dialogue around Scripture pursued in AYM would also affirm the concrete nature of the biblical story. In the same way that Greene emphasizes the physical nature of art objects as significant for promoting concrete ways of being in the world, so too the biblical story presents the account of real people who were themselves engaged in the task of constructing meaning from their lived experience of the world. AYM would emphasize the historical reality of the people of Israel, the person of Jesus, and the early Christian church. The Bible does not offer an abstract philosophy, but a human story anchored in time and place.[75]

By emphasizing the historical dimensions of the biblical story and the promotion of concrete ways of being in the world, AYM would help to overcome the kind of disconnect between faith and practice that is evident in the contemporary evangelical church, particularly among young people. Ward argues that in seeking to communicate the faith in the most effective way, "evangelistic practice . . . has generated a radically foreshortened expression of belief that is based around a small number of doctrinal propositions,"[76] Yet, once the "gospel message" is accepted at the point of conversion, the "everyday believing" evidenced among evangelical Christians emphasizes personal experience. Ward argues therefore that "the theological expression of the 'gospel' has become less and less significant to the day to day walk of faith of Christian communities."[77] As evidence of

---

74. Craddock, *As One without Authority*, 114.

75. It is significant that Pontius Pilate is one of the three human persons named in the Apostles' Creed (along with Jesus, and Mary, his mother). Naming Pilate in connection with the crucifixion of Jesus anchors Christian belief in the concrete reality of the Roman Province of Judea from 26–36 CE.

76. Ward, "State of Believing," 10.

77. Ward, "State of Believing," 10.

this, Ward cites the way worship songs are used as a moment of personal divine encounter. Ward's analysis of the theological content of song lyrics concludes that "the more objective doctrine of the evangelical gospel has been largely replaced in the worship songs by the language of relationship and encounter. The Jesus of the Scriptures has become the more intimate but less well defined 'You' of contemporary Worship."[78] The outcome of this "contemporary believing" is that "it is possible for Christians, and indeed Church communities as a whole to believe one thing at an almost theoretical level and then to live their Christian lives in ways that have little or no meaningful connection to these beliefs."[79] The Christian story has become abstracted from concrete experience.

As AYM invites young people to imagine life in the terms offered in the Bible, youth leaders invite young people to engage in lived reality rather than to retreat into some ephemeral spiritual experience. Adapting the language of poet Marianne Moore, the Bible presents to us "real toads" (Israel and the church, pursuing life in this world, "warts and all") set, not in an imaginary garden, but in a transcendent one.[80] As young people engage with this construal of existence, youth leaders in AYM would prompt them to set the concrete details of their own existence in a similarly transcendent context.

Constructing Meaning

Using Zittoun's language of symbolic resources, AYM would recognize the Bible as a potent source of cultural elements that could be used by young people as resources for negotiating meaning amidst the transitions of adolescent life. With Zittoun, AYM would draw attention to the Bible as "an excellent dictionary of possible aspects of human psyche, conduct, and relationships—from the most luminous to the most hideous."[81] Youth ministry conversations therefore would focus on how various biblical texts speak to the whole range of human experience.[82]

In a valuable parallel to the aims of AYM, Zittoun examines the way the Talmud functioned as a symbolic resource for a group of Jewish young people grappling with the experience of leaving Yeshiva in Israel to return

---

78. Ward, "State of Believing," 11.
79. Ward, "State of Believing," 11.
80. Moore, "Poetry."
81. Zittoun, *Transitions*, 174.
82. In chapter 7 I take up Zittoun's reservations concerning the possibility of the Bible being used as a symbolic resource, given its supposed resistance to diverse uses.

to secular university education in Britain.[83] The rupture experienced by the young people in Zittoun's research is somewhat parallel to that experienced by young people as they move between the structured world of church-based youth ministry and day-to-day teenage life, or when they leave secondary school to move into young adult life, "a move from a sphere where internal and external semiotic systems were isomorphic, to a sphere where these are disjoined: religious persons now have to rely on what they had internalized, without any external support."[84]

Though the Yeshiva experience gave this group of young people a strong corpus of texts, rules, and hermeneutic competencies, they did not draw on these religious resources to make sense of their new secular experience. Instead, they mobilized nonreligious cultural elements. The young people appeared to use religious symbolic resources to maintain identities and to develop some skills, but not for constructing meaning. The one sphere of existence (the Yeshiva) did not provide sufficient avenues for bridging to the new sphere of existence (secular university). The young people found themselves in a new secular situation without the "bridge" spheres of existence that could be offered by mediating adults. Zittoun concludes that "uses of symbolic resources require dynamics of social acknowledgement. When these lack, then people cannot mobilize symbolic resources and expertise deeply attached to a specific sphere of experience."[85] That is, young people not only need to be exposed to a variety of cultural elements, they also need to be shown how others have employed such elements as symbolic resources and instructed in how they might do so for themselves.

The implication for AYM is that young people need to be helped to learn how to use various passages of the Bible as symbolic resources by engaging in formative interactions with adult mentors around the meanings given to various cultural elements. As Zittoun argues,

> the transformation of cultural experiences into usable symbolic resources is likely to occur when two persons interact on a regular basis about a symbolic object, and come to an acknowledgement of what that designates (the shared and objective referent) and a mutual acknowledgement of the fact that it does personally mean/feel for each of them (within each person's internal, embodied representational and emotional world).[86]

---

83. Zittoun, "Difficult Secularity."
84. Zittoun, "Difficult Secularity," 66.
85. Zittoun, "Difficult Secularity," 72.
86. Zittoun, "Role of Symbolic Resources," 352.

Thus, in AYM, youth leaders would engage in regular interaction with young people about various passages of the Bible, drawing out the personal meanings and emotional responses evoked for each person involved. Zittoun argues that "cultural experiences are likely to become internalized as symbolic resources if their meaning for a person, their emotional impact, their links to others have been acknowledged and reflected."[87] The same result does not arise from "paradigmatic discourse" that is limited to objective analyses of texts and explanations of their argument. In order to promote the use of the Bible as a symbolic resource for meaning-making, AYM would aim to develop processes of reasoning that are "associative, metaphorical, and emotionally laden."[88] Bible engagement would therefore be less about learning "the right answer" and more about sharing the ideas, connections, impressions, and feelings that a particular passage evokes for leaders and young people.

Contributions and Questions

This chapter has reviewed Greene's aesthetic theory and the potential of engaging with the various arts to stimulate critical awareness, supply symbolic capital for the task of meaning-making, and promote concrete action in the world. Adopting Greene's understanding of the arts and applying those insights to the processes of Christian spiritual formation, I have added to the outline of what could be called an aesthetic youth ministry. Alongside interacting with creative arts in order to move young people to wide-awakeness in the spiritual realm, AYM would approach the Bible as a work of creative art. Youth ministries would aim to create spaces for young people that are conducive to spiritual-aesthetic experience by promoting open discussion about each one's personal sense of spiritual meaning and purpose. Emphasizing the historical locatedness of the biblical story, AYM would urge young people to pursue action in the world that would embody their developing construals of the spiritual life. In this process, AYM would equip young people to use various biblical texts as symbolic resources with which they might construct meaning of their lived experience. Approaching the Bible as a stimulus and a resource for meaning-making promotes the kind of open-ended, intersubjective dialogue that is at the heart of Greene's proposal for an education in and for freedom.

---

87. Zittoun, *Transitions*, 193.
88. Zittoun, *Transitions*, 193.

Contributions

Focusing on processes of Bible engagement, the main contribution of an aesthetic pedagogy for thinking about spiritual formation in youth ministry is its emphasis on the way young people use the Bible over the content that adult mentors might seek to present. In the same way that Greene identifies art by considering what art does over what art is, so too Christian youth ministry can benefit from focusing on what the Bible does rather than what the Bible is; how the Bible is used alongside how the Bible is intended to be used. Conversations around the actual use of Scripture will be more open-ended, calling on adult mentors to have the skills to shepherd a genuine dialogue with young people and to have the confidence that such open-ended conversation will be spiritually productive. Hughes draws a similar conclusion regarding the "micro-climate" for effective Bible engagement among young Australians: "Space must be given for young people to find the relevance of faith for themselves if they are to own it, and this means placing some trust in them and the Holy Spirit in the process of exploration."[89]

Christian youth ministry therefore will draw attention to the practices of ordinary readers, particularly of young readers.[90] Consonant with the recognition of young people as competent to make their own choices in their spiritual lives, reflecting on youth ministry from Greene's perspective challenges youth leaders to develop skills in identifying those ways that young people are using elements of the Bible as symbolic resources in their construction of spiritual meaning. This highlights the responsibility of youth leaders to be champions of young people, affirming and celebrating even the smallest sign of the movement of the Spirit of God in their lives. AYM affirms the need for adult guarantors in a teenager's efforts of Bible engagement. Erikson pointed to the value for adolescents of father figures who become "guarantors of their established identity,"[91] representatives of the adult world who answer the young person's "plea for being recognized as individuals who can be more than they seem to be."[92] Young people not only need adults to model to them practices of Bible engagement, they need adults who will champion young people and their own attempts at Bible engagement.

89. Hughes, "Bible Engagement," 23.

90. Village, "Bible and Ordinary Readers"; Village, *Bible and Lay People*. Perrin and Bielo, *Bible Reading of Young Evangelicals*, has examined the ordinary hermeneutics of young adults in evangelical churches in the UK. A parallel project could be usefully pursued among mid-adolescents.

91. Erikson, *Young Man Luther*, 120.

92. Erikson, "Youth," 13.

Adult mentors need also to encourage and enable young people to propose new and creative ways of living out their spiritual life in the world. The dialogue around spirituality ought not be content with exploring ideas alone, but needs to promote concrete action in the world directed towards realizing an imagined new future. Youth ministries would therefore need to provide opportunities, resources, and support for young people pursuing a great variety of actions in service of their spiritual convictions. Christian youth ministry should not provide young people with a limited number of choices regarding which outcomes they might pursue. Leaders will not only give young people freedom to choose their own spiritual paths, but also give Christian young people the freedom to choose how they will live out their particular life of discipleship: Will they be an evangelist, a children's ministry leader, an artist, a politician? If youth ministry structures are not able to accommodate the faithful imaginings of young people then the structures themselves need to be questioned and reimagined. Christian leaders need to give up what amounts to an arrogant, and ultimately futile, attempt to dictate and curtail how the Spirit of God might move in the children of God.

Questions

At the same time as affirming young peoples' actual use of the Bible, a Reformed evangelical theology will ask how this approach upholds the authority of Scripture if young people are encouraged to read their own meaning into the text rather than reading meaning out of the text. Is aesthetic pedagogy essentially the Bible engagement equivalent of the chaos at the end of Judges 21, when "all the people did what was right in their own eyes"? If the Bible is regarded as an unstructured, directionless conglomeration of cultural elements that needs to be pieced together to construct meaning, then young people are left without an overarching narrative or theological unity to guide their construction. Greene encourages close interaction with the imaginative visions that creative artists bring to the personal quest for meaning while retaining her personal freedom to significantly modify the vision a particular artist brings. James Wallace's *Imaginal Preaching* is an example of unrestrained use of scriptural images, suggesting that Christian preaching can feature "the images of the text while allowing them to be reworked by one's own imagination and amplified by images of one's own experience."[93] Yet, as Pembroke recognizes, "sometimes he allows his imagination to run quite a distance from the text that he is preaching on."[94] Youth ministry in

---

93. Wallace, *Imaginal Preaching*, 3.

94. Pembroke, "Theological Diagnostics," 8. Pembroke refers to a sermon on

Reformed evangelical traditions will require some way of keeping Bible engagement in AYM from running beyond the text.

Meaning-making as Greene proposes it does not sit under the discipline of any external vision of the world. Works of art are enlisted as creative conversation partners, not as normative authorities. What happens to creative conversation if one of the conversation partners is revered as the authoritative word of God? Bible engagement in a Reformed evangelical framework asks how Christian leaders might lead young people to engage with the Bible not only as the impetus for an exploration of meaning, or as the source of the building blocks of meaning, but also as the framework within which meaning is to be constructed. While engagement with the Bible invites imagination akin to the way interaction with a work of art sparks imagination, the exercise of the imagination once sparked needs to be disciplined by a responsible interpretation of the biblical text.

As at the conclusion of chapter 3, we are back to the question of normativity. Is there any room in Greene's aesthetic pedagogy for normative authority to be given to a particular text or set of texts? How might this claim to authority connect with what Greene sees as an essentially free task? Greene's existentialist philosophy asks the pertinent questions: Why accept this authority? What gives the meaning-making of the biblical authors primacy over the meaning-making of individual persons today? Greene speaks of the way that art mediates an interpersonal dialogue between the voice of the artist and the audience. The artist may have an "expert voice" as one adept at constructing a work that can be presented as a meaningful whole, but ultimately the artist is just another voice in the human dialogue. Yet if the Bible is received by an audience as the word of God, such that engaging with the Bible is in some way mediating a dialogue between the hearer and God in which God's voice is given primacy, then that voice cannot be merely placed alongside all other voices.

However, if the Bible is to be regarded as mediating the authoritative voice of God, what room is left for individuals to construct their own meaning of the world in conversation with this text? To assert the doctrine of divine authorship and inspiration of the Bible appears to imply a singular meaning and interpretation that is at odds with Greene's emphasis on the freedom of individuals to use the text in ways that are personally meaningful. AYM would embrace Tracy's proposal of approaching the Bible as a "classic" expression of the spiritual quest in order to accommodate multiple meanings consistent with aesthetic pedagogy. However, such an approach

Matthew 28:1–10 in which the angel rolls away the stone from Jesus' tomb, where Wallace's theme is "The rock is whatever prevents us from entering the tomb, from dying and being buried with Christ" (Wallace, *Imaginal Preaching*, 72).

appears to embrace spiritual quest at the expense of a traditional Reformed doctrine of Scripture. The objective authority of the Bible as divine revelation has been replaced by the subjective experience of "truthfulness." Chapter 7 will reconsider Tracy's proposal from the perspective of the Reformed evangelical theological tradition.

In short, the questions to be taken up in the correlative conversation are: Is there room in an aesthetic pedagogy for a belief in the Bible as a sacred text that mediates the word of God? And, is submission to the meaning constructed in a particular set of texts authored by someone other than oneself (irrespective of whether that other is human or divine) consistent with human dignity and personal freedom as affirmed in aesthetic pedagogy?

Summary

In this chapter I have explored why Greene places engagement with the creative arts at the center of all teaching and learning. The explorations of meaning-making that Greene aims for (discussed in chapter 3) are stimulated by giving young people the opportunity to have the kind of aesthetic experience in which they become aware of meaningful connections between various parts of their lived experience. Such aesthetic experiences, or aesthetic moments, will be prompted by careful interaction with the creative arts. Perceiving an artwork involves the same work of bringing disparate parts into a meaningful whole, as is required for aesthetic experience; and that same activity is required for constructing meaning of one's experience and proposing imaginative projection for the future.

I have argued that, for Greene, art is not defined by what it is but by what it does. Confronted with the artistic construction arising from the artist's own aesthetic experience, those who are willing to engage closely with the work will be stimulated to critical awareness by enabling them to recognize that the world and their place in it can be constructed in different ways. Following the trails of possibility that artists blaze, we are prompted to construct our own understanding and interpretation of our own worlds. And since artistic works are concrete creations in the world, their existence promotes choices that will pursue concrete actions and ways of being in the world. Essentially, works of art are concrete manifestations of the "expert voice" of the artist. Artists are regarded as expert at recognizing the world as constructed and constructible, expert at combining discrete elements together into meaningful wholes, expert at proposing new ways of acting and being in the world. Engaging with art is another dimension of the human dialogue of meaning-making. But given the expert nature of the voice, interacting with the various arts ought not be left as an occasional dalliance, preserved as a luxury privilege, or dismissed as mere decoration. Interaction with the creative arts need to be at the center of all teaching and learning.

Applying Greene's philosophy to the task of Bible engagement in Christian youth ministry would focus attention on processes that enable aesthetic experiences for young people. Not only would an aesthetic youth ministry engage young people with creative art, it would approach the Bible in a similar way. Adult mentors would use various texts of the Bible to demonstrate to young people how other human beings have constructed meaning in such a way that takes account of the spiritual realities of human existence. Adult mentors would use various texts of the Bible to goad young people to undertake their own explorations of meaning and offer the various texts of the Bible as tools with which they might make sense of their world.

Insights from examining Greene's pedagogy helpfully focus attention on how young people use the Bible. Adult mentors need to be quick to identify and celebrate any instance that demonstrates a young person's readiness to use Scripture as a prompt and guide on their journey of making sense of their world. Adult mentors will therefore look for opportunities to share the meanings they find in the Bible with young people. Teaching young people will be less reliant on analysis of texts and explanation of arguments and more directed towards dialogue around the personal impact of texts, and how those texts have been useful for the leader's own construction of meaning.

Along with these contributions, an imagined aesthetic youth ministry also raises questions in light of a commitment to biblical authority. What is there to keep practices of Bible engagement in aesthetic youth ministry from relativistic eisegesis? Can a text, or set of texts such as the Bible, function both as a pool of cultural elements for use as symbolic resources and as a normative authority over the meanings those resources might be used to construct? In Christian spiritual formation, the Bible is not only a prompt and a catalyst toward personal meaning-making, the Bible is also the frame within which personal meaning is constructed. How then might an aesthetic engagement with the Bible be impacted when those who engage with it are like the Thessalonian church, who accepted the apostolic teaching "not as a human word but as what it really is, God's word, which is also at work in you believers" (1 Thess 2:13)?

Before returning to these theological questions in Part II, the next chapter takes up the question of authority in Greene's philosophy where I argue that, despite claims to the contrary, Greene has definite implied authorities at work in her practice. The second section of the chapter will unpack the actual processes involved in aesthetic cognition—the twin tasks of perception and illumination. Once again, the implications of Greene's pedagogy for Christian spiritual formation will be taken up in a proposed aesthetic youth ministry, focusing particularly on the use of imagination in Bible engagement for spiritual formation.

5

Releasing the Imagination

IN THIS CHAPTER I continue my examination of Maxine Greene's aesthetic pedagogy and the implications of her approach for Christian youth ministry by exploring the imagination as the primary method for engaging with the arts and constructing meaning. So far I have identified Greene's pursuit of education "in and for freedom" by means of arousing aesthetic experience through close interaction with works of art. In this chapter I will examine the instructional and reflective processes that Greene proposes in order to develop aesthetic cognition.

Chapter 3 explored Greene's understanding of freedom as the goal of education. Grounded in her commitment to existential phenomenology, the challenge of human life is to make sense of one's lived experience, recognizing what is "real" as constructed and therefore malleable and open to change. Education involves awakening young people to recognize their freedom to construct their own interpretation of their experience and to prompt them to pursue constructions of meaning in company with others in an intersubjective space. In light of Greene's proposal, I imagined an aesthetic youth ministry that would emphasize the freedom of young people to propose and commit to their individual conceptions of spiritual life. Youth ministries shaped in line with Greene's vision would aim to enable young people to recognize their own agency in constructing their personal spirituality. Youth ministries would look to create spaces of dialogical community, emphasizing the processes of spiritual formation over any preconceived outcome of spiritual life.

Chapter 4 explored Greene's commitment to having engagement with creative arts at the center of the school curriculum by examining her understanding of aesthetic experience and what can be accomplished through interacting with the various arts. Works of art have a particular potency in stimulating critical awareness, supplying symbolic capital useful for personal construction of meaning, and promoting concrete ways of being in the world. Applying Greene's approach to the creative arts to the dynamics of Bible engagement in Christian youth ministry, AYM would pursue dialogue with young people around how the text might be used for constructing meaning in relation to the concrete demands of life.

As in chapters 3 and 4, I begin this chapter with an exploration of Greene's philosophical foundations, examining her understanding of the relationship between personal engagement with the arts and the exercise of external authorities, as well as her understanding of the significance of imagination for awareness, empathy, meaning-making, and transformative action. The second section of the chapter turns to examine the processes of aesthetic cognition in Greene's pedagogy, exploring the twin tasks of aesthetic perception and aesthetic illumination. As previously, the chapter concludes with an imagined AYM and notes the contributions made and the questions raised from applying Greene's educational philosophy to Christian ministry with teenagers.

Authority and the Imagination

At first glance, it would appear that talk of authority has no place alongside Greene's emphasis on imaginative interaction with the creative arts. Imagination and creativity are, by definition, generally understood to be the opposite of authority and control. Artists operate beyond the bounds of conventionality by giving free expression to their personal experience of meaning. Indeed, it could be argued that it is necessary for the arts to operate outside of the systems of social control if they are to stimulate the kind of critical awareness of social constructions that Greene proposes.

Greene explicitly rejects the possibility of appealing to any higher authority to supply answers to our personal questions. While others' thinking may provide useful perspectives through which to consider one's own explorations, they will never substitute for the personal work of philosophy:

> Today there are no guides; there is no higher wisdom to be tapped. Yet there are clues to be found by the individual eager to clarify educational concepts and issues. There are vantage points to be taken by the person concerned to gain insight into his situation as an educator in the midst of a problematic world. Of course, it is useful to find out what philosophers of

different orientations have said and how they have thought about such problems as the nature of man, knowledge, truth, reality, value, and all the other perplexities the sciences can never resolve. But the point of finding out is to learn how to engage in philosophic activity oneself.[1]

Greene regards appeals to higher authority (whether philosophical or religious) as comfortable fictions. They may have been attractive in the past because of their offer of certainty, but that sense of certainty conflicts with the way we have come to understand the world in the scientific age. As such, Greene regards appeals to transcendent authority as inimical to free thought:

> Many people . . . cling to the conviction that something in the universe is "higher" and more valuable than the human drama with all its ambiguities and pettiness. They are convinced (sometimes unconsciously) that an ultimate Reality exists, which a perfected rational faculty as well as religious faith can grasp . . . the notion of an ordered, unchanging universe (even if known only "to the spirit") helped people feel at home in the world. Moreover it enabled people to transcend imaginatively; it gratified, and so it persisted . . . But the teacher should recognize this notion as a perfectly adequate way of making sense in classic times but purely fictive now.[2]

In the words of the Humanist Manifesto II, to which Greene was a signatory, religion (at its best) is able to inspire dedication to ethical ideals and to cultivate "moral devotion" and "creative imagination." However, placing "revelation, God, ritual, or creed above human needs and experience does a disservice to the human species."[3] Greene is willing to recognize religious faiths as another one of the distinctive voices speaking in the human conversation, welcoming dialogue among "women and men of all classes, backgrounds, colors, and religious faiths," where each contributes their distinctive perspective to the shared tasks of constructing a common world.[4] However, religious faith will be welcome at the table if, and only if, it makes no claims to holding a position of authority over any other.[5]

---

1. Greene, *TS*, 20–21.
2. Greene, *TS*, 30–31.
3. Kurtz and Wilson, "Humanist manifesto II," 5.
4. Greene, *RI*, 135.
5. Greene's comments welcoming religious faith to the dialogical community of educators made in 1995 are not a winding back of her humanist convictions made in 1973. As human activities, religions contribute to the human conversation, but do not have any greater authority in that conversation than any other voice. Greene's

It is therefore evident that, despite having her own preferences for how one ought to make sense of the world, Greene was not interested in forcing her own meaning on others. Ayers recalls Greene's insistence on students making their own choices, even though she may have preferred them to agree with her own preferences:

> She chastised and prodded herself for our benefit, insisting on our right, indeed our responsibility to choose: "But still, I can't help myself, I wish you would choose Mozart and not rap." Pausing she added, "But maybe rap is better than Kohlberg in raising sharp moral issues."[6]

Without recourse to external authorities, Greene recognizes that moral standards can only be established by mutual consent. Writing in the aftermath of the 1989 Tiananmen Square protests in China, Greene acknowledges that even though many people in the West believed the forcible suppression of the protesters to be "categorically and objectively wrong," she concludes that "we nonetheless knew on some level that the wrongness of it was not, after all, objectively given."[7] In this Greene does not advocate radical moral relativism, but is simply admitting that the human imagination is able to envision Auschwitz as well as Utopia. Yet, rather than finding a place of security and comfort in "some Truth or Good that rests above and beyond us," Greene invites us to

> turn to the articulation and grounding of what we share, affirming that the roots of what we share are in a lived life and hoping, continually hoping, that the plurality can be enlarged, that more people will become willing to choose as absolute the right of human beings to act in their freedom.[8]

That is, the path to a more humane future for Greene does not lie in imposing moral absolutes, nor even of requiring submission to majority opinion. Greene's hope is in the transformative power of the dialogical space. Transformation results not from one person convincing another to change, but from the new imagination generated from collaboration.

Eschewing control of others in favor of promoting free dialogue does not equate to abandoning conviction or giving up the desire to promote

---

conviction remained consistent with the declaration made in 1973: "humans are responsible for what we are or will become. No deity will save us; we must save ourselves" (Kurtz and Wilson, "Humanist Manifesto II," 6).

6. Ayers, "Doing philosophy," 7.
7. Greene, *RI*, 69.
8. Greene, *RI*, 70.

one's chosen vision of the common good. On the contrary, recognizing that no one social vision is self-evident to all, Greene urges teachers to fight for what they hope for, especially in the face of dominant alternative voices. "Teachers will have to be agents of a system of power if they are to pursue this vision for education in the face of inevitable resistance."[9] There is therefore an authority that each individual exercises, yet one that needs to be wielded without any intention to control others.

Choosing Certain Texts

The authority to pursue liberating visions of education that teachers hold will be particularly expressed in the task of selecting which works of art they will present to their students. There are "certain works" which are able to "interrogate their readers and require them to transform ordinary beliefs and expectations,"[10] certain works "that provoke wide-awakeness and an awareness of the quest for meaning . . . works that engage people in posing questions with respect to their own projects, their own life situations . . . [works] likely to move readers to think about their own thinking, to risk examination of what is presupposed or taken for granted, to clarify what is vague or mystifying or obscure."[11] Not everything that is called "art" has the same pedagogical value to stimulate critical awareness.

Greene directs teachers to select those works that can be held up as examples of meaning-making, those which disclose what is otherwise hidden, and those which challenge audiences to action. Greene particularly values "certain signal works of imaginative literature . . . [which] have a peculiar capacity to disclose to modern readers aspects of our own lived worlds."[12] Teachers should choose those works of art that are able to uncover aspects of experience that have been taken for granted.

Imagination

Along with the authority vested in teachers to promote their educational vision, Greene identifies the freedom granted to students through the exercise of their own imagination. Imagination is one of the necessary "spaces" in which education occurs. Along with public and private spaces,

9. Greene, *RI*, 50.
10. Greene, "Qualitative Research," 71.
11. Greene, *LL*, 165.
12. Greene, *LL*, 23.

the imagination opens up "inner spaces . . . when it discloses untapped possibilities."[13] Imagination for Greene is a "way of knowing" that has a legitimate place alongside rationality.[14] Imagination is both a mode of awareness and a tool for constructing meaning out of what is perceived. While Greene discusses the role of the imagination in artistic creation ("the poetic imagination") as well as in both phases of aesthetic cognition, Greene's chief interest is in "the social imagination"—that is, a vision for society of how things could be otherwise; not just an idea, but how a better society might be actually constructed.

Greene's understanding of what the imagination is and what it does follows familiar lines of inquiry into imagination in Western philosophy. As with many other theorists, Greene offers the fundamental definition of imagination as the "ability to make present what is absent, to summon up a condition that is not yet."[15] Drawing largely from Warnock's historical survey from Hume and Kant through to Sartre and Wittgenstein, Greene affirms the necessity of imagination for everyday perceptual experience as well as for interpretation of that experience. Warnock concludes that imagination is

> a power in the human mind which is at work in our everyday perception of the world, and is also at work in our thoughts about what is absent; which enables us to see the world, whether present or absent as significant, and also to present this vision to others, for them to share or reject. And this power, though it gives us "thought-imbued" perception (it "keeps the thoughts alive in the perception"), is not only intellectual. Its impetus comes from the emotions as much as from the reason, from the heart as much as from the head.[16]

The ability to imagine how things look from another person's perspective enables us to recognize what is present in an experience that we would not have identified otherwise. It is this imaginative mode of awareness that is both necessary for, and released by, attending to and absorbing ourselves in works of art.

Making sense of an artwork involves the imaginative work of identifying connections between its various parts. Constructing meaning out of sense experience, whether of an artwork or of life, is one expression of the basic imaginative capacity to make present what is absent. The parts are present, but the connections between the parts, the whole that makes

13. Greene, "Ambiguities of Freedom," 8.
14. Noppe-Brandon and Holzer, "Maxine Greene," 3.
15. Greene, *DF*, 16.
16. Warnock, *Imagination*, 196.

sense of the parts, is not. Each individual has freedom to make their experience meaningful by imagining a whole within which the individual parts will make sense.

Having made us aware of what is present, Greene also affirms the role of the imagination in creating connections between what we have noticed in order to construct meaning out of what we perceive. Continuing the ideas in Wittgenstein[17] and the Gestalt theorists,[18] Greene recognizes the work of imagination to bring a sense of order to our experience, bringing disparate parts together into meaningful wholes. Greene notes that "imagination has long been conceived as a mode of effective relationships, bringing (as Virginia Woolf once put it) 'severed parts together,' making metaphors, creating new integrations and unities."[19] We create connections between different elements of an artwork in order to make sense of what we perceive, and we create connections between the artwork and our own experience as we realize this artwork as meaningful within the concrete demands of our lived experience. The artwork opens new vantage points for us so that as we reconsider our context from this new perspective, "the fragments of the presented world" are "imaginatively transmuted," opening us to "new visions" and "unsuspected experiential possibilities."[20]

This constructive work is also evident in the work of imagination that proposes alternatives for the future. Here we come to the central concept in Greene's use of imagination: looking at the world as if it could be otherwise. It is the imagination that gives rise to "glimpses of possibility, to what is not yet, to what ought to be;"[21] imagination is "the ability to reach beyond what is to what might be or should be, to open the way to the possible."[22] This constructive work is *social* because the concrete world toward which individual imaginations are directed is an unavoidably social world. Recognizing that humans can imagine, and have imagined, terrible things, Greene finds hope in what she calls a "face-to-face morality," which "finds expression in coming towards another person, looking her or him in the eyes, gazing, not simply glancing."[23] What Greene hopes for is not just for people to be able to imagine something different, but something

17. Wittgenstein, *Philosophical Investigations*.
18. Koffka, *Principles of Gestalt Psychology*; Köhler, *Gestalt Psychology*; Wertheimer, "Laws of Organization."
19. Greene, "Aesthetic Literacy," 137.
20. Greene, *LL*, 187.
21. Ayers, "Social Imagination," 321.
22. Greene, "Artistic and Aesthetic," 79.
23. Ayers, "Social Imagination," 322.

better. In line with her social vision, something better means something that enables one to live in the presence of others, as each constructs meaning in a shared intersubjective space.

In summary, Greene draws on the imagination to make sense of an artwork and to make connections between the artist's vision and our lived experience. This kind of aesthetic cognition releases the social imagination that proposes alternative ways of being in the world in pursuit of Greene's democratic vision. Imagination understood this way is central to both phases of aesthetic cognition to which I now turn.

Aesthetic Cognition in Aesthetic Pedagogy

Turning now to the processes involved in aesthetic cognition, this section explores how teachers make aesthetic experience possible, even probable, for young people. In short, aesthetic cognition refers to a certain kind of active, conscious noticing. Greene, following Dewey, uses active language such as "probing," "going out to,"[24] "reaching out toward," "grasping,"[25] and "answering"[26] to describe the conscious engagement with art objects that she envisages. Aesthetic experience, Greene insists, will not be achieved simply by enabling students to be in the presence of works of art; teachers must foster a deep engagement with them, inviting students to achieve works of art as meaningful against the concrete demands of their context.

Fostering the aesthetic cognition required for this work involves the twin processes of perception and illumination. Phase one involves learning the symbol systems of specific art forms so that a work can be read on its own terms. Greene gives various labels to this phase such as "careful noticing," "faithful perceiving," "educated understanding," and "enlightened cherishing."[27] Phase two allows for the moment of illumination, "the savoring in inner time . . . the seeping down."[28]

Aesthetic Perception

To perceive an art object is to recognize what is present in the object and to interpret it on its own terms. This "careful noticing" is a form of study

24. Greene, *BG*, 13.
25. Greene, *RI*, 26; Greene, "Aesthetic Literacy," 116.
26. Greene, *RI*, 30.
27. Greene, *BG*, 31, 45, 58.
28. Greene, *BG*, 31.

in the sense of a sustained and detailed investigation and analysis of an object. Greene follows Dewey in contrasting this kind of noticing with the casual glance given by tourists as they march through an art gallery "with attention called here and there to some high point."[29] Careful noticing takes time and attention.

In order for students to make sense of the whole, teachers need to enable young people to be attentive to the particular qualities of various art forms.[30] Greene speaks of the need to learn the symbol systems involved in art forms in a way that is akin to learning the grammar and vocabulary of a second language. Students need to "have some acquaintance with figurative language in the case of literature, with the distinctively dynamic images created in dance, with tonal structure and sound relations in music, with plastic and pictorial values in painting."[31] There is a cognitive dimension to learning the conventions of the various art forms, but this needs to be joined by an imaginative awareness that views works of art as artists themselves see them. Taking on an artist's perspective opens us to see what would otherwise be overlooked.

While Greene does not permit reading whatever meaning one chooses into a work of art, neither does she welcome a fixed conclusion about what a work of art "means." Greene's emphasis on the interpersonal exchange with the artist responsible for a particular artwork distances her from "radical" reader-response critics, who regard meaning as solely the result of what the reader decides to bring to the text.[32] Greene recognizes the potential to "read-in" meanings and expressions that are irrelevant to a text and warns readers "not to psychologize or over-intellectualize."[33] Conversely, Greene's emphasis on the need for young people to be personally present in their own task of making sense of an artwork for themselves means that aesthetic perception cannot be "packaged or neatly summarized," since "arguments ... come to conclusions. Works of art do not."[34]

29. Dewey, *Art as Experience*, 56.
30. Greene, *BG*, 10.
31. Greene, *LL*, 180.
32. Vanhoozer, *Is There a Meaning?* 29. Greene's position is more in line with "conservative" reader response critics who regard "meaning as the product of the interaction between text and reader," rather than "radical" critics who "tend to give the reader the initiative in putting questions to the text or simply in using the texts for their own aims and purposes."
33. "It would be a waste of energy to seek out Freudian symbols in *A Midsummer Night's Dream*, as it would be a distortion to reject Picasso's minotaur prints because of Picasso's treatment of women" (Greene, *BG*, 40).
34. Greene, *BG*, 41.

Aesthetic perception requires a work of imagination to apprehend a "complex totality" that is presented to us in various distinct sensory images.[35] The imagination grasps a work of art "in its vital fullness and complexity," not simply by successively linking one piece to another like beads on a string, but by "discovering a vision of wholeness in the making of 'incoherent fragments' becoming coherent in dynamic form."[36]

This kind of imaginative awareness will be enhanced by giving students, and teachers, the opportunity to construct works of art for themselves. Echoing Merleau-Ponty's idea of bodily knowing,[37] Greene notes that there is an understanding of art open to us only through physical involvement with the processes of construction of that art form.[38] Simply engaging with information and explanation cannot accomplish what is available in actual engagement with various art forms. This is not to say that teachers or students have to be accomplished in every form of artistic endeavor on offer; but in at least one context they need to know, from the inside, what it is like to create works of art.

Enabling students to explore artistic mediums for themselves gives students and teachers the opportunity to experience what is involved in taking an imaginative idea, giving it concrete form, and offering it to others as a resource for meaningfulness. This actual and personal engagement with art—to work with paint, clay, words, movement—helps students "come to understand, on some level, that visions are made real when they are transformed into perceptual realities and given intelligible form."[39] The point is not to hone young peoples' skills so that they might create a masterpiece, but to provide an experience of the artistic process: "What is important is the effort to define a vision and to work on giving it expression. An understanding of the struggle, a sense of having been inside it even for a moment, cannot but feed into an awareness of the privileged realities artists create."[40]

To perceive well, therefore, is to be personally present rather than distracted or preoccupied with critical concerns. The aim is to be free to "enter the aesthetic space in which the work of art exists."[41] Whatever value exists in theories of art and art criticism, it is not to prescribe the "right" way of interpreting an art form or to offer a definitive explanation. The insights

35. Greene, *BG*, 12.
36. Greene, *BG*, 13.
37. Merleau-Ponty, *Phenomenology*.
38. Greene, *BG*, 10.
39. Greene, *LL*, 187.
40. Greene, *LL*, 187.
41. Greene, *LL*, 164.

gained by critics and theorists through their greater familiarity with certain kinds of artworks are valuable for directing us to pay attention to various aspects of a work that our unaided vision may have overlooked.

> We do not, of course, erase what we have learned about the arts or about ourselves. It is obvious that such learning, when assimilated, enriches our perception and our pleasure; indeed whatever relevant knowledge we have amassed provides more points of contact with any given work[42]

Different modes of criticism are therefore useful as "perspectives" or "lenses" in order to "multiply the ways of seeing or hearing."[43] These multiple perspectives will guide those who are newcomers to an art form and will also enable those who are more experienced to reflect upon the interpretations and verdicts they have come to. The keyword here is guidance: the theoretical perspective can be called on to assist, but should never be allowed to overwhelm or marginalize the personal. Those who are well-versed in critical perspectives face the challenge of not allowing their knowledge of critical theory to detract from their personal encounter with the artwork.

The work of perception, therefore, is both subjective and objective, and cannot be reduced to one or other of these modalities without loss. The personal experience of perceiving an artwork is aided by insights gained from the established norms of interpretation surrounding particular art forms. There is no suggestion that Greene's emphasis on the creative side of perception is a rejection of the cognitive and rational in favor of the subjective and affective. Greene eschews any division being drawn between the artistic-aesthetic on the one hand and the abstract and the cognitive on the other. Greene's choice to promote the contribution of imagination is a desire to redress imbalance rather than to propose an alternative to what she calls, "the traditional modes of sense-making."[44] Rationality, Greene asserts, is grounded in the pre-rational, "what we perceive before we reflect upon it." This "pre-reflective" knowledge then becomes "the launching place of rationality."[45] Subjective discoveries of meaning ground conceptual knowing, but are not sufficient on their own. What Greene calls "nondiscursive insights" have value, such as for heightening motivation, but they need to be joined by "intelligent understanding of phenomena" in order to "equip

---

42. Greene, *BG*, 16.
43. Greene, "Spaces," 59.
44. Greene, *DF*, 127.
45. Greene, *RI*, 53.

human beings for effective functioning in today's society or for transforming what is given 'in the name of a reality to be produced.'"[46]

This, then, is the first half of aesthetic cognition: a cognitive and imaginative awareness of what is present in a work of art. This awareness is a careful noticing that draws on objective norms to guide and inform personal interpretation. Aesthetic perception demands both intentionality and openness, both of which are hindered by laziness on the one hand and conventionality on the other. As Dewey observes,

> the one who is too lazy, idle, or indurated in convention to perform this work will not see or hear. His "appreciation" will be a mixture of scraps of learning with conformity to norms of conventional admiration, with a confused, even if genuine, emotional excitation.[47]

Overcoming lazy and conventional thinking reveals a tension in the work of educators. On the one hand there is a degree of authoritative direction required to challenge laziness; on the other, teachers need to promote students' freedom in order to enable them to resist conventionality.

Aesthetic Illumination

Having noticed what is offered, the second stage of aesthetic cognition is to immerse oneself in what is perceived. This is the work of illumination. Greene says that the work involved in perception ("labelling, categorizing, recognizing") needs to be joined by "a live, aware, reflective transaction, if what presents itself to consciousness is to be realized."[48] Full engagement with works of art involves "moving inside them through acts of imagination" so that within one's own personal history, the work would be "achieved . . . as meaningful."[49] Teachers lead students to become aware of what is being presented to their consciousness; but that which is presented still needs to be "realized" as meaningful within the students' own experience.

The illuminative phase is when we allow our imagination "to play on what we have perceived."[50] This play of imagination is about "encouraging inventiveness, opening up alternative possibilities."[51] In order for us to "be

46. Greene, *TS*, 16.
47. Dewey, *Art as Experience*, 56.
48. Greene, *RI*, 30.
49. Greene, "Spaces," 59.
50. Greene, *BG*, 11.
51. Greene, "Ambiguities of Freedom," 12.

present" to a work of art, we must move beyond attending to the work in *its* concrete reality and bring the work into contact with *our own* reality. The same imaginative capacity that enables artists to create art objects is used in the work of engaging with and responding to art. The imaginative task in aesthetic illumination is itself a constructive activity of making meaning from what is perceived in the work. Having seen what is present to be seen in an artwork, teachers lead students "to see alternatives, to perceive connections, to create new orders."[52]

Greene is following Dewey's connection between the artistic work involved in producing works of art ("the doing") and the aesthetic work of perceiving and enjoying works of art ("the undergoing").[53] Both the artistic and the aesthetic involve bringing together parts into a unifying whole, and both tasks involve creation and perception. The artist creates with the intention of producing something that will be perceived and enjoyed and therefore will herself be a perceiver in the process of creating. Similarly, those who engage with works of art are not passive; they are involved in an act of creation parallel to the work of the artist. Having noticed what is present in the work, the completion of aesthetic experience requires organizing the elements of an artwork into a whole. Both artist and perceiver are involved in an act of abstraction, "extraction of what is significant . . . a gathering together of details and particulars physically scattered into an experienced whole."[54]

Aesthetic illumination seeks to create space for students to bring together the details and particulars of their experience,—of art and of their life—into a meaningful whole.[55] As noted earlier, there are no guarantees that students will have the kind of aesthetic experience that will move them to take hold of their freedom to make new sense of their world and actively pursue alternative ways of being. Greene acknowledges the "emancipatory potential" of the arts, yet concedes that they "cannot be counted on to ensure an education for freedom."[56] Nevertheless, she holds to the promise that art forms hold an ever-present possibility. Therefore, all that is open for teachers is to try to create situations that make aesthetic illumination more likely; situations that give space for imaginative engagement to

---

52. Greene, *BG*, 32.

53. Dewey, *Art as Experience*, 50.

54. Dewey contrasts perception with recognition. "Bare recognition" takes observations of something and uses them for some other purpose. Perception remains with what is present in the experience and works to bring the elements together. What Dewey names "recognition" is parallel in some ways to what Greene names "perception;" and Dewey's "perception" refers to Greene's perception and illumination.

55. Dewey, *Art as Experience*, 60.

56. Greene, *DF*, 131.

occur. There is a sense of surprise that results from an imaginative engagement that enables students to see things "not as they are." Greene desires to "create more situations in my classroom in which this sort of surprise became palpable—in which persons could truly see alternatives, perceive connections, create new orders."[57] That is, not only does Greene aim for classrooms that make imaginative engagement possible; such engagement needs to be made plain for others to see.[58]

Certain behavioral norms are needed for the kinds of teaching spaces Greene envisages. Mentioned in various places, the norms Greene affirms relate to personal reflection, communal interaction, and sufficient time to accomplish them both. Norms of personal reflection include "thoughtfulness, attentiveness, imaginativeness,"[59] together with time for "privacy, for silences."[60] Yet, because this personal work of meaning-making can only take place in the intersubjective space, the teaching space needs also to be characterized by communal interaction; spaces where persons come together in their diversity.

For all this to occur, along with a certain quality, the teaching spaces Greene envisions also call for a quantity of time. The activities of thought and reflection involved in aesthetic illumination can neither be hurried nor scheduled: "clearly we cannot make that happen; nor can we intrude when people are becoming aware in this way."[61] Whatever "space" aesthetic education functions in, it needs to be an open space that gives time for students to question and choose for themselves. "We can no more institute an aesthetic experience in another person than we can 'learn' another human being. We have to appeal to people's capacities for 'choice and valuation,' to their imaginative capacities, to their ability to take initiatives and attend actively."[62] An outcome that is so dependent on individual choice cannot be tightly scheduled.

---

57. Greene, *BG*, 32.

58. The pedagogical value of making the processes of engagement evident to others is affirmed in Ritchhart et al., *Making Thinking Visible*.

59. Greene, "Spaces," 57.

60. Greene, *BG*, 32. Classrooms marked by such values are the antithesis of the IRF pattern of teacher Initiation, student Response, teacher Feedback (Mehan, *Learning Lessons*; Sinclair and Coulthard, *Analysis of Discourse*). This reflects Greene's emphasis on the freedom and responsibility of the individual to construct their own meaning of their world and their part in it.

61. Greene, *BG*, 32.

62. Greene, "Spaces," 60.

Authority and Imagination in Aesthetic Youth Ministry

How might the activity of Bible engagement in Christian youth ministry be conceived in line with Greene's methodological principles? Taking what Greene says about aesthetic cognition in relation to works of art and applying it without theological critique to how adult mentors lead teenagers to engage with the Bible in Christian youth ministry suggests five key tasks of Bible engagement in youth ministry: selecting biblical texts for aesthetic contemplation, offering the gospel as a possibility for meaning-making, instructing young people in basic skills of biblical hermeneutics, inviting young people to active experimentation with biblical forms of meaning-making, and allowing time and space for illumination.

Selection

In the same way that Greene draws from a particular set of artworks to both defend and illustrate her educational philosophy, so too AYM would openly draw from the biblical canon to defend and illustrate the processes and goals of Christian spiritual formation. The Bible would be regarded as the main resource for the ongoing work of making sense of our experience of life. This idea recalls Griffiths's characterization of the Bible as "a stable and vastly rich resource, one that yields meaning, suggestions (or imperatives) for action, matter for aesthetic wonder, and much else."[63]

There is no qualitative difference between a Christian educator choosing the Bible as the central work of literary art with which to engage their students and Greene's choice to make repeated reference to Camus's *The Plague*, De Lillo's *White Noise*, Flaubert's *Madame Bovary*, and Melville's *Moby Dick*. In the same way that Greene draws on a wide, and ever-widening, collection of artworks while also holding to a familiar core of "signal works,"[64] Christian educators could draw on all manner of works of art that connect in some way with a Christian social imaginary alongside returning again and again to the Bible as the central text of Christian spiritual formation.

If the Bible were to be regarded as a rich resource for meaning-making, AYM would seek to expose young people to all that the Bible has to offer. Even if young people do not yet have full understanding of what they read, holding the Bible in aesthetic space urges youth leaders to follow Augustine's advice for the proper interpretation of the Bible: "The most skilful

---

63. Griffiths, *Religious Reading*, 41.
64. Greene, *LL*, 23.

interpreter of the sacred writings, then, will be he who in the first place has read them all and retained them in his knowledge, if not yet with full understanding, still with such knowledge as reading gives."[65] Brueggemann urges pastors to resist the urge to explain biblical texts in such a way that makes it unnecessary for hearers to do their own work of interpretation and meaning-making. Instead of being "contextualized, placed, or interrelated," Brueggemann argues that texts "need only to be voiced," and that "when voiced, they linger for a while, with power, in our imagination."[66] AYM would aim to read all of the Bible with young people and be content to leave the text to play in their imaginations.

In its aim to expose young people to all of the Bible, AYM would therefore be willing to expose young people to difficult aspects of Scripture along with those that are more readily applicable to contemporary life. As Brueggemann has argued, the church engages with the biblical texts with a degree of "unguardedness" that extends also to those texts which we might otherwise find objectionable, texts we do not like or with which we disagree, because "they are our texts and must be voiced."[67] Indeed "the parts of the Bible that 'do not fit' creedal theology or rational criticism may turn out to be the most important,"[68] since, as Greene argues, the marginalized and overlooked voices are often the doorway to critical awareness and revisioning of dominating imaginations.

In AYM, adult mentors could also direct young peoples' attention to certain biblical texts that seem to be specially geared toward sparking critical thinking and meaning-making. Books such as Psalms and Revelation could be considered particularly suited to prompting the goals of critical awareness and imaginative construction. Brueggemann, for example, advocates using the psalms in order to make sense of the reality of our lived experience.[69] The work involved in praying the psalms calls for an interplay between the words of Scripture and our experience of life.[70] The psalms' expression of the human experiences of disorientation and reorientation connect with the "times when the most elemental and raw human issues are in play."[71] Of all the stages of human life, adolescence is certainly one that brings elemental and raw human

---

65. Augustine, *On Christian Doctrine*, 2.12.
66. Brueggemann, *Texts Under Negotiation*, 61.
67. Brueggemann, *Texts Under Negotiation*, 71.
68. Brueggemann, *Texts Under Negotiation*, 59.
69. Brueggemann, *Praying*.
70. Note Brueggemann's interest in "praying" the psalms rather than on understanding or interpreting them.
71. Brueggemann, "Psalms," 5.

issues to the fore. In such circumstances, AYM would draw on the "rich array of language" in Psalms as "not an exegetical problem to be solved" but as resource for meaning-making by letting "the impressionistic speech touch the particular circumstance" that young people might be facing.[72] In a similar way, Bauckham describes the purpose of the book of Revelation in terms that parallel Greene's aims and methods:

> One of the functions of Revelation is to purge and refurbish the Christian imagination. It tackles people's imaginative response to the world, which is at least as deep and influential as their intellectual convictions. It recognizes the way a dominant culture, with its images and ideals, constructs the world for us, so that we perceive and respond to the world on its terms. Moreover, it unmasks the dominant construction of the world as an ideology of the powerful which serves to maintain their power. In its place, Revelation offers a different way of perceiving the world which leads people to resist and to challenge the effects of the dominant ideology.[73]

In AYM, the book of Revelation would be particularly valuable as a resource for stimulating critical awareness and providing an alternative way of construing present experience. Such construals of human life would not be presented to young people as an authoritative assertion of how things must be interpreted, but rather as evidence that alternative constructions are possible and as an option for how they might choose to make sense of their own lives.

Offer

For AYM to be consistent with Greene's rejection of external authorities and norms, Bible engagement would need to be framed as offering young people a possible rather than a necessary framework for their own construction of meaning. Greene argues that "the disciplines, the organized knowledge structures ought to be offered as possibilities to individual participants, each with the capacity to generate structures that relate to his or her concerns, that clarify what he or she wants to say."[74] In line with Greene's pedagogy, adult mentors in AYM would change the tone of their teaching of the Bible from declaring what is to offering what could be.

---

72. Brueggemann, "Psalms," 8.
73. Bauckham, *Revelation*, 159.
74. Greene, *LL*, 69.

Shifting from declaration to offer is a pedagogical move, not a doctrinal one. Adult mentors do not need to back-pedal on their personal convictions about the authority of the Bible, but in order to honor and to engage young peoples' agency in spiritual life, the biblical world is offered as one way of naming and constructing their experience.

This change in pedagogical tone opens a way for AYM to connect with a group of young people who are each at different stages in negotiating their religious and personal identities. Despite outward labels, youth groups are made up of some young people who confidently identify as Christians, some who don't, some who did, and some who are not at all sure. Yet all of them face the same developmental challenge of exploring and choosing from possible life stories. All of the young people involved in a Christian youth ministry will be facing the challenge of constructing their own way of making sense of their world, whether they have arrived at that task from being raised in a family with strong Christian commitment or not.

Applied to Bible engagement, when leaders declare biblical teachings as what is, the only requirements placed on young people are to understand what is being declared and to choose whether or not they agree, to choose whether they are *in* or *out*. However, Greene argues that offering a binary choice to young people does not inspire the search necessary for learning and removes freedom by "narrowing the space in which they could choose."[75] If Greene is correct, by presenting young people with a simple declaration of "truth" no search is necessary, and only a narrow space for choice is provided. In AYM, offering the gospel as a possible resource for constructing meaning would enable leaders to invite young people on a search that could include considering how this story might be used to construct an alternative interpretation of reality that could transform their lives.

AYM therefore affirms the value of imagination for apologetics evident in the writings of C. S. Lewis. The lesson we may learn from Lewis's approach is that apologetics doesn't need to rely only on deductive argument "but can be construed and presented as an invitation to step into the Christian way of seeing things, and explore how things look when seen from its standpoint."[76] AYM invites young people to "try seeing things this way," asking whether a Christian interpretation of their experience brings things into sharper focus than alternative lenses through which they might imagine the world.

Approaching Bible engagement as offer rather than command would also reframe the way AYM conceives of evangelism and conversion. Greene

---

75. Greene, *DF*, 60.
76. McGrath, "An Enhanced Vision," 416.

would not condone notions of conversion that are grounded in a power imbalance between "the converter" and "the converted." The inherent inequality in such a relationship is the opposite of the dialogical social space that Greene envisages. In AYM therefore, evangelism would focus on offering young people a clear and engaging presentation of the gospel as a possible way of making sense of the world and their place in it. Rather than leaving young people with a choice to make in response to the message presented, AYM would place a priority on adult mentors entering a dialogical space with young people in which adults are open to being shaped by the contributions of teenagers as much as teenagers are open to being shaped by the message their leaders bring. AYM would seek to create a space that looks to enable mutual conversion, as all participants, adult mentors and teenagers alike, are open to new possibilities that arise from their collaboration.

Instruction

The work of aesthetic perception in Greene's theory recognizes the "study" involved to equip young people to read the Bible on its own terms. In the same way that there are certain symbol systems students need to know in order to interact meaningfully with various works of art, there are also basic tools of interpretation that will enable young people to begin to make sense of the Bible for themselves. Providing young people with exegetical tools (such as understanding genre, the conventions of Hebrew poetry, the historical context of the Roman world of the first century) would be important in order to enable them to notice what is there to be noticed in Scripture.

AYM would therefore acknowledge that adult mentors each bring a particular interpretive key to their reading of Scripture. This, Greene would argue, is a necessary aspect of making sense of a work of art. When adult mentors offer to young people a reading of a text or set of texts from the Bible they do so by drawing texts together according to a particular paradigm. AYM is conscious of the presence of various interpretative paradigms through which someone might make sense of the Bible. The point is not to attempt to read the Bible without recourse to a particular paradigm, since to attempt to do so contradicts the task of making sense of the whole. Rather, AYM would be alert to alternative ways to construe the various parts of the text, and invite a dialogue about how different interpretive approaches are more or less useful for shedding light on the task of making sense of our lived experience.

This kind of instruction in interpretive skills functions in AYM as the entry point to an open space for exploration towards making meaning.

Mirroring the emphasis on the processes of spiritual formation over any predetermined outcome, Bible engagement in AYM would place its emphasis on equipping young people with certain skills for reading the Bible over presenting a set of theological "answers."

Experimentation

In order to help young people recognize how various texts of the Bible can be used to construct meaning, AYM could direct adult mentors to find activities that enable young people to write "biblical texts" for themselves. For example, in order to enter into the way the psalms make sense of the experience of suffering, young people could be invited to write their own psalms of lament. Kenda Dean offers an example of how this kind of exercise enabled a group of young people to sense God's presence and strengthened their feeling of belonging to the church community.[77] In Greene's language, these young people experienced an imaginative awareness of what is offered in the psalms of Scripture. Were young people to have an experience of writing their own psalms of lament, they would be invited into an empathetic apprehension of Scripture and thereby be offered a biblically shaped means of responding to their own feelings of anger and complaint. Similar activities could involve inviting young people to write a psalm of praise or thanksgiving, to write a letter to the church in the form of a New Testament epistle, or to express a prophetic oracle in response to a current social issue.

Another imaginative practice that has been proposed for Bible engagement with young people is the writing of biblical fanfiction.[78] Fanfiction are "stories produced by fans based on plot lines and characters from either a single source text or else a 'canon' of works."[79] Popular among adolescents, fanfiction is a contemporary form of revisionist literature with a strong communal element enabled in particular through various avenues of online communication and interaction.[80] Valler sees precedent for biblical fanfiction in the Jewish practice of midrash and proposes encouraging young people to offer their own midrashim on the Bible.[81] Biblical

---

77. Dean, *Practicing Passion*, 216–20.
78. Valler, *Why Jesus Was so into Fanfiction*.
79. Thomas, "What Is Fanfiction?" 1.
80. Hellekson and Busse, *Fan fiction*, 13.

81. Midrash can refer to a specific literary genre or to a general interpretive technique (Bock and Cunningham, "Is Matthew Midrash?"). Following Gundry's argument that the Gospel according to Matthew is a midrash on the Gospel according to Mark (Gundry, *Matthew*), Valler uses the term to mean reworking textual traditions to construct new meaning relevant to a contemporary audience. Gundry's proposal has

fanfiction can function, like midrash, as a way of giving ancient texts new life for a contemporary audience. As producers, not just consumers, of texts, writers of fanfiction explore, remix and reinterpret existing stories.[82] With Valler, Barenblat also likens fanfiction to the Jewish tradition of midrash and notes various ways that a source text is transformed in meaningful ways.[83] Fanfiction can explore what characters are thinking or feeling in a particular scene, speculate on what might have happened prior to or what might happen following a scene, close gaps in the story, explore loopholes in the plot, highlight marginalized voices and perspectives, and examine the story through new lenses to add new ideas or highlight hidden themes. In fanfiction, readers are themselves engaging with the physical processes of writing, constructing new meaning as they do so. Writing biblical fanfiction could enable young people to take the imaginative journey into the biblical world where they are free to explore the issues and challenges that confront them and, in the process, to construct their own meanings and make their own proposals for action.

In any activity of experimentation, AYM would not focus on the quality of the product, but rather recognize how the experience might promote empathetic awareness in young people. In addition, the aim would not be to replace the biblical text with a young person's own creation, but rather to use the experience of experimenting with creating Bible-like texts to help a young person become more aware of what the biblical text offers them. With such empathetic awareness, the text would no longer be merely an object of study but would become a valuable resource for personal meaning-making.

---

met with considerable opposition in New Testament studies. In particular, the question of historicity of the Gospel narratives is not insignificant for central aspects of the Christian story. In Midrash, whether or not these events actually occurred becomes a secondary, if not entirely unnecessary, question. Given the central concern for historicity in the early Christian preaching (Luke 1:1–2; 1 Cor 15:14; 1 John 1:1–3) it is unlikely that the Gospel writers would include midrashic invention in their accounts of Jesus' life (Moo, "Matthew and Midrash"); This does not necessarily undermine the value of fanfiction as a useful form of Bible engagement for young people. It is sufficient to recognize the value of midrash as an interpretive method used in human history without needing to justify it as a Christian practice from New Testament precedent.

82. Fanfiction communities are numerous and diverse. In February 2017, the largest online fanfiction community (fanfiction.net) listed 759,000 Harry Potter stories, 219,000 Twilight stories, 4,600 on *Les Misérables*, and 4,100 on *Pride and Prejudice*. The Bible makes it into the top thirty books with 4,000 fanfiction stories.

83. Barenblat, "Transformative Work"; Derecho, "Archontic Literature."

Illumination

Moving to aesthetic illumination, AYM calls for time and space to be set aside to allow young people to immerse themselves imaginatively in what they have perceived in the Bible. Practices of contemplation, meditation, and reflection affirmed in the contemplative spiritual tradition will be useful for youth ministry in this regard.[84] One such approach pursued with children is Godly Play. Building on the educational theory of Maria Montessori, Berriman's approach creates worship environments for children to explore faith and spiritual experience through wonder and play.[85] Particularly relevant for Greene's approach are the practices of posing "I wonder" questions that open a space for young people to bring their own interpretation and response to God's word.[86] AYM would also provide silent space for young people to choose how they will respond to the biblical story being presented.

One way to foster illumination in AYM would be to encourage young people to memorize biblical texts. Griffiths identifies memorized texts and memorial recall as the ideal mode of religious reading. Committing a text to memory will be deemed worthwhile if the text is recognized as a work "whose potential for being understood and used is both inexhaustible and unconventional, intrinsic to it and endlessly extractable from it."[87] Through memorization, Griffiths argues, religious readers become "textualized" and an "embodiment of the work."[88] Having committed elements of the text to memory, both the specific words of the Bible and the themes derived from them can be readily drawn from memory, reflected upon, and incorporated into a reader's own construction of meaning.

The widespread practice of leading young people in discussion and interaction in Christian youth ministry[89] might seem to meet Greene's focus on creating dialogical spaces that enable illumination. However, for many young people, times of so-called dialogue often involve "a great deal of

---

84. Dean and Foster, *The Godbearing Life*; Yaconelli, *Contemplative Youth Ministry*.

85. Berriman, *Godly Play*; Berriman, *Teaching Godly Play*. Despite Montessori's significant impact on education in the United States of America and their shared concerns, I have not found any indication that Greene interacted with Montessori's educational theory. Greene's discussion of the ideals that have informed American education in *Public School and Private Vision* has no reference to Montessori. This may stem from Greene's connection with Dewey and the critique of Montessori's methods from Dewey's disciple, William Kilpatrick (Beck, "Kilpatrick's Critique"; Kilpatrick, *The Montessori System*; Thayer-Bacon, "Maria Montessori").

86. Hoggarth, *Seed and Soil*.

87. Griffiths, *Religious Reading*, 46.

88. Griffiths, *Religious Reading*, 46.

89. See Morris and Morris, *Leading Better Bible Studies*.

talking by an adult leader and very little talking by youth."⁹⁰ Greene's use of dialogue as a space for personal reflection and imaginative discovery pushes beyond using discussions to increase levels of student interaction around a topic set by the adult leaders. AYM would urge youth ministers to invite young people into genuine dialogue grounded in Buber's "I-thou" relationships.⁹¹ In place of "a time to talk back and forth" (the characteristic of an I-it conversation, focused in things rather than people), "reflecting with the thou requires . . . sharing and listening" such that "the small group begins to share its stories in a nonjudgmental environment."⁹² I-thou conversation honors the freedom of each member to contribute to the dialogue, creating the environment for transformation that Greene envisages.

Contributions and Questions

This chapter has outlined the twin processes of aesthetic cognition: perception and illumination. I have demonstrated how Greene's pedagogy affirms a teacher's authority to pursue their chosen educational vision and affirms students' freedom through identifying the centrality of imagination in aesthetic cognition. Applying Greene's theory of aesthetic cognition to Bible engagement in Christian spiritual formation of teenagers, I have developed further what I have named an aesthetic youth ministry. AYM chooses to place engagement with the Bible at the center of all its processes of spiritual formation. Adult mentors offer the world constructed in the Bible as a possibility of meaning, leaving young people with the freedom to decide whether they might make that meaning their own. AYM gives young people sufficient instruction in tools of biblical exegesis and hermeneutics so that they might be able to read the Bible for themselves and begin to pose their own questions of, and in response to, the text. Included in learning how the biblical text "works" would be opportunities for young people to construct forms of biblical texts for themselves—to write their own laments, to create biblical fanfiction. In addition to these activities that foster careful noticing, AYM leaves sufficient time and space for the imaginative illumination that leads to transformation.

---

90. Arzola, *Prophetic Youth Ministry*, 60.
91. Arzola, *Prophetic Youth Ministry*, 57; Buber, *I and Thou*.
92. Arzola, *Prophetic Youth Ministry*, 59.

Contributions

AYM makes a significant contribution to the practice of spiritual formation in youth ministry by framing a way of holding instruction about what the Bible is together with personal engagement with how the Bible might be used. AYM does more than propose a simplistic "balance" between the two, proposing instead a pedagogical ordering and intention for each aspect of Bible engagement. AYM highlights the ultimate purpose of Bible engagement in Christian youth ministry: to enable teenagers to draw on the biblical text as the norm and guide for their own spiritual life. The aim of spiritual formation of teenagers is personal illumination, and instruction in biblical literacy is a necessary means to achieving that aim. AYM recognizes that while the illumination that leads to transformation can neither be predicted nor controlled, it is still possible to develop the capacity to notice what is necessary for such illumination. Youth ministries need to provide young people with sufficient time and space in which they might experience transformative illumination and imagine new ways of being in the world. Yet in order to make such experiences possible, young people also need to be given adequate familiarity with the biblical text and be equipped with basic skills for how the Bible can be used to construct meaning of contemporary life. The key however is to recognize that instruction regarding the nature of the Bible and principles of interpretation is not the sum-total of spiritual formation, nor even its main emphasis. Objective instruction is preparatory for subjective engagement.[93]

AYM also contributes a reminder of the dignity and agency of young people as able participants in the human conversation. This recognition challenges youth ministers to examine how they conceive of and approach evangelism and apologetics with young people. Processes of evangelism that are manipulative or coercive of young peoples' choices will not only be a violation of their freedom but will also inhibit the possibility for adult members of the church to be transformed through their own interaction with teenagers. As youth ministers take up the responsibility of advocating for young people in the life of the church, youth ministers also need to make space within themselves to be open to be changed through the work of the Spirit of God in young peoples' lives.

---

93. This conclusion resonates with an observation from Dewey about the origins of aesthetic expression: "New ideas come leisurely yet promptly to consciousness only when work has previously been done in forming the right doors by which they may gain entrance" (*Art as Experience*, 76).

Questions

Alongside affirming the freedom of young people to make their own spiritual choices and their freedom to contribute to the spiritual vitality of the whole church, theological critique of Greene's philosophy will ask how a young person's freedom relates to the authority of God expressed in the Bible. In particular, AYM must defend the proposal that "offering what could be" over "declaring what is" is a faithful pattern of Christian ministry consistent with the biblical drama. There are numerous instances in the Gospels and Acts where Jesus and the apostles make clear, even strident, directives concerning how human beings must respond to the person and work of Christ (see, for example, Mark 1:15; Matt 28:18–20; Luke 18:22; Acts 2:37–38; Acts 16:30–31). How might the language of "offer" be recognized as consistent with apostolic instructions to "preach the gospel . . . to reprove, rebuke, and exhort" (2 Tim 4:2)?

Reformed theology also raises the challenge of the need to articulate the relationship between human technique and the work of God in spiritual formation. Following Greene's philosophy, Christian formation would result from young people making meaningful connections between their reading of the Bible (having attended to the objective tools for making sense of this particular text) and the concrete situation of their lived reality. This process takes time and is unpredictable, but it can be achieved by following the required activities of perception and illumination. From the perspective of Reformed theology, this raises the question of the role of the Spirit of God in bringing spiritual transformation apart from the independent use of human wisdom (see 1 Cor 1:18–25). Beyond baptizing Greene's pedagogical process with an opening and closing prayer, Christian theology asks how the human processes of perception and illumination relate to the sovereign work of the Spirit in the work of spiritual formation.

A contrasting question is raised against Christian theology from Greene's perspective: If adult mentors are offering young people a particular reading of the Bible framed by their own chosen frame of reference, even if that reading is offered as "possibility" rather than as "fact," are not young people still being left with a narrowed place in which to choose, which is, according to Greene, ultimately a denial of their freedom? Put more simply, if young people are being invited into a particular construal of meaning offered in the Christian gospel, what place is there for them to freely imagine a preferred future? How could adopting a personal identity shaped by a message of sovereign grace leave room for imaginative exploration of future possibility?

Summary

This chapter completes the survey of Greene's aesthetic pedagogy and the implications for Christian youth ministry if Bible engagement for spiritual formation were to be pursued in line with Greene's vision. In summary, AYM would look to curate environments that enable young people to freely explore questions of meaning and identity in the company of others, young and old, who are themselves facing and pursuing the same challenge. While there can be no guarantee that young people will take on the existential burden of making sense of their lived experience, adult mentors would need to remain committed to giving young people the freedom to make their own spiritual choices, to determine for themselves how they will interpret the world and their place in it, and to pursue their own course of action in the world. Central to the spaces needed for spiritual formation would be exposure to all that the text of Scripture has to offer as an ever-potent resource for meaning-making. Adult mentors would equip young people with cognitive tools for noticing what is present in the Bible and prompt imaginative engagement in order to view their own lives from new perspectives that are opened up by their reading of the text. Time and space would be given to allow young people to explore how they make sense of the text in relation to their world and to pursue visions of how their world could be different in response. Part II of this study will seek to develop each of these ideas in conversation with Christian theology, responding to the various questions raised in the preceding chapters.

Part II

Dialogical Youth Ministry

PART II TURNS TO engage in a theological conversation with Maxine Greene's aesthetic pedagogy with a view to shaping a dialogical youth ministry, an approach to Bible engagement for spiritual formation of teenagers within a culture of expressive individualism.

The analysis of aesthetic pedagogy in Part I has imagined a so-called aesthetic youth ministry, a Christian ministry among young people constructed in line with Greene's aesthetic pedagogy. The conclusions of chapters 3, 4, and 5 have noted various contributions that could be made by AYM. Chapter 3 identified the importance of the processes of spiritual formation, reminding youth leaders that they should not seek to control the outcome of a young person's formation. Chapter 4 highlighted the importance of paying attention to how young people use the Bible in their own work of meaning-making, and therefore of the need for adult mentors to champion the contributions that young people have to make to the life of the church. Chapter 5 revealed a way to hold instruction about what the Bible is together with personal engagement about how the Bible might be used. A significant thread through each chapter is the recognition of the personal agency of young people and the contribution they have to make as active members of the Christian community.

Alongside these contributions, various theological challenges were raised in relation to Greene's pedagogy: Is not Greene's notion of the personal construction of meaning a pedagogical version of human sinfulness that rejects the authority of God? If young people are given the freedom to draw on the biblical text as a resource for personal meaning-making, what will keep them from making the Bible say whatever suits their personal concerns?

How can the notion of offering the gospel as a possibility for meaning align with biblical accounts of more forthright evangelistic appeals? And, what is the relationship in spiritual formation of teenagers between the work of the Spirit and the pedagogical tasks of the youth ministry?

In reply, Greene's pedagogy directs three main questions at Christian theology: How can adult mentors come to the task of spiritual formation with fixed ideas of the outcome they want to see among young people without violating a young person's freedom to explore and make their own choices? If the Bible is regarded as the authoritative word of God, what room is left for the dialogical practices that are central to aesthetic pedagogy? If Christian faith offers young people an identity grounded in the gospel, what room is left for their personal exploration of authenticity?

In the next three chapters I respond to these questions and suggest a secure footing for the contributions to Christian spiritual formation identified in AYM. Chapter 6 recognizes the contemporary quest for authenticity as an appropriate starting point for Christian youth ministry. By adopting an attitude of martyrdom, youth leaders are able to offer the gospel to young people without abandoning their own convictions and without being manipulative of a young person's response. Chapter 7 argues that a conservative theology of the Bible requires youth leaders to engage in open dialogue with young people about biblical interpretation, and that dialogue in pursuit of meaning-making requires applying interpretive rules to discipline engagement with any text, not least the Bible. Chapter 8 offers a taxonomy of various uses of the imagination in Bible engagement, identifies the relationship between the human work of the imagination and the sovereign work of the Spirit of God, and demonstrates that knowing oneself to be "known by God" provides both the space for ongoing exploration of meaning and the relational anchor needed to sustain young people in such quests.

Finally, Chapter 9 concludes the project, drawing together all the threads proposed in chapters 6, 7, and 8, and outlining a practice framework for dialogical youth ministry.

6

Freedom, Authority, and the Martyr's Gift

RECOGNIZING THAT THE WORLD and our place in it is a social construction, aesthetic pedagogy begins with the task of bringing young people to the kind of wide-awakeness that no longer acquiesces to the taken-for-granted but shapes them to take on the responsibility of constructing their own meaning of their lived experience. Applied to the task of Christian spiritual formation of teenagers, an imagined aesthetic youth ministry would aim to enlighten young people to their freedom to make their own choices in relation to the spiritual realm, to enable them to so choose, and empower them to pursue meaningful action in light of their choices.

The conclusion to chapter 3 noted two obstacles that could prove fatal to this study's aim of bringing Maxine Greene's aesthetic pedagogy to Christian youth ministry. From the perspective of Christian theology comes the objection that Greene's aim of enabling young people to construct their own meaning of the world and their place in it sounds like a pedagogical version of the self-centered rejection of God characteristic of human fallenness (Rom 1:22–23). In simple terms, this objection asks, is Greene's pursuit of personal freedom sinful? Clearly this is no trifling objection. If the foundation and guiding principle of Greene's aesthetic pedagogy is to be equated with a Christian doctrine of sin, there will be little hope of pursuing a constructive dialogue regarding pedagogical means and method. If giving young people the freedom to construct meaning is understood as the "problem" Christian spiritual formation is aiming to "solve," this project is hobbled at the starting gate.

The first section of this chapter responds to this challenge by arguing that Greene's project of promoting wide-awakeness and meaning-making, reflecting Charles Taylor's characterization of contemporary culture as the "age of authenticity," is not only an appropriate cultural starting point for youth ministry, it is also an appropriate expression of the theological value placed on personal responsibility. Following on from this, I turn to Nicholas Wolterstorff's vision of shalom as the goal of education as a theological framework within which Greene's pedagogical goals of wide-awakeness and meaning-making can be located.

Not only does Christian theology look with suspicion on Greene's project, so too Greene raises a challenge against approaches to Christian theology which posit a pre-existing meaning embedded in creation by the prior design of God. The question raised asks whether Christian conviction quashes a young person's freedom to explore meaning for herself. From the perspective of Maxine Greene's philosophy, a pre-interpreted world is inimical to the core notion of freedom and moral action upon which aesthetic pedagogy is based. If "the answers" to the meaning of life are given by God, it would see that human beings have the task of comprehending and submitting to the divine will and intention but have no need for (or right to) personal construction of meaning. If a pre-commitment to a Christian framework for meaning is one of the hegemonic mystifications from which young people are to be set free, applying aesthetic pedagogy to Christian spiritual formation becomes self-defeating. The second section of this chapter responds to this challenge by arguing that Christian youth ministry needs to offer the gospel in the form of martyrdom, willing to suffer rejection while resisting the temptations to diminish conviction or permit coercion.

The final section of the chapter outlines three pedagogical principles that arise from the preceding discussion, and that incorporate the contributions of the imagined AYM noted at the conclusion of chapter 3. Three principles are offered towards a dialogical youth ministry: ordering process before outcome, facilitating critically aware choices, and promoting dialogue as an expression of love.

Authenticity and Meaning-Making

Greene's pedagogy is comfortably at home in the "expressive individualism" that characterizes the modern self. The challenge to identify one's true self is expressed in Greene's desire for young people to cast off mystifications and take up the responsibility of constructing their own sense of meaning of their world and their place in it. Not only ought young people be equipped to choose their true self, they must be given freedom to act on those choices. The value placed on choice accords with Greene's identification of moral action with responsible choice. In place of acting "automatically or conventionally" or doing "only what is expected of them,"[1] young people must be enabled to take responsibility for their choices rather than hiding behind the crowd. Greene's emphasis on releasing young people from mystifications, uncovering the cultural stories that are taken for granted, accords with the rejection of external norms as binding in relation to personal identity.

In this chapter I take up the analysis of expressive individualism from Roman Catholic social philosopher Charles Taylor. Taylor's account of the modern secular age has gained wide reception in youth ministry literature as a revealing analysis of the prevailing culture of youth ministry in the Western world today. Interaction with Taylor takes up Root's challenge to explore how the church might testify to the action of God in a secular age of unbelief.[2]

In the analysis that follows, I am using Taylor as a conversation partner with Greene to act in a way akin to Barnabas with Saul in relation to the apostles (Acts 9:26–27). If I attempt to bring Greene to "join the disciples," this project is likely to be met by at least suspicion if not fear; not only is Greene clearly not a disciple of Jesus, but many in the conservative church would not believe her philosophy to be compatible with Christian theology. Rather than bringing Greene to the church, my intention is to use the dialogue with Taylor to bring the church to Greene. Taylor's analysis encourages Christian youth leaders to recognize that they need not fear joining Greene in embracing the culture of authenticity. Authenticity not only presents Christian youth ministry with a necessary cultural starting point, it also embodies moral values consistent with Christian faith.

Authenticity as Cultural Starting Point

Chapter 1 noted that the culture of authenticity is the environment in which Australian youth ministry pursues spiritual formation with teenagers and that such an environment presents significant challenges to Christian faith in its tendency to promote self-focused independence from God. Taylor acknowledges that authenticity is often expressed in debased and deviant forms of narcissistic quests for self-fulfillment without regard for external moral demands and with limited serious commitment to others, resulting in social atomism. Greene likewise decries "negative freedom,"[3] the freedom *from* interference and external control; the freedom that pursues

---

1. Greene, *LL*, 49.
2. Root, *Faith Formation*.
3. Greene, *DF*, 77.

self-dependence and autonomy to the exclusion of relationship with others. Not only are these deviations present, Taylor makes the additional observation that there is an inner tendency in the age of authenticity for expressivism to devolve toward its more debased forms. It is these debased expressions of authenticity that critics are right to reject.

Yet, despite the widespread deficiencies, neither Taylor nor Greene have rejected authenticity as "simply egoism and the pursuit of pleasure" or as nothing more than the spiritual manifestation of economic consumerism. While distancing himself from the trenchant critics of authenticity, the "knockers," Taylor does not by default align himself with the "boosters," who promote the quest for authenticity as the arrival of a new and bright future.[4] While the knockers are too pessimistic regarding the slide to relativism and individualism as inevitable, the boosters have failed to acknowledge the tendency for authenticity to make such a slide at all.

Taylor takes seriously the quest for authenticity as a moral ideal without accepting that everything is as it should be in the way authenticity is being pursued in our culture. Taylor calls for a work of persuasion, aiming to "identify and articulate the higher ideal behind the more or less debased practices, and then criticize these practices from the standpoint of their own motivating ideal."[5] Rather than simply opting for criticism or endorsement, Taylor's goal is to restore cultural practices at the heart of the authenticity project by demonstrating what the ethic of authenticity actually involves:

> The picture that I am offering is rather that of an ideal that has degraded but that is very worthwhile in itself, and indeed, I would like to say, unrepudiable by moderns. So what we need is neither root-and-branch condemnation nor uncritical praise; and not a carefully balanced trade-off. What we need is a work of retrieval, through which this ideal can help us restore our practice.[6]

Taylor challenges commentators to engage in discussions about what authenticity entails rather than over whether authenticity is worth pursuing or not. There is little value in arguing that authenticity ought not be a central feature of our culture, not least because it is an argument that makes the false assumption that, even if won at an intellectual level, there would be any hope of dis-embedding this ubiquitous value from the modern social imaginary. Rather, acknowledging that we find ourselves living in this age and not some other, there is greater value in engaging in discussions about

4. Taylor, *Secular Age*, 481.
5. Taylor, *Authenticity*, 72.
6. Taylor, *Authenticity*, 23.

defining what authenticity properly means, and "trying to lift the culture back up, closer to its motivating ideal."[7] Greene's work in the educational sphere is pursuing the same end and calls other educators to do likewise. This project heeds the call from Taylor and Greene in seeking to articulate an approach to Christian spiritual formation that connects with the ethical ideals of the culture of authenticity.

Accepting expressivism and authenticity as the context given to the church in which to fulfil her mission is not without positive features. Noting that "every dispensation [has] its own favored forms of deviation," Taylor reminds us of the costs presented to spiritual life when personal choice is diminished by expectations of conformity to external demands: "hypocrisy, spiritual stultification, inner revolt against the Gospel, the confusion of faith and power."[8] Former times aroused their own critiques: "The society of the 1950s was castigated as conformist, crushing individuality and creativity, as too concerned with production and concrete results, as repressing feeling and spontaneity, as exalting the mechanical over the organic."[9] Not only does a culture of authenticity avoid past deviations, the new culture of authenticity and expressive individualism has brought significant gains. Both Taylor and Greene recognize the lifting of restrictions on the life-choices available to women as prominent among the social gains brought with the age of authenticity.[10] Indeed, despite the present experience of shallow and undemanding spirituality, Taylor demonstrates not only that the deviations of today are preferable to those of the past, but that personal exploration is not incompatible with a Christian spirituality that chooses to submit to divine authority, and that the core commitments of expressivism align with Christian moral values.

Self-Referential Manner versus Self-Referential Content

Taylor distinguishes two expressions of self-referentiality in order to demonstrate that pursuing an autonomous spiritual quest is not equivalent to exercising an autonomous spirituality. In other words, emphasizing the importance of personal choice in spiritual concerns does not necessarily lead to rejecting expressions of spiritual life that involve submitting to a

---

7. Taylor, *Authenticity*, 73.

8. Taylor, *Secular Age*, 513.

9. Taylor, *Secular Age*, 476. The points of critique of the 1950s that Taylor names are similar to the reasons given by young adults in the United States for why they had left the church (Kinnaman, *You Lost Me*).

10. Taylor, *Secular Age*, 480.

transcendent reality or choosing self-sacrifice for the sake of an external order of meaning. A "self-referentiality of manner" is the stance toward meaning-making that is unavoidable in modern Western culture, whereas a "self-referentiality of matter" is an oft-chosen, but not inescapable, conclusion to the quest.

> [Authenticity] clearly concerns the *manner* of espousing any end or form of life. Authenticity is self-referential: this has to be *my* orientation. But this doesn't mean that on another level the *content* must be self-referential: that my goals must express or fulfil my desires or aspirations, *as against* something that stands beyond these.[11]

Failing to distinguish between these two forms of self-referentiality leads to diametrically opposed responses to the culture of authenticity. Unshakeable critics of authenticity reject all forms of self-referential manner because of their opposition to the self-referential content with which many (perhaps even most) choose to fill it. Unquestioning advocates of authenticity embrace self-referential content (often legitimizing the worst forms of subjectivism) because of their enthusiasm for self-referential manner. Critics and advocates of self-referentiality need to recognize that self-referential content is not a necessary concomitant of self-referential manner.

Taylor argues that a quest for "wholeness" need not be in conflict with a quest for "holiness." As evidence, Taylor highlights the striking popularity among young adults of the Taizé community. The drawing power of Taizé lies partly in the fact that pilgrims are received as searchers who are welcome to express themselves without being confronted by a normative system of belief or discourse with predetermined meaning.[12] Santos's immersive study of the Taizé community offers a similar conclusion:

> One of the primary reasons young people feel free at Taizé is because of the "permeable boundaries" that exist. Young people are given freedom in worship. They are given the opportunity to move toward God at their own pace . . . In Taizé, young people are given space to pursue God. They are given the freedom to sit, wait and listen.[13]

There is a freedom embedded in the process that does not prohibit arriving at an outcome that recognizes some form of authority. Pilgrims participate at Taizé within a clear structure for prayer and Bible reading (including

---

11. Taylor, *Authenticity*, 82. Italics original.
12. Taylor, *Secular Age*, 517.
13. Santos, *Community called Taizé*, 139–140.

rules about when and where pilgrims could drink alcohol). Neither Taylor nor Santos is suggesting that processes of Christian formation remove all boundaries or normative moral frameworks. Yet both are warning against the inappropriateness of attempting to impose external constraints on the outcome of any individual's spiritual quest. In this they both echo Maxine Greene's call for hegemonic narratives of social ordering to be interrogated and exposed, while acknowledging that some people may still choose to live within traditional constructs.

Authenticity as Moral Value

The worthy ethical ideal at the heart of expressivism and the modern quest for the authentic self is a renewed focus on the responsibility of individuals to make choices and to own the choices they make. This more "self-responsible form of life," Taylor argues, "allows us to live (potentially) a fuller and more differentiated life, because more fully appropriated as our own."[14] The religious "pilgrim seeker, attempting to discern and follow his/her own path" is simply the contemporary manifestation of the same "personal, committed form of religious devotion and practice" that has been present throughout the history of Western Christendom.[15] While the existence of viable alternatives invests all forms of belief and unbelief with a certain fragility, there is a welcome strength of commitment that arises from personal choice.[16] The modern secular age is characterized by more conversions from one mode of belief or unbelief to another, as well as by stronger commitments to the various forms of belief or unbelief as a result. Christian youth ministries can celebrate young people's ownership of their choices that comes from accepting the freedom and authority to choose.

Three themes in expressive individualism are notable as reflective of Christian moral values: responsibility for personal choices, the alignment of inner beliefs with outward confession and practice, and individual particularity. The notion of "self-responsibility" is evident in the Gospel narrative in John 21 that comes immediately after Jesus' restoration of Peter following Peter's threefold denial of Christ on the night before the crucifixion. Having received a threefold interrogation of his love for the Lord, and a threefold call to the responsibility of pastoral ministry, Peter turns to

---

14. Taylor, *Authenticity*, 74

15. Taylor, *Secular Age*, 532. Taylor lists the "Calvinist, Jansenist, devout humanist, Methodist . . . the 'born again' Christian" as earlier manifestations of the same "disciplined, conscious, committed individual believer."

16. Taylor, *Secular Age*, 303–4, 556.

another disciple and asks, "Lord, what about him?" (John 21:20). Jesus' answer directs Peter to his self-responsibility to make a choice of discipleship: "'If I will that he remain until I come, what is that to you? You follow me.'" (John 21:22).[17] The terse "What is that to you?" underlines that Peter's focus ought to be on how *he* will (or will not) fulfil Jesus' invitation to discipleship irrespective of the actions or destinies of others. Responsibility for choices, and the freedom to choose, is also affirmed where people are making choices that are contrary to the divine will. Jesus allows the rich young man to turn away from the invitation to discipleship (Mark 10:17–22) and does not chase after him to renegotiate the initial offer. Turning from exegetical to systematic theology, responsibility for real choices is necessary for divine judgment to be morally defensible.[18]

Aligning inner beliefs with outward confession and practice is affirmed in biblical imperatives for faithfulness to extend beyond nominal practices of external religiosity, to require an inward conversion of the heart (Deut 30:6; Joel 2:12–13; Rom 2:28–29). Jesus' rebuke of the Pharisees often revolved around their failure to connect external practices of piety with inner personal devotion (Matt 6:1–18; 23:1–36; Mark 7:1–16). Jesus invited people to a discipleship that aligned beliefs of the heart with outward confession and personal action.

Affirming the value in expressivism that each one must find and follow their own path, Taylor points to Paul's teaching on the variety of gifts given to believers as a precursor to the idea that each individual is given a unique life-path to follow. If each individual is given various gifts, and if specific gifts are correlated with specific vocations, then "the good life for you is not the same as the good life for me; each of us has our own calling, and we shouldn't exchange them. Following you may be betraying my own calling even though you are being faithful to yours . . . We are all called to live up to our originality."[19] Even without affirming the often-deterministic view of vocation in Lutheran and Puritan theology,[20] Christian anthropology affirms the uniqueness of each individual,[21] consistent with modern expressivism.

The objection that Greene's emphasis on personal spiritual discovery could sound like a pedagogical version of Paul's account of sin can,

---

17. In the final imperative "you" placed at the beginning of the instruction is emphatic, (*su moi akolouthei*; σύ μοι ἀκολούθει).

18. Carson cites Calvin's argument, "if a sinful act is done voluntarily that is enough to establish guilt" (*Divine Sovereignty*, 208).

19. Taylor, *Authenticity*, 375–76.

20. Marshall, *A Kind of Life*; Stevens, *Other Six Days*, 73–75.

21. Sherlock, *Humanity*, 157.

therefore, be met by recognizing the ethical ideal at the heart of the contemporary quest for authenticity. Christian theology need not, and ought not, stand in opposition to this culture of expressive individualism. It need not because there is theological merit in affirming the ethical ideal in the quest, of taking personal responsibility for one's choices, and in pursuing inner-outer integrity. It ought not because this is the world in which the church is called to live. Attempts to wind back the clock to a previous age are futile, and attempts to assert external authority in such a way that shuts down spiritual quest will be unlikely to find a welcome audience among those immersed in an expressivist culture.

Wide-Awakeness, Meaning-Making, and the Tasks of Shalom

So far I have argued for the broad acceptance of the culture of authenticity as an appropriate context within which to pursue Christian spiritual formation. In order to consider the specific pedagogical goals of wide-awakeness and meaning-making, I turn to Nicholas Wolterstorff's theological reflection on Christian schools in the Reformed tradition.

Wolterstorff defines shalom as relational and delight-ful. Shalom is about living in rightly ordered relationships, acting with justice and responsibility in those relationships, and doing so with delight:

> The goal of human existence is that man should dwell at peace in all his relationships: with God, with himself, with his fellows, with nature, a peace which is not merely the absence of hostility, though certainly it is that, but a peace which at its highest is enjoyment. To dwell in shalom is to enjoy living before God, to enjoy living in nature, to enjoy living with one's fellows, to enjoy life with oneself.[22]

If shalom is the goal of the kingdom of God, then it will also be the goal of education in service of that kingdom. On such an account, shalom is also the appropriate goal of spiritual formation in youth ministry.

Wide-awakeness and meaning-making can therefore be recognized as pedagogical expressions of the twin tasks inherent in the biblical vision of shalom. While shalom will ultimately arrive as the gift of God, the people of God "are not to stand around, hands folded, waiting for shalom to arrive," but are to recognize themselves as "workers in God's cause, his peace workers."[23] The vision of shalom is offered to humanity with a two-part command: "We

---

22. Wolterstorff, *Reason*, 114.
23. Wolterstorff et al., *Educating for Life*, 104.

are to pray and struggle for the release of the captives, and we are to pray and struggle for the release of the enriching potentials of God's creation. We live under both a liberation mandate and a cultural mandate."[24]

The liberative mandate in shalom grounds the pursuit of freedom expressed in the pedagogical aim of freeing young people from the constraints placed on them by the taken-for-granted social constructs in which they are immersed. Fulfilling the liberative mandate in the pursuit of shalom within a Christian youth ministry needs to involve enabling young people to make their own spiritual choices free from coercion and manipulation.

The cultural mandate in shalom embraces the work of enabling young people to construct their own sense of meaning and purpose in the world. Fulfilling the cultural mandate within Christian youth ministry needs to involve releasing the enriching potentials of God's creation in two ways. First, young people themselves need to be recognized as full of "enriching potentials" created by God. Youth ministry contributes to the release of these potentials for the common good, in service of the church, and to the glory of God. Second, central to what it means to release the potential of young people is to enable them to recognize the enriching potential present in creation. Youth ministry would enable young people to release this potential not only for their own benefit, but for the sake of others, and for the glory of God.

Locating the work of meaning-making within the cultural mandate inherent in the vision of shalom elucidates the relationship between objectivist and constructivist epistemologies noted earlier. The objectivist pole recognizes shalom as a pattern of life revealed by God. God calls to humans to work with God to advance shalom. Conversely, in line with constructivism, human beings are given the responsibility to find their own unique way of living out this call in the world. There are absolute truths that are revealed and personal truths that are constructed. Knowledge is revealed, while understanding is constructed.[25] Constructivism "is not creating something new" but is "putting together ideas in a personally meaningful and honest (and thus 'truthful') way."[26]

This relationship between revealed knowledge and constructed understanding is evident in the creation narratives in Genesis 1 and 2. Genesis 1 presents God as external to, and solely responsible for, all created things. Human beings are not pictured constructing their world through their own storying of their experience. Adam is placed in a garden created by God

---

24. Wolterstorff et al., *Educating for Shalom*, 23.
25. Fennema, "Constructivism."
26. Knowlton, "Shifting toward a Constructivist Philosophy," 121.

(Gen 2:8); he does not create a garden from his own imagining. Yet, also evident in the Genesis narrative is the notion that our human being-in-the-world is constructed, at least in some way, by the way we name our reality and name ourselves in that reality. As Adam names the animals, he is constructing a relationship between himself and the animals and, ultimately, between himself and the woman as his "fitting" partner (Gen 2:19–20).[27] Genesis chapters 1 and 2 picture the freedom of human beings to name their world in a way that is responsive to, and in harmony with, the world God has created for them.

Pursued within the cultural mandate inherent in shalom, DYM affirms the biblical theme that the created order is not bereft of meaning, but is held together in Christ. Christ as the *logos* (John 1:1) refers not only to the origin of creation in the divine word of command (Gen 1:3,6, 9 etc.), but also to the origin of the creation in divine wisdom (Prov 3:19–20). Thus, "in him all things hold together" (Col 1:17), and the Son "sustains all things by his powerful word" (Heb 1:3). Alongside the need to hold on to the "structures" of reality, as emphasized in objectivism, DYM will also acknowledge the "processes" of reality, as emphasized in constructivism. Youth leaders will hold to a moral framework drawn from a reading of Scripture and the Christian tradition as reflecting the God-given structures of reality. Within that framework, youth leaders pursue processes of meaning-making as they invite young people to explore how they will put the various aspects of their lived experience together in a personally meaningful way.

To summarize, the first stage of the correlative conversation has argued that Greene's aims of freedom, wide-awakeness, and meaning-making are not inconsistent with Christian theology. Christian youth ministers can embrace the culture of authenticity as an appropriate cultural starting point, affirming the responsibility each person has before God for the spiritual choices they make. DYM fulfils the liberative mandate in the biblical vision of shalom by endeavoring to set young people free from the taken-for-granted. DYM fulfils the cultural mandate in shalom by enabling young people to determine the meaning they will construct out of the concrete experience given to them by God.

---

27. In the biblical narrative naming is an activity of relationship. When God creates a female, the male constructs his relationship with her through the choice of a name. The Hebrew, *'iššāh* (woman) expresses verbally the connection with the *'iš* (man) that matches the "fittingness" of the woman as a helper for the man.

Freedom and Martyrdom

The second stage of the conversation between Greene and Christian theology considers the converse challenge. Are Christian commitments to divine authority inconsistent with Greene's pedagogy? In particular, how can the Christian commitment to conformity to the likeness of Christ as the ultimate goal of spiritual formation leave room for young people to pursue a personal quest for meaning? This challenge was answered in an imagined AYM by the suggestion that Christian youth ministry could avoid making the gospel an externally imposed system of meaning by shifting the manner in which youth ministers teach the Bible from declaring "what is" to offering "what could be." In order to honor and to engage young peoples' agency in spiritual life, the biblical world is offered as one way of naming and constructing their experience. Yet, the conclusion to chapter 5 noted the need to demonstrate how such an "offer" could be consistent with the directiveness evident in biblical patterns of evangelism. How is the language of "offer" consistent with Paul declaring that "God commands all people in all places to repent" (Acts 17:30), or with the instructions given to Timothy to "preach the gospel . . . to convict, rebuke, and encourage" (2 Tim 4:2)?

The following argument will develop in three stages. First, biblical examples of persuasion made as offers rather than demands reveal that the kingdom of God is extended to human beings who are free to reject the divine gift. Second, I argue that respecting a young person's freedom to reject the gift of Christ expresses the attitude of martyrdom as a way of offering the gospel in order to keep the persuasive rhetoric of Christian faith from becoming coercive, without abandoning the personal conviction of the one who is extending such an offer. Third, in order for youth ministry to be faithful to this call to martyrdom, youth ministers will need to recognize and resist various temptations to abandon that path.

Offering the Gospel

Two instances in the Bible are offered as examples of where the message of the kingdom of God is presented as an offer of possibility rather than as a demand. Jesus' use of parables offers his hearers a way to interpret the world. Through parables, Jesus would draw out those who were interested and turn away those who were not (Mark 4:10–12, 33–34).[28] Paul adopts the same stance, renouncing "shameful secret things, not walking in trickery or falsifying the word of God, but by an open display of the truth, commending

---

28. See France, *Divine Government*.

ourselves to every person's conscience before God" (2 Cor 4:2). Far from being a step away from a personal belief in the Gospel, Paul's stance flows out of his confidence in the work of God. Paul argues that, just as God brought creation into being ex nihilo, and in the same way brought light to Paul's own life as an act of grace, Paul has the same confidence in the work of Christ among his hearers (2 Cor 4:6).

Common to both cases is a readiness to accept that those being offered the divine invitation remain at liberty to refuse. Underlying this readiness is not an ambivalence toward how the kingdom invitation is received, but a trust in God's ability to fulfil his purposes in a way that is compatible with the real exercise of human will.[29] Eschewing human power in the presentation of the gospel is entirely consistent with faith in the promise that God is at work through his word (Isa 55:10–11; 1 Thess 2:13).

Youth leaders therefore need to offer the gospel to young people without suggesting that their relationship with the leader or their participation in the youth ministry is contingent on their acceptance of what is offered. This does not mean that youth ministers suggest that the choice to trust Jesus is without consequence. However, these consequences, whether temporal or eternal, are not to be tools of coercion but would be presented as the burden of choice. DYM will be clear in articulating the choices available, and clear that young people are free to reject what is offered, and clear that young people are responsible for the consequences of the choices they make.

Only as the "martyr's gift" can the Christian rhetoric of persuasion avoid becoming just another violent bid for power. David Bentley Hart's exploration of theological aesthetics from the Eastern orthodox tradition concludes that the Christian claim that Christ imparts his peace without violence can only be expressed in efficacious practice without abandoning the rhetoric of conversion if it is conceived as an act of martyrdom:

> Christian thought learns that its rhetoric must never be a practice of coercion precisely because, in following the form of Christ . . . it is always already placed on the side of the excluded, and must occupy this place as the place of triumph . . . Christian thought finds itself drawn over into the place of the crucified, addressing the nations from this place as the only place where peace is known, seeking to imitate Christ's renunciation of violence. Theology must, because of what its particular story is, have the form of martyrdom, witness, a peaceful

---

29. Carson, *Divine Sovereignty*.

offer that has already suffered rejection and must be prepared for rejection as a consequence.[30]

The "martyr's gift" is the peaceful offer of the gospel that is ready and willing to suffer rejection in imitation of Christ. Martyrdom in this context is not narrowly defined as physical death as a result of Christian witness. It would be dishonoring to those Christian people who have lost their lives for the sake of the faith to equate their suffering with the challenges of discipling teenagers in a local church youth ministry in Australia. However, it is the same commitment to Christian discipleship present in Christian martyrs, past and present, that needs to animate the core commitments of all Christian people, not least of youth leaders. "Christian martyrdom is merely the working out, in a particular circumstance, of the identity in which individual Christians participate."[31] All Christian people are called to follow the way of the cross, living in imitation of the martyr's death suffered by Jesus (Mark 8:34). The essence of martyrdom is not a commitment to death but a commitment to bear witness to Jesus, whether in the face of death or in the face of rejection from teenagers.

Evangelism and apologetics viewed as acts of nonresistance are not an embrace of defeat but a recognition that God's victory comes through suffering, not in place of it. Garrett Green recognizes that "the affirmation implicit in this apparently negative stance is utter faith in the power of God, that power that appears as weakness in this world. God is strong enough to resist all the slings and arrows that the world can hurl against him, and the same is true of God's word."[32]

Martyrdom is not a masochistic delight in suffering, but a gospel faith in the God who brings life in the face of death. Whatever power to persuade that the church holds will only come from the power present in the weakness and apparent foolishness of the cross (1 Corinthians 1:18–2:5).

Resisting Temptations to Abandon Martyrdom

With shame, the church needs to recognize that youth ministries have often become places that have exercised power over young people rather than places where young people have been empowered through Christlike service. The hegemonic mystifications from which Greene hopes young people might break free have often included the coercive rhetoric and confining

---

30. Hart, *Beauty*, 441.
31. Jensen, *Martyrdom*, 3.
32. Green, *Theology*, 136.

structures of the church. Youth ministers need to recognize the particular temptations to abandon the path of Christ so that they might be equipped to take on appropriate postures of resistance. Useful in this regard is Jensen's exploration of the relationship between Christian identity and martyrdom.[33] Jensen explores the nature of Christian identity by examining the four temptations to avoid martyrdom faced by Archbishop Tomas Becket in T. S. Eliot's play, *Murder in the Cathedral*:[34] "the temptation to security,"[35] "the temptation to collaborate,"[36] "the temptation to idealism,"[37] and "the temptation of honor and reward."[38] Of relevance to the present discussion is to consider how these temptations play out for youth ministers to sway them from offering the gospel of peace as an act of peace.

The temptation to security offers would-be-martyrs a way to avoid suffering by finding ways of fitting in with the practical reality they face rather than persisting with a course of action with such dire consequences. "This is a call to be realistic: to live within the given limits of [one's] existence."[39] This temptation comes to youth ministers by enticing them to avoid the challenges involved in awakening young people to the need to make their own spiritual choices. Youth ministers are tempted to avoid the cost of wide-awakeness by allowing and encouraging young people to settle for the taken-for-granted. Rather than face the unsettling challenges involved in meaning-making, youth ministers could simply look for ways to express a sense of Christian faith within the mystifications that surround and hold young people. Youth ministers under this temptation are content to domesticate the gospel according to whatever cultural setting in which the young people they serve are located.[40] For young people who have grown up in the church, youth ministry will not challenge them to take on a greater complexity in their faith commitments. Young people enduring social disadvantage will be offered a few spiritual resources to meet felt needs. Young people enjoying a life of privilege can

33. Jensen, *Martyrdom*. For further discussion of how martyrdom reforms understandings of identity, see Jensen, "In Spirit and In Truth."

34. Eliot, *Murder*.

35. Jensen, *Martyrdom*, 41.

36. Jensen, *Martyrdom*, 75.

37. Jensen, *Martyrdom*, 99.

38. Jensen, *Martyrdom*, 131.

39. Jensen, *Martyrdom*, 48–49.

40. As David White warns, "When the church fails to teach youth to grasp the integrity of the gospel and alternate ways of living faithfully or to provide practical skills for discerning these alternatives, we essentially relegate the gospel to tacit support of the cultural status quo" (*Practicing Discernment*, 45).

add Christianity to their list of merit awards. There is no coercion needed, because no substantial life-change is necessary.[41]

The temptation to collaborate entices would-be-martyrs to fall in line with hegemonic powers by giving up the theological discourse that elicits deadly opposition. Jensen finds contemporary expression of this temptation in Richard Rorty's pragmatic consensus; on this view, the Christian martyr is required to "find a language untainted by the accents of her identity in Christ."[42] This temptation comes to youth ministers in the pressure to give up attempts to persuade young people toward faith in Christ and merely accept whatever spiritual choices young people make in exercise of their freedom (provided those choices are socially responsible). The quest for authenticity moves from an appropriate (and unavoidable) cultural starting point to become both the beginning and the end of the spiritual life. The quest for authenticity itself becomes a hegemonic mystification, particularly in its implied necessary embrace of relativism in relation to the content of spiritual meaning-making. The temptation to collaborate amounts to adopting Maxine Greene's pedagogy for youth ministry without theological critique, adaptation, or nuance. Replacing the kerygmatic dimension of Christian spirituality in favor of free and open dialogue will present little danger of coercion, but the supposed pedagogical gain comes with significant confessional loss.

The temptation to idealism entices would-be martyrs to pursue their own action that is subversive of the powers that oppose them so that they might establish the hoped-for ideal by their own efforts. "The Tempter offers [the martyr] a vision of himself as a self in the full exercise of practical wisdom, responsive to circumstance and with his virtues realized in action for the good of the political community of which he is part."[43] In extreme forms, for youth ministry to give in to this temptation is to embrace coercion as a means justified by theological ends. In doing so the Christian offer of peace is no more than a ruse, a gossamer veil over just another violent bid for power. Less extreme responses that fall for the same temptation include youth ministries that are so predominantly Christian that they effectively exclude alternative construals of life. Youth ministers might construct and direct a group culture with such tightly controlled boundaries that the work of persuasion takes on an air of peace only by the artificial suppression of opposing voices. The appearance that such a youth ministry is not coercing young peoples'

---

41. "People misconceive faith and treat it as a performance-enhancing drug or as a soothing balm rather than as a resource to orient their life in the world" (Volf, *Public Faith*, 28).

42. Jensen, *Martyrdom*, 95.

43. Jensen, *Martyrdom*, 103.

spiritual choices is an illusion; suppressing non-Christian alternatives is simply another way of expressing a violent bid for power.

The temptation of honor and reward chooses to pursue martyrdom for the sake of gaining heavenly glory. "The last temptation is the greatest treason: To do the right deed for the wrong reason."[44] This is the temptation to delight in the suffering that results from faithfulness because of the personal glory that one supposes will follow, rather than delighting in faithfulness despite suffering because of the glory that is given to God as a result of such faithfulness. A youth ministry falling for this temptation might readily preach a conversionist gospel with the expectation that the message will result in rejection from most young people so that they might wear their faithfulness as a badge of personal honor. Such ministries would take refuge in being "faithful but not fruitful." Thus, this final temptation seeks to avoid coercion, not by abandoning persuasion, but by giving up any expectation of success in doing so.

The way of the cross resists all such temptations because it eschews power as it embraces Christ. Martyrdom is not a technique of persuasion. Following Greene's warning against exploiting the power imbalance between "the converter" and "the converted," the way of martyrdom rejects temptations to power and control, inviting youth ministers to know Christ, "to know the power of his resurrection and fellowship in his sufferings, being conformed to his death, and somehow may attain to the resurrection from the dead" (Phil 3:10–11). The way of martyrdom has the power to be transformative, not as an act of personal persuasion on the part of the youth minister, but as an act of testimony to Christ. In pursuing Christlike suffering, youth ministers are themselves "converted" as they enter more deeply into the way of the cross. Where Greene looks for transformation from the collaborative generativity of interpersonal relationships, Christian discipleship finds transformation in interpersonal relationships that announce and embody the presence and promise of Christ.

Towards a Dialogical Youth Ministry

The performative task of this project as a work of practical theology is to propose a dialogical youth ministry as an approach to Bible engagement for the spiritual formation of teenagers that is appropriate to the cultural setting of Australian youth ministry in the age of authenticity. By way of Taylor's analysis of the modern secular age, I have identified Greene's educational philosophy as a pedagogical version of the contemporary

44. Eliot, *Murder*, 52.

quest for authenticity. However, with Taylor, I have affirmed the culture of expressive individualism as both a culturally necessary and theologically appropriate context within which to develop an approach to Bible engagement for Christian formation. DYM pursues wide-awakeness and meaning-making as expressions of the biblical invitation to participate in the tasks of liberation and culture-making towards the vision of shalom. By being willing for young people to choose not to adopt the Christian gospel as the frame within which they will construct their understanding of the world and their place in it, by offering the martyrs' gift, adult mentors are able to affirm their personal faith convictions without undermining a young person's freedom to make their own choices. The final section of this chapter outlines three directives for youth ministry practice to embed and embody these pedagogical aims.

Ordering Process over Outcome

The correlative conversation with Greene's pedagogy drew attention to the importance of process over outcome in young people's spiritual formation. Rather than being committed to a particular outcome for spiritual formation, AYM would concentrate on the processes of promoting critical awareness through open dialogue. In contrast, traditional approaches to spiritual formation of teenagers have largely pursued particular outcomes of Christian maturity (whether expressed as "mature disciples" or "members of a worshipping community" or "knowing the presence of God"), through a wide-variety of processes that are essentially youth-oriented versions of the means of grace. DYM combines the processes of aesthetic pedagogy with the same intention of traditional youth ministry, albeit with a readiness for young people to decide not to choose the intended outcomes. In Taylor's terms, DYM pursues a self-referential process with the hope of young people reaching a non-self-referential outcome. DYM therefore does not require a trade-off between pursuing free process or outcomes accepting of divine authority. Instead, the tension between different forms of religion and spirituality is over the ordering of authority in relation to the freedom of the spiritual quest. Taylor identifies two basic forms of religion and spirituality:

> those which place authority first, and hence are suspicious and hostile of contemporary modes of quest; and those which are embarked on these, and may or may not in the course of searching come to recognize one or another form of authority.[45]

---

45. Taylor, *Secular Age*, 510.

For DYM to be appropriate to the modern secular age as well as an appropriate expression of Reformed evangelical theology, it needs to have a place for freedom in spiritual exploration in harmony with theological authority. The key will be to so order the authority of the Christian tradition that it remains welcoming of contemporary modes of spiritual quest while also promoting an approach to Christian discipleship grounded in trusting submission to the Lordship of Christ. Placing authority in second place to quest is a pedagogical choice that focuses on constructing environments for spiritual formation which may bring young people to a particular awareness (to be wide-awake) through a particular means (dialogue) in order to pursue a particular task (meaning-making). Christian leaders are fully present in these processes as people holding to their own chosen moral convictions, offering themselves and the gospel as a gift of grace.

Facilitating Critically Aware Choices

DYM not only directs youth ministers to enable young people to make their own choices in their spiritual lives, but youth ministers also need to enable young people to be critically aware of the way they make their choices. That is, along with knowing *that* they can choose, and deciding on *what* they will choose, DYM will urge young people to articulate *why* they have so chosen. The mere fact that an individual makes a choice cannot, in and of itself, make that choice meaningful.[46] If choice is all that matters, then the content of what is chosen becomes irrelevant and of no moral significance.[47] Personal choices have moral consequence only in relation to a particular set of values.[48] Greene offers the same imperative to be aware of one's own moral horizon in order to understand one's preferences involved in self-identity: "to understand [one's preferences] is to be able to reflect upon them in the light of some standard, some set of values, some norm."[49]

DYM will help young people apply critical thinking to the Christian imagination as much as to competing alternatives. In Taylor's language, young people need to be alert to both the open and closed stances toward the transcendent as possible "takes" on the nature of reality. Taylor

---

46. Taylor, *Secular Age*, 478–79.

47. See David Bentley Hart: "the liberties to permit one to purchase lavender bedclothes, to gaze pensively at pornography, to become Unitarian, to market popular representations of brutal violence, or to destroy one's unborn child, are all equally intrinsically 'good' because all are expressions of an inalienable freedom of choice" (Hart, "God or Nothingness," 56).

48. Taylor, *Authenticity*, 37; Taylor, "Modern Social Imaginaries," 93.

49. Greene, *LL*, 153.

outlines two basic stances toward the transcendent that one can take in the modern social order. One might inhabit the world as if it is an "open frame with skylights open to transcendence" or as "a closed frame with a brass ceiling."[50] This sense of living in such a way that is closed or open to transcendence is held by most adherents to be self-evident or obvious. That is, most people live within a particular "spin." This is true of the open stance as much as the closed.[51] Closed spin is evident in the "secularism as maturity" story, "that conditions have arisen in the modern world in which it is no longer possible, honestly, rationally, without confusions, or fudging, or mental reservation, to believe in God."[52] Open spin is the realm of various fundamentalisms that assert supernatural beliefs and denigrate those who fail to share the same perspective. In contrast to "spin," what is claimed as natural and obvious should be recognized as a construal, one possible "take" on reality that is neither self-evident nor incontestable. If youth ministers in DYM are to enable young people to make critically aware spiritual choices, it will not be sufficient for them to argue against secular spin by a more forceful assertion of Christian spin. Instead, DYM strives "to dissipate the false aura of the obvious" that surrounds any form of spin.[53] DYM will be willing to acknowledge that Christian faith is one of many possible ways of construing the world.

DYM therefore turns the spotlight of critical analysis upon its own structures and practices as much as on the wider church and the surrounding culture. This requires critical analysis of the systems and structures of youth ministry along with critical analysis of the content of what is taught. Lewis Rambo's classic study of religious conversion describes the influence that teachers exercise as forms of "encapsulation."[54] This is true of youth groups as much as for classrooms, at least in the sense in which they create "an environment in which there can be concentration on the topic at hand, control

---

50. Smith, *How (Not) to Be Secular*, 93.

51. "Our predicament in the modern West is, therefore, not only characterized by what I have called the immanent frame . . . It also consists of more specific pictures, the immanent frame as 'spun' in ways of openness and closure, which are often dominant in certain millieux" (Taylor, *Secular Age*, 549).

52. Taylor, *Secular Age*, 560.

53. Taylor, *Secular Age*, 551.

54. Processes of encapsulation are particularly at work in the "interaction" stage of conversion. Encapsulation processes begin after a convert's initial encounter when their interaction with an adopted religious group intensifies. "Potential converts now learn more about the teachings, life-style, and expectations of the group, and are provided with opportunities, both formal and informal, to become more fully incorporated into it" (Rambo, *Conversion*, 102).

of noise and competing ideas, and minimal interruption."⁵⁵ As Rambo concludes, "the issue is not whether but how people use encapsulation—that is, the degree and kind of encapsulation used."⁵⁶ Preserving freedom does not necessitate removing authority but the careful exercise of it. Youth leaders need to recognize the potential for manipulation and deceptiveness in the formative impact of the "learning environment" of the youth ministry as much as in the explicit teaching and instruction in Christian faith. As Bourdieu recognized, there is a degree of "cunning" that comes from the transformative effect of any habitus arising from "the fact that it manages to extort what is essential while seeming to demand the insignificant."⁵⁷ Given the potential for learning environments to be underhanded in their transformative effect on young people, youth leaders need to help young people become critically aware of the structures of the youth ministry itself.⁵⁸

DYM will also be prepared to acknowledge the appeal to young people of alternative ways of making sense of their experience. Allowing young people to pursue a personal exploration of meaning-making will require taking what Wolterstorff writes concerning the task of a Christian school and applying it to youth ministry:

> The Christian school, without flinching, must acquaint students with the world in which they will have to live out their lives. There can be no denying that this is a dangerous business. To acquaint students with the ultimate loyalties and allegiances of contemporary people in their cultural manifestations is to run the risk of their succumbing to the beckoning attractiveness of such things.⁵⁹

For Wolterstorff, a Christian school has to accept the risk of exploration if it is to prepare Christian young people as witnesses to Christ in the world rather than supposing to pursue Christian mission in isolation from the world. DYM needs to be prepared to face the same risk, allowing young people their freedom to make their own spiritual choices. Wolterstorff concludes his call to lead students in open exploration with the affirmation, "But Christians know their business."⁶⁰ Youth ministers also need to

55. Rambo, *Conversion*, 104.
56. Rambo, *Conversion*, 104.
57. Bourdieu, *Logic of Practice*, 69.
58. "Intentional reflection on practice" is necessary "in order to encourage reflective immersion in practice" (Smith, *Imagining*, 186).
59. Wolterstorff et al., *Educating for Life*, 29.
60. Wolterstorff et al., *Educating for Life*, 29.

be clear about their purpose, grounded in their confidence in the work of God through the gospel.

Dialogue in Pursuit of Love

The primary process of DYM by which youth ministers can facilitate critical awareness among young people is dialogue as an expression of love. There is a mutual contribution to be made here. On the one hand, pursuing Christian love provides a corrective to the potential for the quest for authenticity to slide into narrow self-focus and narcissism. On the other hand, promoting open dialogue in an intersubjective space can provide practices that will embody and embed the Christian ethic of love in lived experience.

Grounded in love, DYM reverses the order of Greene's conception of freedom. Instead of pursuing a freedom where persons act "to make a space for themselves in the presence of others,"[61] DYM directs adult mentors and young people alike to make spaces for others in the presence of the self. Pursuing love creates an encompassing moral value that bends social interactions toward spaces of freedom and openness. Setting love as the primary good by which we evaluate the moral value of other choices supplies an inner corrective for when dialogue and openness leans toward either division and enmity or superficiality and false harmony. The other-person concern in love can help prevent disagreements from becoming divisions by recognizing the opportunity for creative tensions to lead to deeper insight and understanding. In a similar way, loving concern for others can help move a dialogue beyond the safety of social pleasantries to engage with issues of deep interpersonal significance. There is no guarantee that pursuing love will prevent dialogue devolving into animus or trivia, but if either is the outcome it will be because of a failure to hold to the ethical ideal. Youth ministries seek to open spaces where, despite their differences, young people together with adult mentors can come together in a unity of mutual grace.

As well as pursuing love in order to promote dialogue, DYM will also endeavor to train young people, and youth leaders, in the practices of authentic dialogue as a discipline to promote genuine love. While love can promote, but not guarantee, authentic dialogue, promoting authentic dialogue can help direct genuine love and sustain loving practice. Affirming Greene's conclusion that "the person . . . develops in his/her fullness to the degree that he/she is a member of a live community,"[62] by promoting dialogue we recognize that each individual brings a unique perspective on our shared experience. Engaging in dialogue gives us access to additional

---

61. Greene, *DF*, 56.
62. Greene, *DF*, 43.

resources for our individual quests to make sense of our world and our place in it. In dialogue with others the individual finds support, challenge, and guidance in relation to making meaningful choices. In DYM adult mentors have a particular opportunity to guide dialogical practices in pursuit of love by being present with young people in their own authenticity, and as people who show care and concern for those they lead.

Rather than negating or diminishing Greene's advocacy for creating dialogical spaces of mutual concern, pursuing aesthetic pedagogy within a Christian theological frame provides a strong basis upon which this central pedagogical practice can rest. The church is intended by God to be a social space that displays the kind of unity-in-diversity that Greene envisages. That is, the church is intended to be a social space that promotes human freedom. When Paul imagines the unity of the church he sees the variety of gifts in relation to the unity of God. The metaphor of the body (1 Cor 12), and the centrality of love (1 Cor 13) are particularly focused on unity in plurality. As "a finite echo or bodying forth of the divine personal dynamics," the church needs to be the kind of social space that invites young people into the life-giving relations of the Godhead.[63] By promoting dialogue in pursuit of love, DYM can help shape the church to be the sort of community that Greene envisages, one in which,

> persons are likely to choose themselves as committed and as free . . . [to] know what it is to reach out for freedom as a palpable good, to engage with and resist the compelling and conditioning forces, to open fields where the options can multiply, where unanticipated possibilities open each day . . . [to] see the relation between their pursuit and the opening of a public space where persons can appear before one another as who they are and what they can do.[64]

---

63. Gunton, *Trinitarian Theology*, 73.

64. Greene, *DF*, 115. Dietrich Bonhoeffer picks up on how union with Christ promotes a social space that enables people to appear before one another as who they are and what they can do. Bonhoeffer speaks about Christ bringing peace between Christian people because we recognize that our unity is only in and through Christ. Without Christ, Bonhoeffer says, "the way to [other Christians] is blocked by one's own ego" (*Life Together*, 33). The human desire for self-justification, Bonhoeffer argues, imitates the example of the disciples in Luke 9:46 by attempting to establish which of us is greatest. Bonhoeffer says that "from the first moment two people meet, one begins looking for a competitive position to assume and hold against the other" (*Life Together*, 93). Rather than being "who they are," a person will posture and position him or herself to "find the place where they can stand and defend themselves" (*Life Together*, 94). This, Bonhoeffer says, "is the struggle of natural human beings for self-justification" (*Life Together*, 94). Seen in this light, such self-justification is the enemy of a social space that would promote freedom. Instead, justification by grace frees human beings from self-justification for if one has been accepted in Christ, they have no need to establish a ground on which they might make themselves acceptable to others. The grace of the

Summary

Through critical conversation between Greene and Taylor, I have argued in this chapter that the pursuit of meaning is an appropriate goal for Christian youth ministries serving contemporary young people caught up in the culture of expressive individualism. Encouraging, enabling, and engaging with young people in a quest to make personal choices of spiritual meaning recognizes the ethical ideal in authenticity that is consistent with biblical themes of freedom, choice, and personal responsibility. Adult mentors who bring their personal convictions into the dialogue around meaning with young people resist being coercive by taking a posture of offering the gospel as a possibility of meaning, while being prepared for young people to choose to reject what is being offered. The ethic of martyrdom that trusts the promises of God despite the challenges of present experience calls youth ministers to reject temptations to the inappropriate use of power as well as temptations to the unfaithful surrender of their responsibility as agents of divine reconciliation (2 Cor 5:20).

A dialogical youth ministry will therefore direct youth ministry leaders to pursue three key practices. First, while continuing to hope and pray for young people to make choices of meaning that accept the gracious authority of God, youth leaders will equip young people in processes of spiritual formation expressive of the contemporary quest for personal authenticity. Second, by casting a critically reflective eye inwards toward the formative processes of the church as well as outwards toward the various alternative possibilities for constructing meaning, youth leaders will equip young people to make critically aware choices. Third, by pursuing love, DYM can enable authentic dialogue, and by internalizing the value of dialogue, DYM can embody and embed genuine love. Approaching Christian spiritual formation in this way holds together the cultural value placed on personal construction of meaning, Greene's vision of harmonious social life, and Christian convictions regarding divine authority. In DYM, Greene's values and vision can be not only affirmed but held together in a moral framework shaped by the gospel of Christ.

Gospel, Bonhoeffer writes, "confronts us with the truth. It says to us, you are a sinner, a great, unholy sinner. Now come, as the sinner that you are, to your God who loves you" (*Life Together*, 108). Consequently, without the need to pretend to be what they are not or to put on a show of false piety the person justified by grace is free to confess their sins to another believer. It is in "the confession of sin made in the presence of a Christian brother," Bonhoeffer argues, that "the last stronghold of self-justification is abandoned," and a person reaches the "breakthrough to community" (*Life Together*, 110).

7

The Bible, Dialogue, and the Disciplined Imagination

THIS CHAPTER EXPLORES HOW youth leaders could approach the Bible in order to enable and promote open dialogue around meaning-making. Building on the ideas presented in chapter 4 relating to the place Greene gives to engagement with the creative arts, I will consider how what Greene says of the use of creative art in aesthetic education could be applied to the practices of Bible engagement in Christian youth ministry. While I have begun to answer this question in the discussion of Tracy's concept of the "Christian Classic," the particular edge to the following discussion is how an aesthetic engagement with the Bible is influenced by a theological commitment to the Bible as the authoritative word of God.

As was noted in chapter 4, Greene's aesthetic pedagogy finds value for meaning-making only in those works of art that provoke people to critical awareness. Whether or not the Bible is such a text is a moot point, particularly when the Bible is approached as a text with normative authority. Texts of "propaganda" are inimical to what Greene is pursuing because they are "'closed' texts which eschew ambiguity in an attempt to impose their own final, totalized truths."[1] While chapter 4 explored how Zittoun's theory of symbolic resources could be applied to Bible engagement, Zittoun herself expresses reservations about the possibility of the Bible being used this way. While any cultural element could potentially be used as a symbolic resource, Zittoun argues that there is a certain "richness" in some cultural elements that leave them more positively disposed to being used in this way. The

1. Barone, "Maxine Greene," 144.

richness of a cultural element is a measure of "its power to invite various uses . . . its openness to multiple interpretation by people in various sociocultural and historical locations, and the breadth of human questions and issues it might possibly help to reflect."[2] Zittoun questions whether the Bible might "seem more resistant to a diversity of needs, intentions, and uses than, possibly the Bridget Jones diaries."[3] Without commenting on the value of the Bridget Jones diaries, it is apparent that there is a case to be made, at least in the popular imagination, that the Bible is able to serve diverse needs, intentions, and uses when accompanied by a commitment to this text as an authoritative norm for how we interpret the world.

The main argument in this chapter is that a conservative doctrine of the Bible as the "living and enduring word of God" (1 Pet 1:23) can be held alongside the pursuit of free and open dialogue with young people around how they make use of the Bible for their personal construction of meaning. Rather than opting for simple compatibility between these two ideas, drawing on Garrett Green's theological hermeneutics I am arguing a strong case, and in two directions: first, that a conservative theology of the Bible requires a commitment to open dialogue; and second, that the exercise of free and open dialogue requires the discipline of textual boundaries. Garrett Green's emphasis on the role of the religious imagination in the hermeneutical task provides an important bridge between Maxine Greene's emphasis on imagination and the creative arts and practices of Bible engagement in Reformed theology.

Before building this argument, the first stage of the correlative conversation in this chapter will argue that a conservative commitment to the Bible as the word of God focuses attention on the literary qualities of the text, such as the prevalence of metaphor and narrative. Further to this observation, by recognizing that the notion of the "aesthetic" extends beyond the arts or the study of beauty to refer to the bodily dimensions of meaning, I draw attention to the various ways the biblical text appeals to our sense experience. This section affirms that accepting the Bible as divine revelation does not hinder recognizing the Bible as being also a work of human literature. Conservative readers can therefore look to the Bible as a potent impetus and source for constructing meaning, much in the same way that Greene conceptualizes the potential impact of creative art.

---

2. Zittoun, *Transitions*, 175.
3. Zittoun, *Transitions*, 175.

The Art of Scripture

Aesthetic pedagogy is particularly concerned with how an individual might use the biblical texts as works of literature, as tools for interpreting, or making sense of, their lived experience. At one level this claim is non-problematic; since the Bible is undeniably a work of human literary construction, its texts could be used in aesthetic pedagogy in the same way as Greene uses *The Plague* or *Madam Bovary*.[4]

That the Bible is a noted achievement of human literature has long been recognized. Augustine identified the traits of classical writing in the Bible and regarded the literary forms of Scripture as indispensable to determining its meaning. The so-called literary approach to the Bible draws particular attention to its literary qualities (such as genre, the prevalence of narrative, the use of rhetorical devices, the abundance of metaphor, and other sensual imagery), and seeks to apply literary theory as a tool for interpreting the text.[5] The same recognition that the literary forms of Scripture are indispensable to determining its meaning is evident in the attention given to genre and literary style in the exegetical work of Luther and Calvin.[6]

However, in contrast to this widespread affirmation, Reformed evangelical approaches to Scripture, especially ones that affirm "propositional revelation," have often been accused of failing to engage holistically with the Bible's literary qualities. The first task of this chapter is to demonstrate that the evangelical commitment to propositional revelation, far from detracting from the significance of the Bible as literature, actually enhances it.

The Divine Artist

Muriel Porter, long-term critic of the conservative evangelical Anglican Diocese of Sydney, charges the conservative commitment to propositional revelation as "rationalist" and "the direct opposite of holistic spirituality, [which] reflects nothing of feeling, imagination, intuition, or the place of silence in religious meditation."[7] Mining a similar vein, critiques of

---

4. Irrespective of the range of theological opinions on the relation of human and divine authorship of the Scriptures, the Christian tradition has not affirmed solely supernatural accounts of the origins of the biblical texts such as dictation or appearing ex nihilo.

5. Alter, *The Art of Biblical Narrative*; Alter, *The world Of Biblical Literature*.

6. Ryken, "Bible as Literature," traces the history of the literary approach to the Bible, noting in particular the influence of Moulton, *The Literary Study of the Bible*, and Frye, *Anatomy of Criticism*.

7. Porter, *Sydney Anglicans*, 42.

evangelical spirituality, such as this from Greenman, may be clichéd but are not uncommon: "Typical patterns of evangelical engagement with Scripture can easily devolve into an information-oriented rationalism where the Bible is 'word processed' in a mechanical way, rather than being absorbed and digested in a more deeply transformational manner."[8] It would seem that a conservative theology of Scripture is in conflict with an invitation to engage imaginatively with its text.

If a proposition is "a person's assertion that may be true or false,"[9] then much of the content of the Bible is clearly non-propositional, such as the various figures of speech, parables, and extensive use of poetry and narrative. It is not surprising, therefore, that an article with the title "Propositional Revelation the Only Revelation,"[10] authored by Broughton Knox, former Principal of Moore Theological College and celebrated intellectual leader of Sydney Anglicans, has been accused of theological rationalism.[11]

However, while acknowledging the overstatement in the title of Knox's article, the rationalist critique of propositional revelation is largely based on a misunderstanding of what Knox means by "propositional."[12] For Knox a "proposition" refers to "meaningful statements and concepts expressed in words" or "words written meaningfully."[13] Knox's article aims to defend the notion of Scripture as revelation, rather than being merely a witness to revelation or a record of God's revelatory actions in history. Jensen summarizes Knox's position in the simple affirmation, "God speaks."[14]

On this understanding, not only does God speak, but when God speaks, God uses literary art. Thus, rather than the suggestion that a conservative notion of propositional revelation is a hindrance to an appreciation of the literary qualities of Scripture, this approach to the Bible amplifies the significance of those features. The use of narrative, poetry, metaphor, et cetera, are not just human forms attempting to grasp the divine, they are the words through which God chooses to reveal himself to human beings.[15]

---

8. Greenman, "Spiritual Formation," 28–29.
9. Lewis, "Is Propositional Revelation Essential?" 270.
10. Knox, "Propositional Revelation."
11. Osborn, "Realism and Revelation"; Porter, *Sydney Anglicans*.
12. Jensen, *Sydney Anglicanism*, 51.
13. Knox, "Propositional Revelation," 2, 3.
14. Jensen, *Sydney Anglicanism*, 56. See Jensen, *Revelation,* for an extended defence of the essentially verbal nature of Christian revelation. Jensen disputes the suggestion that revelation is personal rather than propositional as a false dichotomy. Personal relationships are established and sustained by words. One can never plausibly say, "I did not believe your words, because they were not you" (Jensen, *Revelation,* 165).
15. How human words might also be God's words is a moot point in Christian

As Thompson notes (in a book dedicated to Broughton Knox), the literary form of Scripture is not a dispensable shell. "If it really is *this text* we are trying to understand, then we must direct our attention there."[16] Paying attention to the particularities of the biblical text such as narrative frame, genre, and canonical shape, are all corollaries of taking the text of Scripture seriously, and taking the responsible reading of that text seriously.

Scripture's Bodily Dimensions

By paying attention to the literary features of the Bible, an aesthetic engagement with Scripture will also seek to connect with the bodily dimensions of meaning present in the biblical texts. Aesthetics is not just about beauty and taste but concerns "all of the things that go into meaning—form, expression, communication, qualities, emotion, feeling, value, purpose, and more."[17] More than engaging in what is "beautiful" or "creative," in keeping with the Greek root *aisthanesthai*, referring to "perception by the senses,"[18] an aesthetic pedagogy will explore the bodily dimensions of meaning-making through our concrete connection with the world.

There is a bodily dimension to engaging with narrative and metaphor because these artistic forms call upon our awareness of, and interaction with, our physical location in time and space. Neuroscientific research has revealed that processing metaphors engages the same parts of the brain responsible for bodily functioning.[19] Interacting with a narrative invites hearers to place themselves physically in the concrete situations the narrative presents. Thus, ruminating on a metaphor or indwelling a narrative are not merely cognitive tasks of analogical reasoning, but are physical acts engaging the senses of sight, taste, touch, hearing, and smell.

---

theology. This project is speaking from and to the Reformed tradition that regards the Bible as the place where "God invests himself in the written Word and . . . even identifies with it, to the point that Scripture becomes a mode of God's own presence" (Bird, *Evangelical Theology*, 196). There is a work of divine superintendence in the work of inspiration such that the words chosen by the human authors of the Bible are the words that God intended to be used to convey his self-revelation. "God is himself the author of the instruments he employs for the communication of his messages to man and has framed them into precisely the instruments he desired for the exact communication of His message . . . If God wished to give his people a series of letters like Paul's, He prepared a Paul to write them, and the Paul He brought to the task was a Paul who spontaneously would write just such letters" (Warfield, *Revelation*, 91).

16. Thompson, *Clear and Present Word*, 121.
17. Johnson, *The Meaning of the Body*, 212.
18. Smith, *Imagining*, 116.
19. Lacey et al., "Metaphorically Feeling."

The bodily dimensions of meaning are an expression of the "creational conditions" of embodiment and sociality.[20] We live in a material creation with the capacity (and necessity) of interacting physically with this creation and receive this materiality as the "very good" gift of God (Gen 1:31). The biblical revelation repeatedly affirms that God meets us in the physical constraints of our body and the historical particulars of human community. It is therefore significant that Paul calls the Roman church to present as a living sacrifice their bodies rather than just their minds or souls (Rom 12:1). The cognitive work of renewing the mind is to have physical consequences for the presentation of the body.

As well as paying attention to the bodily dimensions of interacting with biblical imagery and narrative, an aesthetic engagement with the Bible will also be aware of the bodily dimension involved in Bible reading itself. The Bible is a book intended to be read aloud in public worship.[21] Thus the bodily dynamic of reading aloud and listening to what is read places the contemporary worshipping community in the same position as Adam and Eve (Gen 3:9), Abraham (Gen 12:1), Moses (Exod 3:4), and Isaiah (Isa 6:8), among many others; that is, human beings being addressed personally by the living God. Reading from the Bible in Christian worship is therefore in itself a way of enacting the biblical story.[22] An aesthetic engagement with the Bible will pay attention to the way the physical dynamic of listening to the public reading of Scripture reinforces the identity of God's people as those who hear and respond to the divine call.

As an aesthetic engagement with the Bible looks to enact what we read, it will also draw our attention to how the text involves our bodies in that action. The significance of the body in God's purposes for humanity is affirmed in the doctrines of creation, the incarnation of Christ, Christ's bodily resurrection as first-fruits of our own bodily resurrection, and the promise of the new creation. It ought be no surprise, then, that the Scriptures make frequent reference to bodily posture in worship: to stand (1 Sam 1:26; Mark 11:25), sit (2 Sam 7:18), bow down (Ps 95:6), kneel (Ps 95:6; Eph 3:14), raise hands (Ps 63:4; 1 Tim 2:8), lift one's eyes (Ps 123:1), clap (Ps 47:1), shout (Ps 66:1), sing (Ps 33:1; Eph 5:19). Various postures embody various theological values. Since the meaning embodied in postures is neither self-evident nor

---

20. Smith, *Imagining*, 33.

21. References to reading the scriptures in Christian worship (Col 4:16, 1 Thess 5:27, 1 Tim 4:13, Rev 1:3) all use the word *anagnōnai*, which most commonly refers to the official practice of reading aloud in a group of people.

22. Smith, *Desiring*, 195. David Smith describes similar attention to posture and the cultivation of particular virtues in relation to reading texts in educational settings ("Reading Practices," 52).

static, theological significance arises from ongoing dialogue between action and Scripture,[23] but not in such a way that the actions become superfluous. That the postures described in the Bible are often regarded as expressions of culture, and therefore as dispensable, reflects the cognitive bias in Western Christianity. In contrast, Luther often spoke of the physical postures of prayer, affirming the connection between bodily posture, the attitudes of the heart, and the words of the mouth.[24] An aesthetic engagement with the biblical text regards references to posture as elements of the text that are integral to exploring the meaning of the text itself.[25]

The first conclusion of this chapter, therefore, is to note that an aesthetic engagement with the Bible, paying attention to the literary qualities of the text along with bodily dimensions of meaning contained in the text, is entirely consistent with conservative approaches to the Bible as the living word of God. Valuing propositional, or verbal, revelation focuses our attention on the text that we have received as God's chosen vehicle of self-revelation. A conservative doctrine of Scripture ought to lead to a joyful interaction with the variety of literary forms and bodily connections present in the Bible as the gift of God, with the promise of growing in personal knowledge of God as we do so.

It is clear, then, that the Bible contains the aesthetic materials useful for meaning-making in a way that bears some resemblance to Greene's use of creative art. As a concrete artefact of human literary achievement, with its frequent use of metaphor and narrative that anchors this text in the physical reality of our lived experience, the Bible carries features of creative art that Greene regards as necessary for promoting wide-awakeness in the world. What remains to be established is whether the potency of those raw materials

---

23. Westerfield Tucker, "Knee-Bowed and Body-Bent."

24. Haemig, "Practical Advice on Prayer," quotes Luther's comments on Psalm 118:5 in which Luther involves the whole body in the act of prayer: "We read: 'I called upon the Lord.' You must learn to call. Do not sit by yourself or lie on a couch, hanging and shaking your head. Do not destroy yourself with your own thoughts by worrying. Do not strive and struggle to free yourself, and do not brood on your wretchedness, suffering, and misery. Say to yourself: 'Come on, you lazy bum; down on your knees, and lift your eyes and hands toward heaven!' Read a psalm or the Our Father, call on God, and tearfully lay your troubles before Him. Mourn and pray, as this verse teaches . . . Likewise Pss 141:2: 'Let my prayer be counted as incense before Thee, and lifting up of my hands as an evening sacrifice!' Here you learn that praying, reciting your troubles, and lifting up your hands are sacrifices most pleasing to God" (*LW*, 14:60).

25. Haemig, "Practical Advice on Prayer," 29. This connection between theoretical truths and bodily action underlies Vanhoozer's identification of Christian life as fundamentally "dramatic": "The Christian way is not something one can behold (*theōreō*) or contemplate with the mind's eye only. Doctrine seeks not simply to state theoretical truths but to embody truth in ways of living" (Vanhoozer, *Drama*, 15).

is able to withstand the imposition of a theological tradition with an authoritative message. The remaining sections of this chapter turn to consider how the value of the Bible as an aesthetic resource for meaning-making is influenced by theological commitments to the Bible as an authoritative norm for how human beings might make sense of the world.

The Bible Requires Dialogue

Chapter 4 recognized Tracy's notion of the classic as a way of finding a space for open dialogue with the message of the Bible that is accessible to the public beyond the church. Yet what Tracy's account of Scripture purports to gain in enabling a dialogue about spiritual meaning in line with Greene's vision seems to come from diminishing the significance of the divine origin of the biblical text. In arguing that a conservative doctrine of Scripture requires a commitment to open dialogue, I first need to explain why I consider Tracy's argument to be an insufficient solution.

In place of Tracy's proposal, I argue from Garrett Green's theological hermeneutics that a conservative doctrine of the inspiration and authority of Scripture not only permits open dialogue and quest for meaning, but requires it. Receiving the Bible as the word of God presents readers and hearers with a "hermeneutic imperative" inviting us into a "hermeneutic space" of open-ended meditation and ever-potent reflection. I establish the necessity of dialogue as the central practice of such hermeneutical spaces by recognizing the hermeneutic imperative as a gift of God's grace to the church.

Reconsidering the Classic

Tracy regards the Bible as the normative expression of how the Christian community experienced, and continues to experience, the "event and person of Jesus Christ" as the "Christian classic."[26] As suggested in the conclusion to chapter 4, if we were to apply Tracy's notion of the classic, without critique, to Bible engagement in teenage spiritual formation, youth ministers would invite young people to engage with the Bible as a human text that has been hailed as spiritually significant in the past, and that holds the promise of being spiritually significant for them in the present. Youth leaders would therefore invite young people into a conversation space, recognizing a plurality of questions along with a plurality of possible interpretations.

---

26. Tracy, *Analogical Imagination*, 233.

Understanding the theological task as reflection on publicly accessible "classics" offers a welcome invitation for youth ministry. According to Tracy's proposal, theology "can be done by anyone who can read and think and who is even mildly sensitive to the universal ambiguities of the human condition."[27] Such a description includes many, if not all, young people. Where Bible engagement is cast as interacting with a classic expression of human spiritual expression any young person can join in dialogue about spirituality in relation to Jesus and the Bible, whether or not he or she has come to a place of personal faith.

However, while Tracy's approach to the Bible accords with Greene's love of questions, open dialogue, and freedom to construct one's own meaning, it does so at the expense of traditional doctrines of divine revelation and biblical authority. Tracy's revisionist model of theology argues that a theologian "cannot allow his own—or his tradition's—beliefs to serve as warrants for his arguments."[28] Theologians nevertheless "believe that they can provide evidence to fair-minded critics inside and outside Christianity for the meaning and truth" of the Christian understandings of God, Jesus Christ, and revelation.[29] Yet by making the conclusions of theology accessible to the public beyond the church, Tracy has so emphasized the human accessibility of this text that it obscures the work of the Spirit in revealing the word of God to human creatures. Tracy's project is a modern variant of the "accommodationist theology" that endeavors to "present Christianity in a form acceptable to the enlightened sensibility of modern people by removing its offensive 'positivity.'"[30] Tracy's notion of the classic aligns with Kant's twin projects in *Religion within the Limits of Reason Alone*:[31] a philosophical task to describe a rational faith stripped of the inappropriate and unnecessary clothing of the historical religions, and an apologetic task to argue that Christianity can be recognized as the manifestation of a rational faith.[32]

Absent from Tracy's approach to theology is any imposition of external authority on the interpretive conclusions drawn, whether by an academic

---

27. Portier, "Theology and Authority," 594.
28. Tracy, *Blessed Rage*, 7.
29. Tracy, *Blessed Rage*, 9.
30. Green, *Theology*, 60. Garrett Green's use of "positivity" is picking up Kant's contrast between a "natural religion," based on the nature of things and thereby accessible by the exercise of unaided human reason, and "positive religion" that depends upon the authority of an external source.
31. Kant, *Religion*.
32. Christianity as a religion is, according to Kant, "objectively a natural one though subjectively a revealed one" (Kant, in Green, *Theology*, 33).

theologian or an inquisitive teenager.[33] Speaking out of his Roman Catholic tradition, Portier seeks to recast Tracy's approach in such a way that permits church authority to exercise some corrective function over theological opinion.[34] From my Reformed tradition I ask the same question in terms of how Tracy's proposal permits Scripture to exercise a corrective function over how young people might construct meaning.

Garrett Green's critique of Tracy as an exemplar of the accommodationist endeavor clarifies the challenge for Bible engagement within an aesthetic pedagogy. How can a "positive" Christianity be consistent with the pedagogical imperative of openness to personal exploration and discovery? The following argument draws on Garrett Green's notion of the hermeneutic imperative as an answer to this challenge.

Hermeneutic Imperative

Garrett Green argues that there is a "hermeneutic imperative" in both Scripture and creation, such that to do "good theology" means to always be involved in an ongoing task of interpretation. Green argues that "to read the Bible as scripture is to interpret it—and to interpret the world and oneself at the same time."[35] That is, the hermeneutic imperative arises as a direct implication of receiving the Bible as sacred Scripture, not despite it.

As I have argued above, the Bible's wealth of imagery and literary forms establish an obvious connection between Bible engagement and the interaction with works of art in aesthetic pedagogy. Beyond the appeal to the imagination, there is a "surplus of meaning" in biblical language which leaves the interpretive task ever incomplete.[36] Connecting in particular with Maxine Greene's focus on creative art, the hermeneutic imperative arises from the fact that "God has chosen to reveal himself not in transparent doctrines appealing to pure reason but in opaque symbols and narratives that appeal to the imagination."[37] Though the task of theology is "conceptual," requiring

---

33. Green, *Theology*, 30.
34. Portier, "Theology and Authority," 595.
35. Green, *Theology*, 176.
36. Green, *Theology*, 173.
37. Green, *Theology*, 182. Garrett Green offers further argument for the surplus of meaning from Ricoeur's theory of symbolic language (from which the language of "surplus of meaning" is drawn), Derrida's theory of the inherent instability of signs, and Barth's theology of the inability of human words to ever fully articulate God's word. I have restricted the argument here to connect with Maxine Greene's focus on literary art.

"the articulation and interpretation of the religious imagination,"[38] concepts cannot replace symbols without potential loss of meaning.[39] Important as theological abstraction is to Christian faith, it can never replace the biblical text from which such abstractions are drawn.

That interpretation of the Bible needs to have an open-ended character arises also from the theological conviction that this text is the personal revelation of a personal God. Accepting the Bible as divine revelation does not lock interpretation into "an authoritarian appeal to a single textual meaning."[40] In the same way that Greene emphasizes the interpersonal exchange between artist and audience in engaging with works of art, so too a Reformed theology of Scripture emphasizes that to engage with the Bible is to engage, in some way, with God. As Trevor Hart recognizes, since speech and texts are modes of human engagement, reading is not a matter of dealing with an impersonal object but engaging with what an author has said. So too with the Bible. Thus, "when I take up the Bible . . . I am dealing with St. Paul, and by way of dealing with him, I am, awesomely, dealing with God."[41] Therefore, recognizing God as "a free agent who cannot be manipulated or treated as a mere object"[42] establishes the necessarily interpersonal nature of reading the Bible as holy Scripture. Bible readers therefore should recognize that "just as I cannot 'interpret' you as though you were a finished product or a fixed text, so *a fortiori* I cannot treat the Word of God as simply given, fixed, and available to my understanding."[43] As a personal word from a personal God, the task of interpreting the Bible will always be incomplete.

Eugene Peterson identifies three ways that Bible readers have depersonalized the biblical text: by reading for intellectual challenge, practical instruction, or personal inspiration. To do so is to use the text for our own purposes leaving us free of having "to deal with a personally revealing God who has personal designs on you."[44] Peterson refers to C. S. Lewis's comments on engaging with works of art:

---

38. Green, *Imagining God*, 71.

39. Ricoeur states his position more strongly, that "real metaphors are not translatable" and that any paraphrase "is infinite and incapable of exhausting the innovative meaning" (Ricoeur, *Interpretation Theory*, 52). Garrett Green states a more cautious conclusion, that "the paraphrase of a metaphor is *indefinite*" since "whether it is infinite is something that cannot be known in advance" (*Theology*, 174).

40. Green, *Theology*, 173.

41. Hart, "Imagination and Responsible Reading," 338.

42. Green, *Theology*, 176.

43. Green, *Theology*, 176.

44. Peterson, *Eat this Book*, 30.

> A work of (whatever) art can be either "received" or "used." When we "receive" it we exert our senses and imaginations and various other powers according to a pattern invented by the artist. When we "use" it we treat it as assistance for our own activities . . . "Using" is inferior to "reception" because art, if used rather than received, merely facilitates, brightens, relieves or palliates our life, and does not add to it.[45]

Lewis's distinction between "use" and "reception" of a work of art is echoed in Griffiths's contrast between consumerist and religious reading. Religious reading is to read "as a lover reads, with a tensile attentiveness that wishes to linger, to prolong, to savor."[46] It is a reverential reading, where the work read is considered "an object of overpowering delight and great beauty," a work that "can never be discarded because it can never be exhausted. It can only be reread, with reverence and ecstasy."[47] In stark contrast, "consumerist reading" is to read in order "to extract what is useful or exciting or entertaining from what is read, preferably with dispatch, and then to move on to something else."[48] Consumerist reading reflects the casual glances given to artwork that Greene decries. Consumerist reading is inimical to dialogue as well as disdainful of the authors of the text, both human and divine.

The way Griffiths describes the way religious readers view sacred texts bears many of the hallmarks of Maxine Greene's descriptions of the way works of art can be used for promoting wide-awakeness in students:

> the work read is understood as a stable and vastly rich resource, one that yields meaning, suggestions (or imperatives) for action, matter for aesthetic wonder, and much else. It is a treasure-house, an ocean, a mine: the deeper religious readers dig, the more ardently they fish, the more single-mindedly they seek gold, the greater will be their reward. The basic metaphors here are those of discovery, uncovering, retrieval, opening up: religious readers read what is there to be read, and

---

45. Lewis, *An Experiment in Criticism*, 88.

46. Griffiths, *Religious Reading*, ix.

47. Griffiths, *Religious Reading*, 42. An example of such reverential reading is found in Pope Francis's preface to a German edition of the Bible for young people: "If you saw my Bible it might not draw your attention. You might say, 'What? That's the Pope's Bible? What an old, worn-out book!' You might even be tempted to buy me a new one, one costing a thousand euros maybe. I would not take it. I love my old Bible. It has been with me for half of my life. It has seen my joy, and has been wet by my tears. It is a priceless treasure. I live of it [sic], and would not give it up for anything in the world" (Wooden, "Through Thick and Thin").

48. Griffiths, *Religious Reading*, ix.

what is there to be read always precedes, exceeds, and in the end supersedes its readers.[49]

The richness of sacred texts with their promise of endless reward resonates with Greene's view that works of art can open spaces for continual conversation and discovery. Sacred texts, on Griffiths's analysis, offer constructions of meaning as well as proposing concrete action in the world. There is "aesthetic wonder" offered in sacred texts which resonates with the aesthetic experience Greene seeks through engagement with works of art. With strong echoes of Greene's advocacy of engaging with works of art to stimulate the work of meaning-making, Griffiths describes reading sacred texts as providing "tools and skills" for believers that can be used "to interpret the world."[50] Dialogical youth ministry regards the Bible as this kind of sacred text, mediating an interpersonal exchange, and inviting a never-complete work of interpretation.

Regarding the Bible as the kind of sacred text that Griffiths describes, and recognizing Garrett Green's notion of the hermeneutic imperative, will therefore involve holding the Bible in a "hermeneutical space."[51] Though not identical, a hermeneutical space for the Bible is akin to the aesthetic space within which Maxine Greene directs us to hold works of art. For Greene, entering an aesthetic space involves setting aside theoretical prescriptions that suggest the "right way" to interpret an artwork so that one can give oneself over to the alternate world being offered by the artist. In a similar way, Garrett Green identifies Vroom's "hermeneutical space" with Hans Frei's suggestion that "a good interpretation of a text is one that has 'breathing space' . . . in which finally no hermeneutic allows you to resolve the text. There is something that is left to bother; something is wrong; something is not yet interpreted."[52] Holding the Bible in hermeneutical space means to remain open to exploration and the expectation of new discovery.

God's Good Gift

Faithful engagement with Scripture as the word of God involves aesthetic encounter and quest for meaning as envisaged in Maxine Greene's educational philosophy. This is no grudging concession. The hermeneutic imperative ought not be regarded as "simply a problem to be endured, a

---

49. Griffiths, *Religious Reading*, 41.
50. Griffiths, *Religious Reading*, 19.
51. Green, *Theology*, 182; Vroom, "Religious Hermeneutics."
52. Frei, "Conflicts in Interpretation," 353.

perhaps inevitable but nonetheless lamentable consequence of our finitude," but rather received with gratitude as "a sign of God's grace, a source of joy and hope for believers."[53]

To approach the Bible in hermeneutical space means to always come with a readiness to hear something new. This promise of newness is, Garrett Green argues, the intended outworking of the great Reformation principle of sola scriptura:

> not a backward-looking traditionalism but rather a hopeful confidence that God will continue to shed new light from scripture. A church whose central activity is the interpretation of scripture is not the guardian of a timeless deposit of faith but rather the *ecclesia semper reformanda*.[54]

What is true of the Bible as the living word of the Living God is true also of the world that God created, precisely because it is a world created by this God. The world is in need of interpretation not only because of the noetic effects of sin. In the Genesis narrative Adam was invited into the work of meaning-making before the fall. Adam and Eve were dependent on God's special revelation to navigate the world (Gen 2:16) even before their minds were darkened by sin, the implication being that the meaning of creation was not self-evident even in the prelapsarian state. That the world is both interpretable and in need of interpretation is not the result of sin but of creation. The world has been created by God and designed to be understood only in relation to God:

> The Lord God has created a world, so say the biblical witnesses, that is an enigma, a surd, apart from its divine origin and destiny. Seen in its godly relationship, the world does not become comprehensible so much as interpretable. It remains mysterious without being meaningless. Indeed, its meaning depends on the divine mystery at its heart, so that its meaning is not given but is rather a task, a quest.[55]

That is, contrary to the possible objection that accepting a biblical interpretation of human life and existence would obstruct young people from pursuing personal quests for meaning, the opposite is true. Accepting the world as the intentional creation of a personal God does not mean that we are given "all the answers." Rather, we are offered the promise that there are "answers" to be found. At the heart of the universe is not meaningless

---

53. Green, *Theology*, 177.
54. Green, *Theology*, 177.
55. Green, *Theology*, 183–84.

absurdity but the God to whom nothing is secret or unknown, and who chooses to make himself known to human beings.

Recognizing the Bible as the living word of the Living God therefore invites us to acknowledge that we will never come to the end of knowing God's self-revelation, and to glory in that realization. Proverbs 25:2, standing at the head of a small collection of wisdom concerning the King, connects God's work "to conceal things" with the task of kings "to search things out." Both tasks are signs of glory: God is glorified by the mystery with which he has cloaked both himself and the world, while human beings (of whom the King is the prime representative) are glorified by the way they search out the meaning that God has embedded in all that God has revealed. Faithful engagement with the Bible as the word of God therefore invites us to embrace the quest, to "love the questions" as Maxine Greene urges; but not just to settle for quest as all that we have to hope for in a world that offers no final answers. We are invited on a quest by a good and gracious God who offers himself to us in mystery in order that human beings "should seek God, in the hope that they might feel their way toward him and find him" (Acts 17:27).

God's Good Gift for the Church

One step in the argument remains in order to establish the conclusion that a conservative doctrine of the Bible as the living word of the living God requires dialogue. So far I have followed Garrett Green's argument for recognizing the hermeneutic imperative in the Bible as stemming, not only from the literary form of Scripture, but fundamentally from identifying the Bible as the personal word of God. This need for interpretation, of the Bible and of the world, can be received with joy as a good gift from a wise and generous God. Human beings are not simply given the answers but are invested with the capability and dignity of searching them out. All of this has established the need for exploration and quest, but not yet of dialogue.

In order to establish the necessity of dialogue, it is necessary to argue that the hermeneutic imperative is God's good gift for the church. "Scriptural interpretation," Garrett Green argues, is not "an activity to be engaged in by isolated individuals, for the Christian imagination, the organ of scriptural interpretation, is forged in communal experience."[56] In the same way that many members together make up one body (1 Cor 12:12), so also many readings of Scripture can build together toward an increasingly adequate

---

56. Green, *Theology,* 184.

grasp of God's word to us.[57] These theological concerns match the value Maxine Greene places on dialogical community. Interaction with others can both challenge one's existing interpretations (especially where existing interpretations are simplistic and unexamined), and provide alternative perspectives as resources for constructing meaning.

DYM will be especially concerned to open a space for young people to participate in the church's dialogue, and to empower and equip them to do so. Greene's particular concern for allowing previously silenced voices to be heard in the mutual conversation shares common roots with the concern of liberation theology to promote the voices of the poor and marginalized. Inasmuch as the hermeneutic imperative "resists attempts at interpretive closure," Garrett Green notes the necessity of humility in reading the Bible, since "the message has been 'rigged' in such a way that the powerful and the arrogant are bound to miss its point."[58] Such concerns are particularly apt for youth ministries that seek to nurture the interpretive contributions of young people, often considered as "the parts of the body that are thought to be weaker" (1 Cor 12:22), who are often looked down upon because they are young (1 Tim 4:12).

Dialogue Requires Discipline

Not only does a conservative theology of the Bible require Christian communities to share in open dialogue in the shared quest for meaning, open dialogue requires the discipline of boundaries. Such boundaries, I will argue, are necessary for engaging in dialogue in relation to any work of creative art but are especially important for engaging with the Bible. At the conclusion to chapter 4, I raised the question from Christian theology, asking of Greene, what will keep an open exploration of personal meaning in relation to the Bible from devolving into a consumerist reading that imposes our own meaning onto the text? Responding to this question by building a case against hermeneutical relativism is not only a theological concern for conservative Christian communities with an interest in defending their traditions. There is also a political dimension of this discussion, as Volf argues: "The Bible is a potent text, and over the past two thousand years has been interpreted in seriously nefarious ways . . . [as] sufficiently imaginative minds . . . interpret texts to mean virtually anything."[59] For the sake of the church and for the common good, there is

57. Vanhoozer, *Is there a Meaning?* 420.
58. Green, *Theology*, 185, citing Luke 10:21.
59. Volf, *Captive to the Word*, 27.

pressing need to prevent free and open dialogue from becoming simply an "anything goes" approach to biblical interpretation.

Garrett Green's theological hermeneutics is intended to chart a theological course through polarized options of "authoritarian appeal to a single textual meaning" on the one hand, and "hermeneutical relativism that undermines all scriptural authority" on the other.[60] I have engaged his argument to avoid the Scylla of authoritarianism, and must now demonstrate how this affirmation of open dialogue will not send us into the Charybdis of relativism.

Transformative Interaction with Others

Maxine Greene argues that disciplined boundaries are necessary if engagements with the creative arts are to be transformational interactions between artist and audience. If an audience were to impose an interpretation on a work of art that disregarded the contribution of the artist, the opportunity for transformation through a dialogical encounter with another person is lost. As W. H. Auden famously quipped, we should not ask whether someone has read any good books lately but instead, "Have you been read by any good books lately."[61] While it is possible to use a text to construct whatever meaning one chooses, irrespective of whether or not such an approach can be deemed intellectually or ethically appropriate, to do so is to pursue an individual activity rather than an interpersonal exchange. Without interpersonal exchange, an individual's construction of meaning will be impoverished.

Before any individual can exercise their freedom to determine how they will interpret their world and their place in it, Greene's pedagogy directs them to interact with others in the intersubjective space. When an interpersonal exchange is being mediated through engagement with a work of art, individuals need first to hear the construction of meaning that is being offered in the artwork under consideration. There will need to be some discipline applied to any dialogue about meaning lest the text becomes a wax nose and thus of no value as a resource for meaning-making. Without first hearing what is being said, there is no opportunity to agree or disagree, to be challenged or helped.

---

60. Green, *Theology*, 173.

61. In Medcalf, "Eliot, David Jones, and Auden," 526. Perhaps less well known is the aphorism on which Auden's reply seems to have been modelled, "You cannot criticise the New Testament. It criticises you" (Auden and Kronenberger, *The Faber Book of Aphorisms*).

Rules for Interpretation

Greene's understanding of the nature of works of art carries various implications for employing hermeneutical rules that will bring discipline to open dialogue. First, being attentive to a particular work of art involves not only paying attention to the details of the work itself, but also learning something of the nature and use of the specific symbol-systems of that art form. Second, audiences need to approach works of art as meaningful wholes, engaging with all that the artist constructed rather than isolating one element from among many. Third, and most importantly, interpretive boundaries should not be externally imposed critical perspectives but should arise from careful consideration of the work itself.

DYM applies these same principles of setting interpretive boundaries to reading the Bible.[62] While the precise nature of hermeneutical rules have varied in different times and places,[63] the fact of such rules has been more constant.[64] Application of hermeneutical rules has been particularly emphasized in theological traditions stemming from the Magisterial Reformation.

The goal toward which we aim, even while acknowledging our inability to achieve it perfectly, is an approach to reading the text that is more and more shaped by the text itself. This "hermeneutical spiral"[65] is gained through "apprenticeship" both to the interpretive tradition of the church, and fundamentally, to the interpretive practices of Scripture.[66] DYM will primarily seek to lead young people in dialogue that is characterized by a constant return to the biblical text so that any interpretation offered is one that can be established, evaluated, and critiqued by reference to the features of the text. However, in order to maintain discipline without shutting down the possibility of alternative approaches, the constraints laid down by the text need to be conceived of as boundary markers rather than fetters, the guidelines as design principles rather than blueprints.

---

62. Philosophical hermeneutics has pursued similar rules for interpretation, exemplified in Dilthey and his successors (Makkreel and Rodi, *Dilthey Selected Works IV*). Gadamer (*Truth and Method*) rejected Dilthey's quest for objectivity, focusing on interpretation as event rather than method. Reformed evangelical hermeneutics has not followed Gadamer's more subjective path.

63. Developing largely in the contrasting strands of the Alexandrian allegorical approach and the Antiochene literal approach; Reventlow, *History of Biblical Interpretation*; Thiselton, *Hermeneutics*.

64. Hart, "Tradition, Authority," 185.

65. Osborne, *Hermeneutical Spiral*.

66. Starling, *Hermeneutics as Apprenticeship*.

Disciplined Imagination

Therefore, when we consider the work of imagination in constructing meaning in response to the Bible, DYM will speak not simply of imagination, but of "disciplined imagination." In his analysis of the prophetic imagination exercised by the Hebrew prophets, Brueggemann draws attention to the way they presented a new way of looking at their world that was deeply anchored in the normative narratives of Israel.[67] The prophetic imagination is not only free, but also disciplined.[68] In a similar way, Bauckham's study of the book of Revelation notes that a commitment to faithful use of the imagination does not imply giving in to radical subjectivity. The faithful imagination cannot neglect the reliability of the Bible as a source of necessary information:

> We should not construe the notion of different imaginative ways of perceiving the world in the vulgarly postmodern way that reduces all significant truth to matters of personal preference and ends in nihilism. Revelation gives us no warrant for mistaking images for truth itself, but it seeks images that conform to truth and seeks to use images in a way that conforms to truth.[69]

Applied to Bible engagement in DYM, open dialogue is not only to be set free and consistently applied to Scripture, it is also to be directed by and anchored in Scripture.

One example of how an open space for imagination can be held together with a commitment to the authority of the source text can be found in the practice of fanfiction discussed in chapter 5.[70] Writers of fanfiction not only create their own stories but also respond to the stories created by others. One of the key roles in responding to stories is to guard the integrity of the source text, often referred to as the "canon." For example, when writing about a character that appears in the source text (referred to as a CC, "Canon Character"),[71] the story may be critiqued as being "OOC" meaning "out of character" if the character has been made to say or do something that

---

67. Brueggemann, *Prophetic Imagination*.

68. "Prophetic utterance, under the discipline of the Torah, erupts in emotive possibility that is not constrained by our reasonableness" (Brueggemann, *The Practice of Prophetic Imagination*, 25).

69. Bauckham, *Revelation*, 160.

70. This is the case for mainstream fanfiction. Other, more "transgressive practices" use source texts as launching points for entirely novel creations (Thomas, "What Is Fanfiction?" 7).

71. In contrast to an OC, "Original Character," a character created by the fanfiction author that does not appear in the source text.

is deemed to be inconsistent with their presentation in the source text.[72] Practices such as these are consistent with the concerns of DYM that dialogue be disciplined by the biblical text. Youth leaders might therefore question whether a young person's imaginative construction in response to the Bible is OOC—out of character with other elements of the biblical story.

The Bible in Aesthetic Space

What, then, are the practices of Bible engagement with teenagers that will embody and embed these pedagogical principles in Christian youth ministry? What are the implications for Christian youth ministry if engaging with the Bible as the living word of the Living God requires open dialogue about biblical interpretation and construction of meaning? What are the implications of establishing appropriate boundaries to bring discipline to such dialogue? The final section of this chapter describes four features of DYM in order for it to function as a hermeneutic space in which young people and adult mentors can engage together in open and disciplined dialogue with the Bible.

Return to the Text

Youth ministries as hermeneutic spaces will be characterized by their constant return to the biblical text. Chapter 5 argued for the need to expose young people to all that the Bible has to offer in order to equip them with multiple resources for meaning-making. In addition to this purpose, a continual reading, and re-reading, of the Bible is required so that whatever interpretations of the Bible are offered are ones that can be established, evaluated, and critiqued by reference to the features of the text itself.

Not only will practices of Bible engagement in youth ministry seek to acquaint young people with the whole range of biblical characters and stories, prayers, prophecies, proverbs, et cetera, they will also seek to construct a sense of how all these individual features can be held together as a meaningful whole. Thus, Brueggemann's instruction to simply allow individual texts of Scripture "to linger for a while, with power, in our imagination" is valuable to an extent. The danger is that emphasizing "little texts" and allowing them to have a voice that is not dominated by others can lead to "proof-texting" that justifies anything as "from the Bible."[73]

---

72. Joyous202, "OC, OOC, and CC."
73. Hart, "(Probably) The Greatest Story Ever Told?" 203.

Each particular text is both informed and restrained by its wider biblical context. Reading a text "on its own" is not to set it free from the tyranny of context but simply to choose some other, often unacknowledged, context or set of factors.[74] Bible engagement in DYM will expose young people to the individual texts of the Bible as well as guiding them to discern the whole within which the parts are understood.

Sober Expectations

Guiding the dialogue in youth ministries as hermeneutical spaces will be sober expectations of what can be achieved by this activity. DYM recognizes that the biblical text, like any piece of interpersonal communication, is both determinate and indeterminate. To settle on one of these descriptors over the other is fatal for meaningful dialogue. Exclusively determinate readings that suppose a single and fixed meaning, one that is available to readers who apply the required tools and skills, make a "presumption of 'presence'" (that is, the presumption that the meaning is present in the text itself) but do not account for "the elusiveness of that presence."[75] On the other hand, exclusively indeterminate readings "mistake the elusiveness of presence for absence."[76] As adult mentors lead young people in Bible engagement, it will be important to establish, and constantly reinforce, the expectation that meaning is elusive but not absent. DYM aims therefore for clarity rather than comprehensiveness; confidence rather than certainty.

One significant implication of holding these expectations is to welcome an open space for doubt as a legitimate expression of faith. The opposite of faith is not doubt, but unbelief. In Jesus' post-resurrection encounter with Thomas, Thomas is not challenged to stop doubting, but to not be an unbeliever (John 20:27).[77] Matthew 28:17 describes the disciples' meeting with the risen Christ in Galilee, noting that, when they saw him "they worshipped, but

---

74. Absolving Bible teachers of responsibility for what the hearers will do with a text once they have fed it into "the zone of imagination" naïvely ignores the considerable power exercised by those church leaders with the responsibility to select which texts they will present to the congregation. "There could be a significant danger that, rather than facilitating a genuinely 'democratic' imaginative exercise, we simply allow the substitution of the ideological preferences of individual 'fund managers' for the wider voice of the church catholic" (Hart, "(Probably) The Greatest Story Ever Told?" 204).

75. Hart, "Tradition, Authority," 194.

76. Hart, "Tradition, Authority," 195.

77. *mē ginou apistos alla pistos* (μὴ γίνου ἄπιστος ἀλλὰ πιστός). When Thomas hears the report of Jesus' resurrection, he declares that he "will not believe" (*ou mē pisteusō*, οὐ μὴ πιστεύσω) without firsthand evidence. Jesus' words contrast belief and unbelief rather than faith and doubt.

some doubted."⁷⁸ While it is possible that Matthew is describing two groups of response (the worshippers and the doubters), it is more likely that those who doubted were a subset of those who worshipped.⁷⁹

That the church has not been welcoming of doubt and doubters is one of the reasons given for the exodus of young adults from the church:

> Young Christians (and former Christians too) say the church is not a place that allows them to express doubts. They do not feel safe admitting that faith doesn't always make sense. In addition, many feel that the church's response to doubt is trivial and fact focused, as if people can be talked out of doubting. *How can the Christian community help this generation face their doubts squarely and integrate their questions into a robust life of faith?*⁸⁰

DYM offers at least a partial answer to Kinnaman's challenge. By inviting young people into a dialogue around the Bible with the expectation that meaning will be elusive, DYM validates the faith experience of those who wrestle with doubt. At the same time, the expectation that meaning is not absent challenges young people who have taken on a position of doubting as an escape from further investigation or as a way of avoiding personal challenge. Wrestling with doubt is not the same as apathy or unwillingness to explore.

Beyond simply allowing a place for doubt, DYM welcomes the challenge that doubters can bring to overly-confident and unjustifiable expressions of certainty. The kind of dialogue pursued in DYM does not require all young people to cast doubt on all their beliefs (to do so would be to undermine the expectation of presence), but it will challenge young people to consider how they might hold their beliefs in light of the genuine questions from others.

Humility and Conviction

Youth ministries crafted as hermeneutical spaces will need to be marked by the virtues of humility and conviction. Holding and contributing one's personal construction of meaning with humility will keep dialogue from becoming argumentative or antagonistic. Yet if contributions are not made

---

78. *idontes auton prosekunēsan, hoi de edistasan* (ἰδόντες αὐτὸν προσεκύνησαν, οἱ δὲ ἐδίστασαν).

79. There is a syntactical parallel in Matthew 26:67, where *hoi de* (οἱ δέ) is used to identify a smaller subgroup of a larger group who have been subjects of the preceding verbs (Nolland, *Matthew*, 1262).

80. Kinnaman, *You Lost Me*. 93.

THE BIBLE, DIALOGUE, AND THE DISCIPLINED IMAGINATION   159

with conviction, dialogue devolves into superficiality or the pluralism of contradictory positions.

Humility and conviction align with the twin works of the Spirit in restraining and enlivening the interpretive task. The restraining work of the Spirit urges readers to do justice to the text by allowing the text to speak rather than attempting to make the text say what one wants it to say. Readers come to the text humbly acknowledging that they cannot stand over the text: "Humility is the virtue that constantly reminds interpreters that we can get it wrong . . . [and] enables the reader to wait upon the text, to participate in the covenant of discourse, and, if need be, to empty oneself for the sake of the text."[81]

The enlivening work of the Spirit prompts readers to bring vitality to the text by seeking to make sense of it and apply it to new contexts. Readers who bring their various interpretations with conviction can be evidence of the work of the Holy Spirit enlivening the text for the good of the church. Hermeneutical conviction recognizes that "while absolute knowledge is not a present possession, adequate knowledge is."[82] Thus, conviction recognizes the value in particular interpretations, while humility resists claiming that any one interpretation has said all that needs to be said.

Always More to be Said

DYM therefore accepts that, whatever one has been given to say, there is always more that could be said. Greene makes frequent reference to Warnock's conclusion regarding the purpose of education as to never give people the opportunity to be bored, where boredom is defined as "succumbing to a feeling of futility, or to the belief that they have come to an end of what is worth having."[83] Bible engagement needs to have the "feeling of infinity" that Warnock describes as "the belief that there is more in our experience of the world than can possibly meet the unreflecting eye, that our experience is significant for us, and worth the attempts to understand it."[84] DYM aims to never give young people the suggestion that there is nothing more to be gained from engaging with the Bible.

In the same way, for those who have chosen the Christian tradition as the large story within which they construct the meaning of their experience, there is, as Greene observes, always more in our experience of the world

---

81. Vanhoozer, *Is There a Meaning?* 464.
82. Vanhoozer, *Is There a Meaning?* 465.
83. Warnock, *Imagination*, 203.
84. Warnock, *Imagination*, 202.

than what we know or can predict.[85] I often recall the jaded reply from a teenager in response to starting a new Bible study series on the letter to the Romans, "I've already done Romans"! I suspect Greene would respond by saying that even if you have "done" it once, there is always more; there is always possibility. There is more to hear from the letter to the Romans, there is more to hear from what others hear in Romans, and there is more to consider of how our shared understanding of the message of Romans engages the ever-changing circumstances of life.

For Warnock, as for Greene, this need for constant discovery is grounded only in the experience of human limitation, not, as Warnock maintains, as "an item in a creed."[86] Greene and Warnock are largely correct in their observation of human experience. Notwithstanding vast numbers of people numbed by boredom, human experience has mostly been about discovery and possibility. There has, on the whole, always been more. However, in a Christian imagination, human limitation and the ongoing possibility of discovery is not simply an expression of our experience but is chiefly grounded in the nature and work of God. The Christian understanding of infinity is an experience that confirms the creedal declaration, "I believe in God." Christian faith embraces wonder because it looks to God, and the revelation of God in Christ, in whom we believe "all the treasures of wisdom and knowledge are hidden" (Col 2:3).

Paradoxically, in the Christian imagination infinity has a beginning and an end—"the fear of YHWH is the beginning of wisdom" (Prov 1:7) and "Christ is the end of the law" (Rom 10:4). Jesus is "the Alpha and the Omega, the first and the last, the beginning and the end" (Rev 22:13). Naming God as beginning and end of all things does not mean human beings are able to grasp either; the experience of coming to know God will be unending. But naming God as beginning and end does provide a starting point and a goal for the human quest. There is freedom in the search, but it is a search that begins in God and what God has chosen to reveal of himself to his creation.

Summary

This chapter has added to the argument in support of applying Maxine Greene's aesthetic pedagogy to practices of Bible engagement for the spiritual formation of teenagers. I have argued that a commitment to Scripture as the authoritative word of God is not opposed to interacting with the Bible to promote the kind of open dialogue concerning meaning-making that Greene pursues. On the contrary, a conservative theology of the Bible

---

85. Greene, *RI*, 22.
86. Warnock, *Imagination*, 202.

requires that a faithful engagement with this text would open generous spaces of exploration and discovery. There is no need for Christian leaders of young people to abandon or sequester their personal convictions about the normative authority of Scripture in order to involve young people in an aesthetic engagement with the Bible.

The argument has built in three stages. First, I have affirmed the literary qualities of the Bible and the bodily dimensions of meaning present in the Bible as being consistent with the qualities Greene values in the creative arts. Next, I have argued that even when the Bible is approached as a text that offers an authoritative direction for how we would make sense of the world, receiving the Bible as the personal word of the Living God carries a hermeneutic imperative. Reading the Bible as Scripture requires engaging in open dialogue. Thirdly, I have argued that in order to meaningfully engage with a work of creative art, dialogue needs to be disciplined by the interpretive boundaries evident in the work itself. Therefore, the theological commitment to the Christian reading of Scripture as a regulated reading is not an a priori imposition of meaning on the text that shuts down dialogical exploration. Rather, as an apprenticeship to the hermeneutical principles proposed by the text itself,[87] through the history of the interpretive activity of the church, the disciplined imagination is free to interact with others in open and constructive dialogue.

The final section noted four features of a youth ministry that is shaped by these conclusions. As a hermeneutical space for young people to engage with the Bible, youth ministries need to be marked by a constant return to the biblical text in order to direct the interpretations being offered. Youth ministries need to build in the expectation that the meaning to be gained from dialogue with the Bible will be elusive, but not absent. Such dialogue will be maintained by exercising the virtues of humility and conviction. And, though DYM does not necessarily expect to reach a resolution to the search, the dialogue it engages in rests on a sure starting point reaching toward a definite goal.

Close to the surface in all of this discussion has been the role of the imagination in the way we interpret the Bible and make sense of our experience in light of our interpretations. As Garrett Green explains, "for Christians, the chief point of imaginative contact with God is Holy Scripture, that epic of positivity whose narratives, poetry and proclamation are able, by means of their metaphoric inspiration, to render God himself to the faithful imagination."[88]

Chapter 8 turns to consider the role of the imagination in the dynamics of Bible engagement in more detail.

87. Starling, *Hermeneutics as Apprenticeship*.
88. Green, *Theology*, 185–86.

8

Imagination, Bible Engagement, and Being Known by God

IN THIS CHAPTER I come to the specific question of the role of the imagination in the dynamics of Bible engagement in a dialogical youth ministry. Picking up from the place that Maxine Greene gives to the imagination in the twin processes of aesthetic cognition as presented in chapter 5, this discussion is particularly concerned with how the use of the imagination is influenced by taking the Bible as a divinely inspired normative authority for spiritual life. This chapter begins with a theological account of the imagination in light of Maxine Greene's proposal. Second, I explore the relationship between the human work of imagination and the sovereign work of the Spirit of God in the processes of spiritual formation, drawing in particular on Garrett Green's notion of the paradigmatic imagination. In the third section I draw out two implications of this analysis for the practice of youth ministry, thinking about the place of imagination in the processes of meaning-making and the task of Christian proclamation. The final section of the chapter responds to the question raised from Greene's pedagogy to Christian theology of how adopting an account of personal identity offered in the gospel can be consistent with the emphasis in aesthetic pedagogy on ongoing imaginative exploration. I argue that the Christian offer of being "known by God" is not only consistent with a spirituality of personal exploration, it provides a relational security that is both able and necessary to relieve the existential burden that accompanies the personal quest for meaning and identity.

A Theological Taxonomy of the Imagination

Chapter 5 summarized key aspects of Greene's understanding of the imagination's function: enabling empathy, constructing meaning, and proposing alternate futures. Imagination is essential for empathy by enabling us to view life from another person's perspective. Imagination enables us to construct meaning by connecting the parts of our experience into meaningful wholes. Imagination enables us to propose new ways of making sense of our experience by reconstructing the parts into alternate frames, and thereby to envisage new ways of being in the world. Each of these uses of imagination express the ability to see "how things could be otherwise," whether taking on another's perspective (through an empathetic dialogue or engaging a work of art), or by proposing a new perspective of meaning or action. The initial aim in this chapter is to reflect on Greene's conception of the nature and role of the imagination by locating it within a taxonomy that distinguishes various uses of the imagination in relation to the Bible.

Acknowledging that any taxonomy has an inherent degree of reductionism, I propose the role of the imagination in Bible engagement to involve identifying connections, creating new connections, building empathy, and proposing alternative realities.[1] These uses can each be understood as sub-movements of the overarching task of imagining a Christ-conformed life. The boundaries between these different uses of the imagination are less distinct than a diagram with hard edges allows. Nevertheless, we could diagram the relationship between the uses of imagination as follows (Figure 1):

---

1. Various authors speak also of a prior, broader use of imagination in relation to the way humans perceive the world around us. Coleridge defined the primary imagination as "the living Power and prime Agent of all human Perception" (*Biographia Literaria*, 304). Warnock identified the use of imagination for perception as the power "to represent things previously experienced" and "to construct images of a certain form, blueprints, as it were, for all future and possible reproductive images" (*Imagination*, 33). Used in this way imagination becomes an omnibus term for various mental process including intuition and memory. How imagination is understood within the philosophy of perception is beyond the scope of this project. For the present purpose, when imagination is given such a broad meaning it loses any sense of meaningful application.

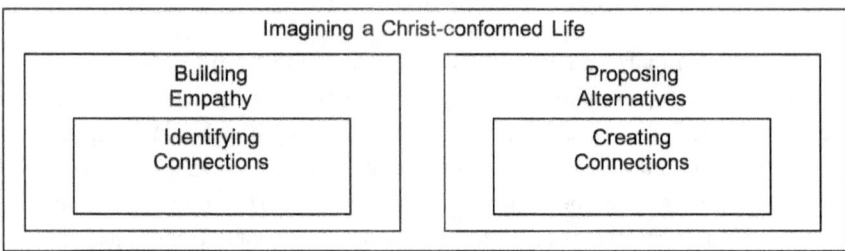

Figure 1.

On the basis of this taxonomy, Greene's pedagogy can be analyzed as fostering learning communities that build empathy so that individuals may exercise their ability to create new connections of meaning and propose alternative realities. Engaging with the creative arts encapsulates these imaginative processes of dialogical meaning-making by inviting students to identify connections of meaning in an artwork, to build an empathetic appreciation through indwelling the work, enhanced by their own acts of artistic creation. Greene's ultimate goal is for young people to pursue meaningful action by imagining a life shaped by their freely chosen construction of meaning.

Identifying Connections

Engaging with the Bible as a work of creative literature carries an obvious need for the work of imagination. Noting the prevalence of metaphor, symbol, and myth in the Bible, Avis argues that Christianity "lives from the imagination."[2] Searle concurs that the literary forms in the Bible "demand an active use of the imagination."[3]

Ricoeur extends the idea of a metaphor ("the collision between two semantic fields in a sentence") to apply "not only to words but to whole sequences of sentences."[4] Imagination is used in the work of "metaphorisation" that perceives "something else, something more" from the connections of signification between isolated texts. A characteristic role of the imagination is to interpret the "grammar" of a biblical text (including the mechanics of the Hebrew, Aramaic, and Greek languages along with cultural references and intertextual connections) by bringing the various parts together into a

2. Avis, *God and Creative Imagination*, 8.
3. Searle, *Eyes of Your Heart*, 47.
4. Ricoeur, "Bible and Imagination," 161.

meaningful whole. Imagination is "the activity of the mind which . . . presents to the 'mind's eye' coherent and meaningful wholes for consideration . . . the faculty which makes sense of things, locating particular bits and pieces within larger patterns."[5]

This use of the imagination to identify and construct patterns of "meaningfulness" in what we read is evident in approaches to reading the Bible that might not ordinarily regarded as being at all imaginative. For example, the "principlizing" method seeks to identify unifying theological principles in a biblical text, and then "to [re]state the [biblical] author's propositions, arguments, narrations, and illustrations in timeless abiding truths with special focus on the application of those truths to the current needs of the church."[6] Though this process is largely considered to be merely intellectual, identifying theological principles involves an imaginative work that identifies concepts drawn from the various elements of the text.

Andrew Root's description of Bible reading as a "fundamentally imaginative activity" also looks to the imagination to identify connections.[7] With Barth, Root focuses his attention on how Scripture witnesses to God's action in the world. The text of Scripture supplies the characteristics of the category of experience named as "divine action"; the work of imagination is directed to our experience in the world in order to connect those aspects of our experience that constitute divine action. Thus, while both Kaiser and Root apply the imaginative work of identifying connections to reading the Bible, Kaiser focuses on connections in the world of the text, Root on the world in front of the text.

Creating Connections

Alongside using imagination to identify meaningful connections in existing data, we also use imagination to create something new. This use of imagination, particularly associated with the creative arts, is Coleridge's "secondary imagination," that human ability to draw from the elements or fragments of what has been perceived and reassemble them in order to create something new.[8] By *identifying* connections imagination enables us to interpret an existing metaphor, and by *creating* connections imagination enables us to invent new metaphors.[9]

    5. Hart, "Imagination and Responsible Reading," 319.
    6. Kaiser, *Toward an Exegetical Theology*, 152; Kaiser, "A Principilizing Model."
    7. Root, *Unpacking Scripture*, 102.
    8. Coleridge, *Biographia Literaria*.
    9. The distinction between these uses of imagination lies more in the purpose of

Using the imagination to create new connections is affirmed in the romantic tradition as "our gateway to God," and the products of such creativity as "conduits for transcendent experience."[10] Kaufman regards the task of imagination as bringing together descriptive terms from human experience as "building blocks [for] putting together its conception" of God.[11] In a similar manner, McFague's "metaphorical theology" regards the theologian's role as a "poet-philosopher" who exercises her imagination to construct new metaphors, "nontraditional, unconventional, novel ways of expressing the relationship between God and the world," in order to "express Christian faith for our day in powerful, persuasive ways."[12]

Reformed theology has not taken up the romantic notion of the revelatory power of imagination, seeing in this approach an eclipse of divine sovereignty and a diminishment of the authority of Scripture. Rather than being a source of revelation, the creative imagination is exercised in response to, or directed by, Scripture. For example, speaking about representations of the ascension in Western art, David Brown notes that "because the artistic tradition is concerned to engage, there is much more emphasis on the potential relevance of the doctrine to the viewer, listener or reader, and so as much concern with the impact on us as on Christ."[13] Imaginative creativity understood as a response to divine revelation encourages reflection on how theological concepts are personally appropriated.

Building Empathy

The imagination enables us to build empathy by imagining ourselves in someone else's shoes. This capacity is particularly evident in the enduring power of stories in human culture to develop awareness and understanding of alternate experience. Helping young people engage in imaginative

what is imagined than in the mental activity undertaken. Any act of conceptualizing meaning is creative in some sense since it involves more than simple reproduction. The meaningful connections being identified in the mind are a new creation. Conversely, new connections are not created ex nihilo. Our imaginings are always combinations of pre-existing parts: we are able to imagine a seven-legged orange elephant, but we cannot picture an object in four-dimensional space or a color beyond the visible spectrum. Nevertheless, there is a meaningful distinction to be made between using the imagination to interpret an existing construction such as a written text or work of visual art (identifying connections) and the imagination in the prior work of constructing such artefacts (creating connections).

10. Levy, *Imagination*, 10.
11. Kaufman, *Theological Imagination*, 29.
12. McFague, *Metaphorical theology*, 35.
13. Brown, "The Ascension," 257.

experimentation by interacting with literature liberates them from the limitations of their own experience as well as relieving them of the burden of making premature commitments to concrete action. Reading stories can "enable teenagers to move forward in experience to consider what lies ahead, to contemplate experiences as it were 'by proxy' before encountering them directly."[14] Ricoeur's description of literature as "a vast laboratory for thought experiments"[15] is amplified in C. S. Lewis's observation that "my own eyes are not enough for me, I will see through those of others . . . Literary experience heals the wound, without undermining the privilege, of individuality . . . in reading great literature I become a thousand men and yet remain myself."[16] Reading literature helps form the moral imagination by enlarging human experience:

> It offers readers vicarious experiences of persons, places, and circumstances that may be different than their everyday lives. It cultivates their empathetic capacities and their ability to identify with characters. It enables them to follow the course of decisions and actions over time and to develop the ability to assess characters.[17]

The work of imagination to build empathy is critical because of the fundamentally interpersonal dynamic of engaging with written texts as the media of human exchange. Using the imagination for building empathy is needed to both discern and to indwell any written text. Even though cultural groups share a public language, no language is truly common, "since the ways in which we deploy the language which we inherit and inhabit, and the sense of the things which we say . . . are marked . . . by other levels of our particular personhood."[18] In order to understand the other we need to pay attention to the subjective dimension of their communication as well as the objective "grammar" of our common language. Imagination is needed to make sense of the grammar of a text and needs to be combined with a work of imagination to engage with how the originator of a text has personally used the common language. This subjective dimension of interpretation requires the use of the imagination to develop empathy with the one with whom we are communicating.

---

14. In Howard, "The Importance of Pleasure Reading," 48.
15. Ricoeur, *Oneself as Another*, 148.
16. Lewis, *An Experiment in Criticism*, 140–41.
17. Osmer and Salazar-Newton, "Practice of Reading," 65.
18. Hart, "Imagination and Responsible Reading," 312.

By building empathy, the imagination is necessary for making an interpersonal exchange become "a genuine meeting of persons,"[19] and for our own personhood to be modified by that meeting. Like Greene, Hart argues that training in the art of understanding is facilitated by learning how to engage with imaginative literature. In language that would not be alien to a passage from Greene, Hart says that the work of a creative writer

> enlarges our vision, tracing patterns, threads and connexions which stretch out beyond the horizons of our known world, and leading us out (as we trace them with him) into the complex structure of things until, at last, we find ourselves in quite unfamiliar territory, our imagination stretched, sometimes to breaking point.[20]

The use of imaginative language in the Bible can be seen to serve a similar end. Rather than simply giving an illustration of a doctrinal point, the use of poetic language is used by the biblical authors to draw their audiences into a personal experience of God's presence.[21] Such empathetic imagining is at the heart of the Ignatian spiritual exercises.[22] The meaning offered in the text is a precursor to the opportunity to meditate on the text and imagine oneself into the construction of the world offered by the text.

Proposing Alternatives

The work of imagination to build empathy is closely related to the work of proposing alternatives; having come to see how things are for others, we are also able to consider how things might be otherwise for ourselves. Proposing alternatives is to building empathy as creating connections is to identifying connections. There is an imaginative capacity used for entering an existing "story" that can be distinguished, without separation, from the imaginative capacity used for creating a "new" story. Reading fiction not only helps to

---

19. Hart, "Imagination and Responsible Reading," 326.
20. Hart, "Imagination and Responsible Reading," 316.
21. Selby, *Not With Wisdom of Words*.

22. The fifth contemplation in the second week of the exercises invites readers to place themselves within the biblical narrative and "with the imaginative use of the five senses" to reflect on the incarnation and the nativity: "Look in imagination at the persons, meditating and studying in detail the situation in which they find themselves, drawing some profit from the sight . . . Listen to what they are saying or might say . . . Smell the indescribable fragrance and taste the boundless sweetness of divinity . . . Touch by kissing and clinging to the places where these persons walk or sit" (Saint Ignatius of Loyola, *Spiritual Exercises*, par. 121–25).

develop identity (through an exercise of sympathetic imagination) but is able to "remake" reality and lead to transformation:

> Fiction has the power to "remake" reality and, within the framework of narrative fiction in particular, to remake real praxis to the extent that the text intentionally aims at a horizon of new reality which we may call a world. It is this world of the text which intervenes in the world of action in order to give it a new configuration or, as we might say, in order to transfigure it.[23]

Having indwelt an alternate reality by way of the imagination, the experience leaves us changed:

> Upon our return we discover that, while we are the same person we were, our personhood has nonetheless been transfigured in some way by the experience. We have seen and tasted more of reality that we had previously, and the texture and colour of our own world presents itself differently as a result.[24]

It is this imaginative work of proposing alternatives that is expressed in the prophetic imagination of the Hebrew prophets: "What the prophetic tradition knows is that it could be different, and the difference can be enacted."[25] In a similar way, the Apostle Paul reads the Hebrew Scriptures with a poetic imagination. Finding in Scripture "a rich source of image and metaphor," Paul's imagination proposes an alternative vision that "enables him to declare with power what God is doing in the world in his own time."[26]

These uses of the imagination are central to the dramatic metaphor that views the Christian life as an improvisation of the biblical drama. In the absence of a script to follow, we use our imagination to picture how we may participate faithfully in the drama through improvising our role as the people of God.[27] Reflecting the notion of the "disciplined imagination," improvisation does not mean making up whatever one feels like doing or saying. Improvisation is not about being outrageous but appropriate. To improvise well is to participate in the biblical drama in a way that is fitting, appropriate to the overall drama and our particular place in it.[28]

---

23. Ricoeur, "On Interpretation," 185.
24. Hart, "Imagination and Responsible Reading," 316.
25. Brueggemann, *Prophetic Imagination*, xxi.
26. Hays, *Conversion of the Imagination*, xvi.
27. Balthasar, *Theo-drama*; Bartholomew and Goheen, *Drama of Scripture*; Lash, *Theology on the Way to Emmaus*.
28. Potter, "Living in the Moment"; Wells, *Improvisation*.

Imagining a Christ-Conformed Life

Imagining a Christ-conformed life draws on each use of imagination as sub-movements in an all-encompassing use of imagination directed to the whole of life. There is an imaginative work being done when one moves from imagining various aspects of one's experience through the experience of others to adopting particular stories or visions as expressive of an overall identity. Instead of proposing how things may be otherwise in relation to discrete events in our life, we use our imagination to consider how the overall shape and direction of our lives could be different.

This encompassing work of imagination is central to Garrett Green's proposal that Christian formation involves seeing the pattern for human life in relationship with God in the person of Christ. Christ is offered to all human beings as "the image of God" in the sense that his life is a paradigm of the faithful human life. The Christian goal of being "conformed to the image of Christ" (Rom 8:29) involves "shaping one's life after Christ's life, patterning one's own living according to the pattern of his story, following the example of Jesus. The imago Dei is thus restored . . . in the 'narrative shape' of the Christlike life."[29]

Garrett Green echoes Balthasar's description of Jesus as "the concrete categorical imperative" and "the formally universal norm of ethical action" as a result of Jesus' life of faithfulness.[30] John Chrysostom speaks in a similar way of the life of the apostles: "You have a most excellent portrait. Proportion yourself to it."[31]

When Scripture is understood as providing the content of the Christ-conformed life, it functions as the "social imaginary" of the kingdom of God.[32] Operating primarily at the subconscious, intuitive level of the imagination, the Bible offers a collection of stories, laws, songs, prayers, proverbs, promises, genealogies, letters, and visions as a way of construing the world that shaped the people of God, as well as Jesus' own life of faithfulness. "It is precisely by responding to the various illocutions in Scripture—by believing its assertions, by trusting its promises, by obeying its commands, by singing its songs—that we become 'thickly,' which is to say covenantally, related to Christ."[33] As the church engages these Scriptures, it imagines what sort of people told these stories, sang these songs, prayed these prayers, hoped in these promises. The

---

29. Green, *Imagining God*, 101.
30. Balthasar, "Nine propositions on Christian Ethics," 79.
31. Hall, "Reading Christ into the Heart," 154.
32. Taylor, "Modern Social Imaginaries."
33. Vanhoozer, *Drama*, 68.

invitation to discipleship invites Christians to imagine what sort of people the church would be if they were to do the same.

That the social imaginary often operates at an unconscious level is pursued in James Smith's work on the power of bodily actions to transform behavior. Drawing extensively on Merleau-Ponty's notion of "bodily knowing" and Bourdieu's notion of "habitus," Smith draws attention to the power of ritual, both sacred and secular, to shape our desires by enlisting the imagination.[34] Smith is using a particular definition of imagination as our unconscious understanding of our surroundings that is embedded and carried in our bodily comportment to the world and our narratival construals of the world.[35] Smith grounds his analysis in a theological anthropology that understands human persons as defined by love and desire. Smith is concerned to reposition Christian education as a holistic process that engages our bodies, our desires, and our imaginations, rather than one that is concerned for abstract, disembodied ideas.[36] A narrowly cognitive approach to learning, Smith argues, betrays a truncated anthropology. In contrast, Smith pursues the pedagogical implications of an Augustinian model of human persons as "embodied agents of desire or love."[37]

While this encompassing use of the imagination could be simply regarded as the cumulative effect of the other uses of imagination writ large, the point of distinguishing it is to connect with the whole-of-life transformation envisioned by Christian formation. Christian tradition regards the all-encompassing claims of Christ (Col 1:15) to call for an all-encompassing transformation (1 Thess 5:23), which requires an all-encompassing imagination that envisions Christ as the goal of transformation (2 Cor 3:18).

Imagination and the Work of the Spirit

The preceding analysis has affirmed the various uses of the imagination in Maxine Greene's pedagogy as relevant also for engaging with the Bible as Christian Scripture. In doing so, the question raised at the conclusion of chapter 5 becomes more apposite: how does the human work of imagination relate to the sovereign work of the Holy Spirit in the work of spiritual formation? If the transformation that arises from engaging with the Bible were wholly ascribed to the human work of imagination, the resulting model of Christian spiritual formation would have no place for the gift of divine grace.

34. Merleau-Ponty, *Phenomenology*; Bourdieu, *Logic of Practice*.
35. Smith, *Imagining*, 17–18.
36. Smith, *Desiring*, 39.
37. Smith, *Desiring*, 47.

Greene's pedagogy allows for a certain unpredictable serendipity in the way interactions with the various arts prompt students to wide-awakeness and effect substantial transformation of their lived experience. That the outcomes of aesthetic engagement are uncontrollable is left to the vagaries of human experience rather than the working of any external influence or power. In contrast, the Christian doctrine of grace affirms that the divine-human relationship is initiated and enabled by God rather than through human effort alone. This is not to say that human action has no effect on spiritual outcomes. For all its emphasis on God's sovereignty, Reformed theology does not assert a notion of divine control that renders human action as meaningless or robotic. But neither does God's sovereignty work in such a way that God's actions are secondary, mere responses to human initiative. Rather than asserting divine sovereignty over human freedom, or asserting human freedom over divine sovereignty, Reformed theology asserts a compatibilism between God's sovereign will and action and human responsibility for real choices.[38] Human technique and the work of God in spiritual formation need to be integrated with each other. Divine action cannot be reduced to adding a note of blessing to human accomplishments. Conversely, human action cannot be reduced to arbitrary actions where the outcome of formation is entirely the result of the inscrutable work of God.

The key to distinguishing the work of the Spirit from the human activity of imagination in spiritual formation lies in identifying the imagination as the locus of the Spirit's work rather than providing the content of saving relationship with God. I draw this conclusion through Garrett Green's analysis of imagination as the point of contact for divine revelation.

The Paradigmatic Imagination

Garrett Green's concept of the "paradigmatic imagination"[39] identifies the imagination as the locus, but not the content, of the revelatory work of the Spirit of God. Garrett Green develops this conclusion by drawing on Kuhn's theory of the role of paradigms in scientific discovery.[40] Kuhn

---

38. Compatibilism differentiates between constraining and non-constraining causes. A constraining cause forces someone to act contrary to their will. This deprives someone of their freedom and hence removes any sense of responsibility for their actions. A non-constraining cause is sufficient to make someone make a particular choice, but not in a way as to go against their own will, desires, or wishes. A non-constraining cause allows someone to act in freedom and establishes personal responsibility (Carson, *Divine Sovereignty*; see also Packer, *Evangelism and Sovereignty of God*).

39. Green, *Imagining God*, 69.

40. Kuhn, *Structure of Scientific Revolutions*.

argues that scientific revolutions come about from the adoption of a new paradigm rather than because of new data, and therefore scientific observations do not have "meaning" in themselves but are given particular meaning from the paradigm in which they are interpreted. That same dynamic of meaning-making within certain paradigms is at work in human life in general. We make sense of our world by adopting paradigms, or patterns, that provide a meaningful "whole" into which we can fit our experience of life. Adopting new patterns of meaning is the work of what Garrett Green calls the "paradigmatic imagination," the human capacity for making and recognizing patterns. This aligns with Maxine Greene's recognition of the "whole" within which the disparate parts of experience or a work of art are given meaning.[41]

Connecting the notion of paradigmatic imagination to the dynamics of Christian faith, Garrett Green's central thesis is that "the point of contact for revelation is formally the paradigmatic imagination and materially the image of God."[42] The imagination is the locus of revelation, the "place" in the human where God's revelation occurs, while the content of the revelation remains an act of divine grace. When God graciously chooses to reveal the image of God in Christ to a person, it is by her imagination that God's revelation will be grasped.[43]

Distinguishing the imagination as the locus of revelation from the image of God as the content of revelation enables Garrett Green to reject natural theology on the one hand and positivism of revelation on the other. Garrett Green develops his argument in terms of the debate between Barth and Brunner concerning the point of contact (the *Anknüpfungspunkt*) between divine grace and human experience. With Brunner, contra Barth, Christian theology must be able to describe what happens when human beings receive divine revelation, and do so in a way that makes sense to

---

41. Greene, *TS*, 18, 20.

42. Green, *Imagining God*, 85.

43. Trevor Hart reaches the same conclusion as Garrett Green through reflection on a Christian theology of hope. The Christian hope, Hart argues, is something "surprisingly new" that arises out of the resurrection of Christ as the paradigm event rather than in the latent capacities of human experience and history (Hart, "Imagination for the Kingdom of God?" 66–67). Hope therefore draws on the human capacity to imagine how things-could-be-otherwise. Yet, for hope to be directed to the eschatological vision inaugurated by the death and resurrection of Christ, our imaginations need to be captured by the Spirit of God. Christian hope grounded in the promise of God appeals to, seizes and expands the imagination. Hart concludes therefore with the suggestion that the imagination may be "the primary locus of God's sanctifying activity in human life" (Hart, "Imagination for the Kingdom of God?" 76).

"theological outsiders as well as insiders."[44] Conversely, with Barth, contra Brunner, any account of the point of contact between the human and the divine must preserve the ground of revelation in the free grace of God rather than in some humanly-generated potentiality. As the locus of revelation, the paradigmatic imagination is not a human accomplishment that predisposes individuals as recipients of divine grace. Rather, the imagination is a basic human ability. "One of the things that people do is to imagine, and one of the things they imagine is what theologians have called revelation."[45] The imagination is therefore "the anthropological point of contact for divine revelation. It is not the 'foundation,' the 'ground,' the 'preunderstanding,' or the 'ontological basis,' for revelation; it is simply the place where it happens—or better, the way in which it happens."[46] God reveals himself to the imagination;[47] but human imagination, whether the imaginative faculty itself or the images, ideas, or patterns that the imagination creates, cannot produce saving knowledge of God.

Garrett Green identifies the content of God's revelation as the *imago Dei*, the image of God, which he defines as the ability to "imagine God *rightly*" or "to have real knowledge of God."[48] Rather than asserting what the image of God is, Garrett Green identifies what the image enables human beings to do. The image of God makes God accessible to the human imagination: "Adam in the garden could imagine God as he truly is. Whatever may be its 'nature,' its function is to enable us to imagine God."[49]

The impact of sin on humanity does not remove the capacity to imagine, but it does prevent human beings from imagining God aright. "The possibility of imagining God and therefore of imagining themselves in a right relationship with God has been obliterated by their own doing, by the 'evil imaginations' of their hearts."[50] The image of God remains post-fall only in the formal sense of the imaginative capacity, but the image of God as the paradigm by which human beings might make sense of the world in a way that is faithful to all that God is and has done has been lost.

In Garret Green's account of the imagination, the image of God is restored in the "narrative shape" of the Christian life. Christian formation refers

---

44. Green, *Imagining God*, 34.

45. Green, *Imagining God*, 40.

46. Green, *Imagining God*, 40.

47. Noting of course that God's work of revelation through the imagination is part of the communal activity of interpretation undertaken by the church rather than an isolated activity of each individual.

48. Green, *Imagining God*, 87.

49. Green, *Imagining God*, 87.

50. Green, *Imagining God*, 89.

to God's work of impressing his image on believers. By the illuminating work of the Spirit, Christians are those people who see the person and work of Christ revealed in Scripture as the paradigm through which they will interpret the world and its relation to God. Jesus is the form to which Christian people are being conformed by the transforming work of the Spirit:

> Externally, God takes shape in Christ, in whose image the imagination of the apostles is transformed, and who in turn give shape to the scriptures. Internally, the imagination of the reader or hearer of the Word is transformed by being conformed to the image of Christ. The chain of imaginative transformation extends still further: the transformed (sanctified) Christians (who are the "body," the physical shape, "of Christ") go on to impress the *imago* further through the pattern of their activity in the world.[51]

Where Jesus' life is offered to human beings as representative and substitute, human life shaped by his life turns from trusting their own righteousness to receive the righteousness that is by faith in Christ (Phil 3:9). Where Jesus' life is offered as the image of God, human life shaped by his life will seek to have the same mindset as Christ (Phil 2:5). Where Jesus' life is offered as the incarnate Son of God who speaks the words of God (Heb 1:1–2), human life shaped by his life will trust and obey the law of Christ (Gal 6:2). In other words, a human being is transformed when the life of Jesus becomes the paradigm within which she interprets her experiences of life and the pattern according to which she shapes her life.

Implications for Dialogical Youth Ministry

Two implications for the practice of youth ministry arise from identifying the imagination as the locus rather than the content of revelation. If "the field of action is the imagination,"[52] then adult mentors could aid the spiritual formation of young people by affirming the significance of the imagination for all human knowing in general, and the priority of imagination for biblical interpretation in particular.

---

51. Green, *Imagining God*, 102.
52. Green, *Imagining God*, 150.

Imagination for Meaning-Making

By affirming the central place of the pattern-recognizing and pattern-forming work of the imagination in all aspects of human learning and knowledge, youth leaders will help to undermine Feuerbach's influential idea that because religious belief involves the imagination it is therefore "fiction," in contrast to scientific belief which involves reason, and is therefore "true."[53] By recognizing the role of paradigms in shaping understanding, "imagination turns out to be not the opposite of reality but rather the means by which manifold forms of both reality and illusion are mediated to us."[54] Young people will be helped if they are able to see that imagination is operative in scientific understanding as much as in religious belief.

Youth leaders do well therefore to use the word "as" in order to affirm the constructed nature of reality as Maxine Greene has argued. Garrett Green takes the word "as" to be the "copula of imagination" in that, "the paradigmatic imagination is the ability to see one thing *as* another."[55] Christians are people who hear the Bible *as* the word of God. Exclusive humanists live life *as* contained within an immanent frame. "As" acknowledges that the way we are making sense of the world is a "take" rather than assuming the "spin" that our way of construing reality is "obvious."[56] Accepting that alternative takes are construals is in contrast both to the conservative theological attempt to declare what "is" true and the liberal embrace of a mythic "as if" that dispenses with the necessity of making truth claims. "As" becomes the "key to the logic of religious belief,"[57] and not just of religious belief, but of all human constructions of meaning.

The first task of Christian apologetics therefore is to "level the playing field"[58] by pointing out that secularism and other systems of belief are imaginative constructions of meaning as much as is religious faith.[59] Helping young people learn to distinguish "take" from "spin," to use "as" in place of a naïve or violent "is" or in place of a defeatist "as if," promotes the wide-awakeness that Greene affirms. Brueggemann asserts a similar conclusion using language that incorporates Taylor's "take," Garrett Green's

---

53. Green, *Theology*, 93–103.
54. Green, *Imagining God*, 83.
55. Green, *Imagining God*, 73.
56. Taylor, *Secular Age*, 551.
57. Green, *Imagining God*, 139.
58. Smith, *How (Not) to Be Secular*, 120.
59. Smith describes Taylor's account of secularism as "a level playing field. We're all trying to make sense of where we are, even why we are, and it's not easy for any of us" (Smith, *How (Not) to Be Secular*, 120).

"as," and Maxine Greene's social construction. In Christian worship and gospel proclamation,

> we imagine [the world] differently. We "take" it all differently. When we "take" it and imagine it differently, we can (and will) act differently, personally and publicly. Our alternative "as" asserts that the world is much more supple than we had been led to discern. We therefore take a position of advocacy for God's assured newness.[60]

Imagination and Proclamation

Alongside helping young people exercise their imagination in the task of meaning-making, Christian youth ministry will also invite young people to direct their imagination to the biblical story. Developing young peoples' imaginations enables them to participate in meaning-making as the central process of spiritual formation; offering young people an imaginative engagement with the Bible invites them to choose Christian faith as the content of spiritual formation.

Affirming the imagination as the locus of divine revelation adds theological weight to the importance of engaging with the literary qualities of Scripture as discussed in chapter 7. The prevalence of metaphor, symbol, and narrative in Scripture is more than a quirk of the specific cultures within which the texts were written. The imaginative material of Scripture is the precise form that corresponds to the imagination as the place in the human person where God chooses to meet us, affirming the role of imagination as "a means of communicating truth."[61] Garrett Green describes Christian proclamation as "an appeal to the imagination of the hearers through the images of scripture" and that therefore, "the preacher's task is to mediate and facilitate that encounter by engaging his or her own imagination, which becomes the link between scripture and congregation."[62]

Approaching teaching the Bible as an appeal to the imagination relieves youth leaders of the burden of responsibility for the outcome of their teaching and preserves the freedom of young people over their own imaginations. Echoing Maxine Greene's note about the lack of control that teachers have over the outcome of their students' engagement with the arts, Brueggemann writes similarly of the preachers' task:

---

60. Brueggemann, *Texts Under Negotiation*, 56.
61. Searle, *The Eyes of Your Heart*, 47.
62. Green, *Imagining God*, 149.

> No one, not the preacher or the interpreter, has any access to this zone of imagination or control over the outcome... For that reason, the pastor or interpreter is enormously free from anxiety about and responsibility for the outcome with the listener to the text. The minister is not the one who must worry about the future, health, or obedience of the listening church. It is the pastor's simple task... to make sure the text is offered as input in the liveliest way possible. Beyond that, the subjects themselves must answer for the process.[63]

While offering the biblical text in "the liveliest way possible" may not be as simple as Brueggemann suggests, he is right to relieve preachers and youth ministers of the burden of responsibility for the outcome of their teaching. Youth ministers thereby have no need for anxiety, and no reason for overweening pride.

However, if the responsibility for constructing meaning in one's spiritual life is left solely with young people themselves, we have simply transferred the burden from one set of shoulders to another, and ones that are often far less able to bear its weight. Aesthetic pedagogy does well to affirm the agency and privilege of young people to construct their own sense of meaning and to interpret the biblical text for themselves. However, in order to best enable young people to take up this privilege, aesthetic pedagogy needs to also provide resources that will enable them to fulfil the task.

Relieving the Burden of Meaning-making

How may adult mentors relieve young people of the personal burden involved in the task of meaning-making and the quest for authenticity, without also removing from them the privilege of making their own spiritual choices and exploring their own sense of identity? This question poses a counter-challenge to the question raised in chapter 5 concerning whether adopting a sense of identity offered in the gospel is able to preserve the freedom of young people to explore personal identity. On the one hand, the gospel offers security and assurance, but seems to preclude quest and exploration. On the other hand, a personal search for meaning and authenticity offers quest and exploration, but with a significant degree of anxiety concerning the outcome. I contend that by offering security and assurance, the Christian gospel is able to promote quest and exploration. Thus, I argue that adopting the relational security that is offered in the gospel is no obstacle to the core values of aesthetic pedagogy but rather is a way of enhancing them.

63. Brueggemann, *Texts Under Negotiation*, 63.

IMAGINATION, BIBLE ENGAGEMENT, AND BEING KNOWN BY GOD   179

It is at this point that the gap between Greene's philosophy and DYM is at its widest. Greene recognizes the anguish involved in exercising personal freedom.[64] But, rather than relieving this burden, her goal was always to acknowledge points of resistance, arguing that it is necessary to confront obstacles in order to learn and grow. DYM shares this conviction, but recognizes that the challenge of personally constructing meaning can be so great for young people as to become debilitating. Brain has noted the burden of stress and dissatisfaction that accompanies the secular spirituality pursued by many young Australians.[65] When more than one in four 16- to 24-year-olds in Australia have suffered a mental disorder in the previous twelve months,[66] there is a pressing need to help young people better cope with the challenges of adolescent life. While Greene would not advocate for one particular paradigm of meaning over another, DYM will invite young people to consider how the Christian gospel can provide a secure context within which the quest for meaning can be navigated more successfully.

The notion of an assured hope, one that is secured by the promise of God and affirmed in the resurrection of Christ in the past,[67] could seem to suggest that there is no driving need for action in the world.

> If the eventual outcome is secure regardless of our striving or lack of it towards the goal of our hope, if redemption does not rest on our fashioning of the conditions for the coming of the kingdom, then surely the more economic and comfortable option is to sit back and wait for it all to happen.[68]

As an alternative, Hart suggests that the model of hope proposed by Ernst Bloch[69] is more able to promote purposeful action. Hope is an "activity of the imagination which lays hold intuitively of something which may or may not actually come to pass, but the potential for which lies genuinely within the latent capacities of the system or process of human history."[70] The question that Hart poses in light of Bloch's proposal arises equally from Maxine Greene's pedagogy:

---

64. Greene, *DF*, 5.
65. Brain, *Engage!*
66. Australian Bureau of Statistics, *National Survey of Mental Health and Wellbeing*.
67. "Because he has raised Christ from the dead, therefore the fulfilment of his promise is certain" (Moltmann, *Coming of God*, 145).
68. Hart, "Imagination for the Kingdom of God?" 69.
69. Bloch, *Principle of Hope*.
70. Hart, "Imagination for the Kingdom of God?" 61.

> Is not Bloch's model with its element of risk and genuine responsibility on the part of those who strive for the utopian future more likely to generate the sort of enthusiasm and effort necessary to see the kingdom at least approximated in this world?[71]

Similarly, is not Greene's model, with its emphasis on the personal responsibility of young people to construct meaning for themselves, more likely to generate the effort needed for transformative learning than promises of assured meaning to be found in the gospel? Recall Greene's adage, "a rock is an obstacle only to someone who wants to climb the hill. Not caring, the traveler merely takes another path."[72] Greene affirms Sartre's recognition of the "anguish" that is linked to freedom: "The person who chooses himself/herself in his/her freedom cannot place the onus on outside forces, on the cause and effect nexus. It is his/her interpretation or reading of the situation that discloses possibility."[73] If Christian assurance removes the anguish that accompanies choice, will it also remove the impetus to pursue transformative action?

Such a challenge can only be sustained by a misunderstanding of the place of hope in the Christian gospel. First, this challenge suggests that the transforming power in Christian life is fear rather than hope. On the contrary, the source of transformation lies in the power and energy of hope rather than in the fear or anxiety that comes from a risk of failure. The same is true of Greene. The anguish of responsibility for action is not the stick that drives change; rather, learning is inspired by the hope that freedom can be attained in community with others.

Transcendent Guarantor of Hope

From this perspective then, Hart turns the original question on its head and asks in return whether transformation actually requires some "transcendent guarantor of the outcomes of hope" in order to motivate transformative action:

> If, in the final analysis, our hope is rooted in the latent potential of the present, including our own potential to act and thereby generate the conditions for its eventual realization, then it is difficult to see just how we can escape the despair which

---

71. Hart, "Imagination for the Kingdom of God?" 70.
72. Greene, *DF*, 5.
73. Greene, *DF*, 5.

accompanies the juxtaposition of our self-knowledge and the demands which the road to self-redemption makes.[74]

Greene admits that there are no guarantees that her pedagogy will result in actual transformation, and urges teachers not to give in to despair.[75] Yet Greene offers no resources to resist despair beyond the expectation that what has happened in the past in other circumstances may happen once again in new circumstances. In contrast, resources for persevering in transformative action can be found in the gospel ordering of promise and demand:

> Because the gift is offered freely and does not rest on the adequacy of our response, it actually liberates us from the culture of fear and anxiety, and thereby sets us free to act with radical confidence, confidence which is free to make mistakes because it knows they will not result in rejection. Failure itself is forgivable and redeemable.[76]

In the same way that the logic of the gospel sets us free "from the burden of having to become the condition for the realization of the kingdom,"[77] so too the promise of relationship with God secured by the prior work of Christ offers to set young people free from the existential burden of responsibility for the outcome of their quest to identify and express their authentic self. Thus, rather than shutting down responsible action in the world, the assurance of meaning and purpose offered in the gospel can liberate young people to pursue meaningful action within the security of the divine promise.

Taylor notes the presence of an "ontic doubt about meaning itself" as "integral to the modern malaise."[78] The challenge facing young people today is quite different to the one that shaped the doctrines of justification and grace in the Reformation:

> The problem of the meaning of life is therefore on our agenda . . . either in the form of a threatened loss of meaning or because making sense of our life is the object of a quest. And those whose spiritual agenda is mainly defined in this way are in a fundamentally different existential predicament from that which dominated most previous cultures and still defines the lives of other people today . . . The existential predicament in which one fears condemnation is quite different from the one

---

74. Hart, "Imagination for the Kingdom of God?" 70.
75. Greene, *LL*, 51; Greene, *DF*, 131.
76. Hart, "Imagination for the Kingdom of God?" 71.
77. Hart, "Imagination for the Kingdom of God?" 71.
78. Taylor, *Secular Age*, 303.

where one fears, above all, meaninglessness. The dominance of the latter perhaps defines our age.[79]

In such an environment, Christian faith can offer young people the possibility that accepting the reconciling love of God in Christ could be for them an experience of relational security that comes as a gift rather than as a task requiring human effort. While Greene would contend that such an approach amounts to a foreclosure of a young person's search, I argue otherwise. The security that comes from the gracious gift of relationship with God does not remove the need for ongoing spiritual quest, since the relationship with God being offered is one that opens possibility by inviting ongoing personal exploration of authenticity. The Christian gospel offers young people the security of being "known by God."

Known by God

Despite relatively few references, the idea that God's people are "known by God" is a fundamental theme of spiritual identity in the Bible.[80] God's knowledge of human beings appears less than twenty times compared to several hundred references to human beings knowing God. However, the theological importance of the theme is demonstrated by its appearance at critical points in the biblical story:

> in the Old Testament, Abraham (Gen 18:19), Moses (Exod 33:12), David (2 Sam 7:20), Jeremiah (Jer 1:5) and the nation of Israel (Amos 3:2; Hos 13:5) are all known by God; and in the New Testament being known by God defines Christian existence (Gal 4:8–9; 1 Cor 8:3), is a criterion of the last judgement (Matt 7:23 ["I never knew you"]; 25:12; cf. Luke 13:27) and is a measure of eschatological glory (1 Cor 13:12 ["then I shall know, even as I have been fully known"].[81]

Rosner notes that these references to being known by God in the Bible are linked to three related ideas: to belong to God, to be chosen or loved by God, and to be adopted as the child of God. These are not three different ideas, but more specific versions of the same reality: "To belong to God is to be chosen by him. And we belong to God not just as his people, but more specifically as his children."[82]

79. Taylor, *Sources of the Self*, 18.
80. Rosner, *Known by God*.
81. Rosner, "Known by God," 208.
82. Rosner, *Known by God*, 97.

Rosner develops the biblical theme of being known by God as an expression of personal identity that carries important psychological benefits.[83] Finding one's identity in being known by God offers significance that comes from God's gracious beholding rather than from personal achievement or capacity; we receive comfort and protection from the security of divine care; and we receive moral direction from being included in God's story. In particular, being known by God offers security amidst the uncertainty of the age of authenticity: "Receiving one's identity as a relational gift, rather than solely striving for it as an individual achievement, is an attractive alternative to the identity angst of a postmodern world where a stable and secure sense of self can be so elusive."[84]

Applied to youth ministry, these conclusions would direct adult mentors to accompany young people in dialogue around meaning and the quest for the authentic self, and to do so with the offer of understanding oneself as a person who is known and loved by God. Christian identity through union with Christ is offered as a gift to receive rather than a task requiring human effort.

Often however, discussions of Christian identity so emphasize overarching theological themes that individual concerns are neglected, if not eclipsed entirely. For example, Rosner gives a "resounding, Yes" to the question of whether a Christian person should aim to be "who you are," but the ideal self is described only in communal terms: "Believers in Christ are to be true to themselves, that is, their new selves in Christ. The Christian life is about knowing who you are in relation to God."[85] The "defining moment" for any Christian, "that point at which the central character of a person is established," is the crucifixion of Christ, and their shared "signature move ... that behaviour that sums up and expresses a person's identity," is love.[86] Without wanting to diminish the immense theological significance for Christian self-understanding of being united with Christ and therefore to be characterized (individually and as a community) by Christ-imitating love, this theological prescription can be taken to undermine the significance of individual concerns and personal discovery.

It is therefore important to distinguish between finding collective identity[87] in being known by God, and finding personal identity through personal exploration and discovery. The two are complementary and

83. Rosner and McLean, "Theology and Human Flourishing."
84. Rosner and McLean, "Theology and Human Flourishing," 65.
85. Rosner, *Known by God*, 235.
86. Rosner, *Known by God*, 242–44.
87. Melucci, "The Process of Collective Identity"; Whooley, "Collective Identity."

inseparable. There is a collective identity that all Christian believers share, but this does not preclude individual expressions of identity that cannot be established simply by locating oneself within the gospel story. Christians are together known by God and are individually called to authentically express their new life in Christ. The former enables the latter, and the latter arises out of, and lives into, the former.

Rosner lists eight practices of Christian life that help a believer to confirm their "identity" as someone known by God, all of which reflect and reinforce collective identity.[88] Four of these are communal practices: baptism, communal singing, saying the creed, and the Lord's Supper. In these practices, individual believers join in unison with the church catholic to express shared truths of Christian identity. The remaining four practices are also communal to the extent that they are activities that believers share in with others, but are individual in the sense that the precise manner in which each believer engages will be—and I would add, needs to be—unique. The way that any individual Christian participates in congregational gatherings, reads and hears the Bible, prays and lives life in response to the gospel, will be uniquely shaped by their personality, relationships, and circumstances. In each activity a believer will display the shared "signature move" of Christlike love, but the precise manifestation of that life of love is up to each one to explore and discover. All those who choose to find identity in being known by God, continue to exercise personal responsibility, striving for consistency between their inward and outward expressions of faith, as they seek to identify their individual giftedness and choose action that will bring their personal charism to serve God, God's people, and God's world.

DYM locates the quest for personal meaning-making within the collective identity of being known and loved by God. By doing so, young people are offered a collective identity to receive as a gift without diminishing the need and opportunity for ongoing exploration and discovery of their personal identity. On the contrary, a collective identity received as a gift has two benefits: it invites young people into a space that bends authenticity towards love rather than narcissism, and it offers a space of security that can help relieve the existential burden of meaning-making.

Receiving collective Christian identity as a gift promotes love by freeing young people from a preoccupation with themselves. Webster argues that

> my freedom is in part my freedom from final responsibility for maintaining myself . . . having been liberated from the anxious toil of having to be my own creator and preserver. Evangelical

---

88. Rosner, *Known by God*, 246–61.

> freedom is rooted in a security given to me ... That security is such that in Christ I am inviolable, and so free from concern for my own preservation ... [expressed as] a profound lack of self-preoccupation, a confidence which has its roots in the sheer objectivity of my condition as one set free by God.[89]

It is in this way that affirming the gift-nature of Christian identity promotes love:

> Free for fellowship with God, I am thus free also for human fellowship. If freedom is self-governance, it is the end of love; if however, freedom is the restoration of my identity in company with my fellows, then I am free to act in support of my neighbor's cause.[90]

That is, if a young person accepts the gospel offer of understanding themselves as someone who is known by God, and this not of their own doing, but the gift of God (Eph 2:8), they can find a place of security. The security of being known by God does not remove the opportunity for engaging in a quest of self-discovery, but does remove the existential burden for being responsible for the successful outcome of the search. Free from that burden, young people are released from the need to be preoccupied with themselves and enabled to turn towards others in love.

The youth ministry community will therefore become a space that offers a shared sense of meaning in the world, expressed in communal practices such as baptism, communion, and communal singing. Within that shared space, individuals encourage and support one another in their personal quests to discover how each one might live out their new life in Christ. Such exploration is likely to present many unanswered questions and uncertain conclusions. Yet, the uncertainty need not be accompanied by angst since, even if a young person has little idea of where she belongs or what she has to contribute, she can be confident in the promise that she is known by God and can find security and freedom in that gift.

Summary

This chapter completes the theological conversation in response to Maxine Greene's aesthetic pedagogy. A proposed taxonomy of the uses of the imagination in Bible engagement affirms the role Greene gives to imagination in the processes of aesthetic cognition. Responding to the question raised

---

89. Webster, *Confessing God*, 225.
90. Webster, *Confessing God*, 226.

from Christian theology against Greene's pedagogy in chapter 6, I argued that the imagination is the locus of the revelatory and transforming work of the Spirit. A dialogical youth ministry looks to stimulate young peoples' imaginations in constant dialogue with the meaning offered in the gospel so that they would be "in the right place" for when God chooses to reveal himself to them. In response to the question raised from Greene's pedagogy against Christian theology in chapter 6, I argued that the assurance and security that comes from adopting a sense of collective identity as a gift from God is able to promote personal exploration and quest by relieving young people of the burden that comes from shouldering responsibility for making sense of their world. All that now remains in this project is for the concluding chapter to draw together all the threads of DYM proposed in chapters 6, 7, and 8 in order to outline a practice framework for Bible engagement in Christian youth ministry.

9

A Practice Framework for Dialogical Youth Ministry

THIS FINAL CHAPTER BRINGS together the various threads of the preceding discussion to propose a practice framework for dialogical youth ministry. DYM begins by accepting expressive individualism as the cultural context in which the church is called to serve young people, affirming the core value of the modern quest for authenticity as a reflection of the Christian ethic of personal responsibility. Youth ministry undertaken in this context will affirm the teenage quest for meaning-making and seek to move young people to be wide-awake to taken-for-granted interpretations of physical and spiritual reality. Alerting young people to alternative constructions of meaning opens the door for them to construct new meaning and imagine how things could be otherwise. DYM offers young people a dialogical space where they are challenged and enabled to engage with others as they each exercise their freedom to pursue personal explorations of meaning. Participation in such spaces of dialogue and freedom provides young people opportunities to observe, consider, and experience life shaped by the gospel of Christ. Shaped by their belief in the beauty and goodness of Christ, adult mentors eschew attempts to manipulate or control the outcomes of each person's spiritual quest as they offer the gospel as a possible paradigm for meaning-making, being prepared for young people to choose alternative paths. At the center of all of the formational practices of DYM will be various avenues of engagement with the Bible. Adult mentors invite young people to imagine how the Christian gospel could be a possible way of making sense of all the dimensions of their human experience. The message of God's grace, that they could be known by God, offers young people a place of security within which they are free to explore and discover how they might personally live out the new life in Christ.

In light of this approach to Christian spiritual formation, I propose a practice framework for Bible engagement in youth ministry comprised of three sections. First, I describe the intended outcomes of youth ministry: that young people would be wide-awake to "spin," that young people would embrace spiritual formation as an ongoing task of human life, and that young people would gain an elementary level of Christian literacy and experience. In light of these intended outcomes, I identify testimony as an evidential practice to demonstrate whether or not young people are moving toward these goals. Second, the practice framework details the means by which those aims will be fulfilled. Given my focus on the dynamics of Bible engagement, this section concentrates on practices of reading, indwelling, and embodying the biblical text. In addition, DYM seeks to achieve its aims by honestly engaging with belief systems other than Christianity, and through the use of dialogue as a source of content as well as a means of engagement. Third, I identify love, humility, and conviction as the preeminent values by which such youth ministry is shaped and sustained.

Aims and Purpose

DYM places questions about meaning at the top of the agenda for the spiritual formation of teenagers. The fundamental purpose of youth ministry is to move young people to be wide-awake to the possible construals of the spiritual life, and to invite them to engage in a quest of meaning-making in dialogue with one another in the context of the Christian faith.

DYM affirms both freedom and authority in spiritual formation, but orders them such that personal quest is the starting point, and Christian commitment a possible conclusion. That young people would come to recognize and welcome the authority of Christ is desired, but not required. "Truth" is not abandoned in favor of "quest," but questions of what is good, and what is true, take second place to engaging in the process of discovery and personal meaning. Traditional youth ministries could be characterized by pursuing questions of truth and goodness, focused either on the personal spiritual dimension (who is good, how good do I need to be, how can the bad be redeemed?) or the social action dimension (what is right, what ought be done to overcome injustice, oppression, and exclusion?). Traditional apologetics focuses on questions of truth and authority (did Jesus really rise from the dead? Is the New Testament reliable?); and mission, particularly in Reformed contexts, focuses on evangelistic decisions, emphasizing personal commitment to a set of beliefs. As I have argued in chapter 6, young people immersed in the modern quest for authenticity are likely to disengage from this kind of discussion because it narrows the space within which they are able to exercise personal choice.

Youth ministries focused on meaning-making enter into dialogue with young people about what makes the most sense of most of their experience. Youth ministers will not only aim for young people to develop a cognitive understanding of Christian belief, but will invite them to an imaginative exploration, asking "what if" they were to adopt this way of making sense of their world? Under the broad aim of meaning-making, DYM identifies three key learning outcomes for youth ministry: that young people would be wide-awake to "spin," that young people be willing to pursue a life-long process of formation, and that young people would develop a basic level of Christian literacy and experience.

Wide-Awake to Spin

The first learning outcome for youth ministry is for young people to be made aware of, and able to identify, "spin." DYM aims to help young people accept alternate beliefs as possible "takes" on meaning and purpose, rather than claiming certain systems of belief or unbelief as self-evident or non-contestable. In James Smith's words, the aim is to "level the playing field" between the various systems of belief and unbelief available to young people.[1] Exposing spin applies to its Christian forms as much as to forms of secularism or other religious beliefs. DYM directs youth ministers to reject special pleading, but instead to expose Christian faith to the same critical examination as any other proposal for meaning. Acknowledging Christian faith as one of many possible construals of reality is not made as a step toward relativism. It is rather a recognition of the pluralistic landscape within which young people negotiate their commitments of faith.

Challenging spin offers a way forward for engaging with Christian young people who have entered adolescence from a childhood experience of Christian faith. Some young people come jaded, as they begin to think that the Christian faith they developed as a child is not up to the task of seeing them through adolescent life. Others come with misplaced overconfidence in the understanding that served them as children but is less likely to meet present and future challenges. DYM directs youth ministers to problematize and defamiliarize Christian faith for Christian young people

1. Smith, *How (Not) to Be Secular*, 120.

in order to move them toward greater personal ownership of their choices and more mature understandings of the faith.

For example, an affluent, Bible-belt dwelling teenager who has grown up with a simplistic understanding of the message "God is good, all the time; all the time, God is good" may be challenged to consider how that refrain would sound on the lips of the persecuted church, or how it might sound to her in more difficult personal circumstances (on the unemployment queue, after the loss of a loved one, or in a family break-up). She might be encouraged to imagine what it would be like to join in this chant as a member of the persecuted church in North Korea. Reading the book of Lamentations, or Psalm 88, could be used to challenge simplistic notions of how God's people experience life and introduce more mature reflection on the relationship between faithfulness and suffering. As in Psalm 73, young people could be challenged to consider moving from a mechanistic equation of righteousness leading to blessing (Ps 73:1: "Surely God is good to Israel, to those who are pure in heart") to a more complex sense of the divine presence (Ps 73:28: "For me it is good to be near God").[2]

By problematizing Christian experience, the intention is not to sow doubt and breed insecurity; to do so would amount to spiritual abuse. Rather, by providing both a challenge to naivety and the resources available to meet the challenge, DYM seeks to grow a more mature faith, one that is wide-awake to a wider range of human experience.[3] Young people can hold their chosen beliefs with greater commitment because they are consciously self-chosen in the face of considered alternatives.

Pursuing Ongoing Processes of Formation

Maxine Greene's aesthetic pedagogy does not regard wide-awakeness as a stage through which one passes but the state in which productive dialogue about meaning is made possible. In the same way, DYM aims to build an expectation in young people that the process of spiritual formation will

---

2. Brueggemann argues that Psalm 73 stands at the theological centre of the book of Psalms, expressing the movement from obedience (Psalm 1) to praise (Psalm 150) "by way of candour about suffering and gratitude about hope" (Brueggemann, "Bounded by Obedience and Praise," 72). Candour about suffering is one way of problematizing Christian spin.

3. DYM seeks to move young people into their Zone of Proximal Development: "the distance between the actual developmental level as determined by independent problem solving and the level of potential development as determined through problem-solving under adult guidance, or in collaboration with more capable peers" (Vygotsky, *Mind in Society,* 86).

be an ongoing task of human life. The need for ongoing exploration and discovery rests on four key convictions. First, because the Bible is received as the personal word of the living God, no one can expect to "master" the meaning of this text in the same way that no one can expect to gain an exhaustive understanding of another person. That the Bible is received as the personal word of a divine and eternal being simply underlines this conclusion. Second, the life experience against which we are seeking to interpret the Bible is constantly changing; while one day a young person is grappling with how to relate to a new group of friends, two months later she may be facing the death of a grandparent or questioning government policy on foreign aid. Third, each individual comes to each act of interpretation and meaning-making in a unique place, having been shaped, in ways small and large, by each new experience of life; what a young person may have drawn from the Bible when she was fourteen is likely to be different to what is available for her now that she is sixteen. Fourth, even if the life changes experienced by one individual are so minor as to be insignificant to herself, life changes in the experience of other members of the group, or the addition of new members to the group, changes the dialogical space in which meaning-making is pursued. The combination of each of these factors means that the process of meaning-making in relation to the Bible in dialogue with others will be an ongoing journey.

DYM aims to build an expectation in young people that the work of spiritual formation is never complete in this present age. Meaning-making is not a task that some people complete sooner than others, after which they can move on to "higher pursuits." Spiritual formation is not an adolescent stage that one moves through. DYM pursues meaning-making for spiritual formation as the basic activity of human life.

Elementary Christian Awareness

The third learning outcome in DYM is that young people would attain a basic level of Christian literacy and gain an authentic experience of Christian community. DYM refuses the option of coercing and pressuring young people to make the choice of Christian faith. However, this does not require youth ministries to give up any goals relating to Christian content. Youth ministers are unable to dictate a young person's choices, but they can seek to build a young person's awareness and understanding of what is available for her to choose from. In this regard youth ministry contributes to the common good by providing the opportunity for young people to gain a sympathetic awareness of Christian faith and practice.

DYM aims for young people to be able to give an accurate articulation of the basic contours of Christian faith. Elementary Christian literacy would include familiarity with the Gospel narrative, with gospel proclamation, and gospel life. A graduate of the youth ministry ought to have engaged with at least one of the four Gospels and be familiar with the life and ministry of Jesus, his actions and teaching, his passion and crucifixion. DYM aims for young people to recognize these features of the Gospel narrative as historically defensible even if they do not accept them as theologically meaningful.

In addition to these aspects of the historical record, DYM aims for young people to be aware of the gospel proclamation that Jesus' tomb was found empty on the third day (Luke 24:1–3), that the eyewitnesses to his death claimed to see and touch his resurrected body (Matt 28:8–10; 1 Cor 15:5–8) and to witness his ascension to heaven (Acts 1:9). Even if a young person does not believe these claims, she needs to know that Christian people do.

To these core aspects of gospel proclamation would be added the message of grace (Eph 2:8), the invitation to repentance and forgiveness of sins, and the promise of the indwelling Holy Spirit (Acts 2:38). Even if a young person does not choose Christian faith for herself, she needs to be made aware that the Christian hope for salvation is grounded in the generous gift of God rather than on the accomplishment of human effort.

Along with being aware of the gospel promise, youth ministry will also aim for young people to appreciate the characteristics of gospel life. Whether or not a young person chooses to pursue a gospel-shaped life, she ought to be aware that the invitation to Christ is an invitation to a life of self-giving love, in imitation of Jesus' own act of self-giving love (1 John 4:10–11). Even if a young person does not believe that Christians have lived up to the instruction and example of Jesus, it will be good for her to know that Christians are called to love God and neighbor (Matt 22:37–40), to love even their enemies (Matt 5:44), and to not look to their own interests but to the interests of others (Phil 2:3).

Testimony as Evidential Practice

Given these aims for youth ministry, DYM will provide numerous opportunities for testimony as "evidence" of a young person's move toward (or away from) these goals. Testimony is an evidential practice that gives a young person the opportunity to articulate their changing patterns of belief and action. Testimony is a way of communicating to youth ministers and other stakeholders whether the various activities pursued in the youth ministry are effective in meeting the intended aims of the ministry. Testimony will also communicate to the young people themselves, as pieces of evidence of where they are up to in their journey of spiritual formation.

Amanda Drury's extended study of the practice of testimony in adolescent spiritual development highlights the formative impact of giving teenagers the opportunity to articulate their understanding of how God has been at work in their lives. Drury draws from Ricoeur's understanding of testimony as a report on what someone has seen or understood, "not perception itself but the report, that is the story, the narration of an event."[4] Testimony therefore is a practice that constructs meaning out of one's experience; "testimony always contains some kind of interpretation."[5] Testimony is an expression of the creative imagination to construct a narrative from one's experience, and a work of paradigmatic imagination that brings the various parts of one's experience into a meaningful whole. Whether spontaneous or ordered, delivered in formal or informal settings, testifying is a central practice of DYM.[6]

Extending Drury's proposal, DYM will also provide young people the opportunity to speak of their understanding of God's absence in their lives as much as God's presence. In line with the broad aims of spiritual process outlined above, having young people who are not yet believers articulate their reasons for their continued unbelief (or alternate belief, or partial belief, et cetera) contributes to the aim of wide-awakeness for the whole group. For the young person testifying to their experience of unbelief, they are challenged to grow in self-awareness and self-knowledge by reflecting critically on their spiritual journey to date. For other young people, hearing a considered account of unbelief provides an opportunity to build empathy and contributes to problematizing simplistic notions of faith. The same can be said about opportunities for young people to articulate doubt. Testimony does not need to always be couched in positive terms. Giving space for honest expression of the low points on the spiritual journey as well as the mountain top experiences, and recognizing that most journeys involve all manner of twists and turns, is a way of affirming that the task of meaning-making and spiritual formation is rarely straightforward, and never complete.

Adult mentors have a significant part to play in developing young people's ability to testify well. Drury concludes her study by recognizing the

---

4. Drury, *Saying is Believing*, 123.
5. Drury, *Saying is Believing*, 21.
6. Drury identifies four types of testimony based on whether the testimony is spontaneous or "ordered" (i.e., written, or previously prepared), and the setting in which the testimony is delivered, whether formal (such as in a church service or youth group meeting) or informal (such as personal conversation). Drury, *Saying is Believing*, 153.

need for teenagers "to be nurtured to see the world through a spiritual lens that allows them to live in a state of perpetual Advent, looking for the ways in which God interacts with their stories."[7] Adult mentors will only be able to do this for young people if they are themselves alert to the presence of God in their own lives. In Maxine Greene's language, it is only adults who are wide-awake who are able to move young people to wide-awakeness.

Content and Means

In order to achieve these learning outcomes, DYM looks to three intersecting sources of content for the teaching and learning program in youth ministry. Chief among these is the Bible, received as the living word of the Living God. This discussion of the means of DYM will focus in particular on the role of the imagination in the dynamics of Bible engagement. Alongside the Bible, DYM will also look to include other ways of making sense of the world, alternative "takes" on understanding spirituality and human life. The third "source" in DYM is dialogue, where dialogue is not primarily a process of engaging other sources, but is rather providing, in the intersubjective exchange of perspectives, further material to both prompt and fund personal constructions of meaning.

Bible Engagement

Identifying the Bible as providing the primary content of DYM is not simply to reassert the theology of *sola scriptura* as an epistemological foundation. The focus of my argument has not been to defend the theological conviction that the Bible be regarded as the authoritative norm of the word of God. Instead, my aim has been to demonstrate that such a conviction is not inconsistent with pursuing an aesthetic pedagogy, and to explore the performative implications of this conclusion.

DYM does more than direct youth ministers to make sure they include a "Bible talk" at some point in the youth ministry program, or to ensure that the Bible talk is given a place of prominence among all the other elements of the program. Rather, engaging with the Bible needs to be the flavor of all the processes of teaching and learning in the youth ministry.

The centrality of BE in youth ministry arises from the aims of DYM outlined earlier in this chapter. DYM does not affirm the centrality of the Bible simply because of its theological importance, but because of its

---

7. Drury, *Saying is Believing*, 167.

pedagogical usefulness for accomplishing specific aims and purposes. Engaging with the Bible is to be central to youth ministry because engaging with the Bible is a potent resource for promoting wide-awakeness, for challenging personal construction of meaning, for prompting concrete action, and for teaching basic Christian literacy. If youth leaders are convinced of the aims of DYM, and of the value of BE for accomplishing those aims, then determining the actual practices of BE will be less of a challenge.

BE in DYM will at least recognize the variety of avenues by which youth leaders bring the Bible to teaching and learning in youth ministry. This will be especially important in church traditions that place great importance on preaching as the central teaching practice of the church. One Bible talk in the middle of a youth gathering is not able to achieve all that BE in DYM is intended to accomplish. Peter Adam's critique of "pulpit-restricted" ministry applies equally to youth ministry:

> We need to see preaching as part of that ministry of the word. Otherwise we shall try to make preaching do what it cannot easily achieve. Not only will God's people suffer because they do not receive other ministries of the Word, but our preaching will suffer as we force it into an alien mould.[8]

Therefore, DYM will look for multiple ways to tell, explore, and embody the biblical story. This will involve engaging with the Big Story of salvation history and the overarching narrative structure of the Bible, as well as presenting the small stories, the parts that make up the whole.[9] The Bible will not only be read, but its words and themes will be sung, prayed, used as the inspiration for works of art, dramatized.

Three interrelated processes engage the imagination in the dynamics of BE: reading the text, indwelling the text, and embodying the text. These three processes are a reworking in two ways of the twin processes of aesthetic cognition (perception and illumination) in Greene's pedagogy. First, I have distinguished three processes in contrast to the two identified previously by separating out the work of embodying the text. I have done this in order to highlight the concrete and active dimension of aesthetic pedagogy in contrast to the reflective and mental work of interpretation and illumination. This, I suggest, is a way of enhancing the central place that Greene gives to concrete action that may be obscured by only referring to tasks of perception and illumination that can be heard as referring to purely internal activities. I have taken the work of active experimentation with various art forms from the

---

8. Adam, *Speaking God's Words*, 75.

9. See Middleton, "A New Heaven and a New Earth"; Goldsworthy, *Christ-Centered Biblical Theology*.

task of aesthetic perception, combined it with the ultimate task of performing new, or renewed, action, and included the influence of engaging in Christian practices as a habitus of spiritual formation. Second, where the previous demarcation of twin tasks can seem to imply a necessary order, beginning with aesthetic perception before engaging in aesthetic illumination, I am here distinguishing three *interrelated* processes in order to express the recursive and cumulative effect of these ways of engaging with the Bible.

Before outlining each process in more detail, I need to defend the emphasis on "the text" in the proposed descriptions. Griffiths expresses his preference to refer to literary "works" rather than texts. To speak of a "work" carries the implication that there must have been some work of composition or construction. Griffiths notes that though the sense of construction is evident in the Latin root *texere*, to weave, it is all but absent in postmodern literary theory that promotes the idea of textual autonomy. Griffith's prefers the labels "'work', or 'literary work' . . . to emphasize the importance of human agency and human labor."[10]

My use of "the text" of the Bible is not to ignore the existence of the authors, both human and divine. Rather, the intention is to focus attention on the words of the biblical books themselves as a prior step to our interpretations of those words. Admittedly reading the Bible in translation will already involve at least some degree of interpretation. Yet, notwithstanding this caveat, there remains a meaningful distinction between the words that make up the Bible itself and the interpretations that individual readers and various theological traditions will make out of those words. Engaging with the biblical text identifies a step prior to how one makes sense of or uses that text against the concrete demands of their lived experience.

The language of "engaging the text" becomes slightly more problematic when I speak of indwelling or embodying "the text." While it makes sense to speak of reading a text, it would be more usual to speak of indwelling or embodying the meaning discerned from reading the text. However, I have avoided speaking of indwelling and embodying "the meaning of the text" in order to move away from "interpretive monism," while also avoiding speaking of indwelling or embodying "*a* meaning of the text" in order to reject an unbounded "interpretive plurality."[11] My intention is to help young people indwell and embody the meaning they are discovering in the text as they work together in a recursive process of exploring how that meaning might fit with both the text and their lived experience.

---

10. Griffiths, *Religious Reading*, 23.
11. Vanhoozer, *Is there a Meaning?* 416–17.

Reading the Text

The foundational process of Bible engagement in DYM is to read the biblical text. Youth leaders invite young people to engage with the Bible as a sacred text that offers resources for aesthetic wonder, challenging readers to make sense of this text, and of the world in light of its message. DYM exposes young people to this text in the conviction that it is through this text that God has promised to speak. Reading the text involves exposing young people to the biblical text and equipping them to notice what the text has to offer.

Exposing

It is not possible to present to young people the Bible in its entirety in any one sitting. Nevertheless, recognizing this text as a meaningful whole requires that it be presented in toto, rather than being dissected to be received piecemeal. Attempting to make the gospel more readily accessible to young people by disseminating it as a more manageable collection of short verses does not provide young people with the text as a whole and thereby deprives them of the resource by which they might go about constructing their own interpretation of the text and their world.

Exposing young people to all of Scripture will at least mean engaging with whole books of the Bible as coherent literary constructions of intentional interpersonal discourse with an identifiable illocutionary and perlocutionary force.[12] Further, since the church has gathered these books together in the belief that it is their combined witness that faithfully presents Christ to the world, youth ministry needs to expose young people to all of the books of the Bible, enabling them to explore and discover intertextual connections of meaning.

In light of low levels of biblical literacy among young people, exposing young people to the whole Bible will require a Bible-reading plan over an extended period of time. While programs for reading through the Bible in a year are common, for many young people the demands of such a program will present too great a challenge. Yet over a three-year program of reading it will be possible to expose young people to at least the key parts of each of the major books of the Bible.

---

12. Resources such as Fee, *How to Read the Bible*, or Mackie, "Eat this Book," are examples of resources designed to give young people an introduction to books of the Bible as meaningful wholes.

While I differ with Root in regard to his emphasis on identifying divine action as the purpose of theology,[13] I agree with his insistence that "the way to get young people engaged with the biblical text is to make the task of our study of Scripture not about learning the Bible, but about seeing the God to whom the Bible witnesses."[14] I affirm therefore Root's invitation to rename "Bible study groups" as "Bible reading groups" in order to more accurately represent the purpose of such groups: to give young people the opportunity to actually read the Bible, rather than a more narrow focus on increasing biblical knowledge. Building biblical literacy through Bible study depends on the prior work of building biblical awareness through Bible reading. Biblical awareness provides the resources for the personal construction of meaning needed to establish biblical literacy in the heart and hands rather than just the head.

DYM pursues Bible reading with an "attitude of receptivity appropriate to the presumption—maybe always only a provisional assumption—that it is a site of God's self-revelation."[15] Because it is God's work to reveal himself to young people, youth leaders have no need to make Scripture more accessible or relevant whether by dumbing it down, stitching it up, or sticking to the safe paths. Rather than avoiding those parts of Scripture that seem to make no sense, youth leaders will be open to embrace them as places that not only invite dialogue and exploration with young people, but also allow God to make himself known to them. Volf's conclusion is apt:

> We can continue to engage the text without suppressing puzzlement or even negative judgment, while patiently waiting for the sense to emerge, either as a result of a new insight or a personal transformation. In our encounter with the Bible, tarrying in persistent non-understanding is often the condition of possibility of genuine disclosure, in which we hear more than just the echo of our own internal voice.[16]

Not only will youth leaders trust the promise that God will speak through his word (Isa 55:10–11; 1 Thess 2:13), they will also trust that God is at work in young people enabling them as they make choices of meaning. As they

---

13. Root, *Taking Theology to Youth Ministry*; Root, *Christopraxis*. Root's Barthian theology understands God's enduring presence in the world in terms of divine action; my own Calvinist perspective emphasises God's enduring presence in terms of divine promises embodied in Christ and mediated by the Spirit.

14. Root, *Unpacking Scripture*, 96.

15. Volf, *Captive to the Word*, 34.

16. Volf, *Captive to the Word*, 35.

do so, perhaps it will be the imagination of young people that God will use to bring fresh, even new, disclosures of truth.

Noticing

Not only will young people need to be exposed to the entirety of the biblical text, they will need to be given instruction in the "grammar" of this text, the interpretive cues necessary to enable them to explore and discern the meaning being offered in the text. This expresses the theological conviction that a Christian reading of Scripture needs to be regulated by the *analogia scriptura* and the *analogia fidei,* and parallels Greene's recognition of the need to provide students with sufficient instruction in the various ways that the creative arts communicate meaning.[17]

Where the Bible is received as the collection of enscripted discourse that God uses for establishing, expressing, and directing the covenant relationship between God and his people established in Christ, there are three main aspects of the "grammar" of the text in which young people need to be instructed. As enscripted discourse, young people need to be enabled to notice the text as a work of human literary construction, including things such as genre recognition, socio-cultural context, and use of imagery. As covenant documents, young people need to be familiar with the salvation-historical movements of the biblical story: whether the three-part creation, fall, redemption scheme,[18] or the six acts of the biblical drama of creation, fall, Israel, Christ, the church, the eschaton.[19] Finally, in light of the unity of the canon and the climax of the covenant in the person and work of Christ, young people need to recognize

---

17. Greene argues that students ought to "have some acquaintance with figurative language in the case of literature, with the distinctively dynamic images created in dance, with tonal structure and sound relations in music, with plastic and pictorial values in painting" (Greene, *LL,* 180).

18. Wolters, *Creation Regained.*

19. Bartholomew and Goheen, *Drama of Scripture.* Vanhoozer, *Drama of Doctrine,* and Wright, *New Testament and People of God* offer five-act versions of the drama. Wright suggests creation, fall, Israel, Jesus, the church; Vanhoozer, creation, Israel, Jesus, the church, new creation. Wright's proposal benefits from distinguishing the fall as a separate act to creation (the fall is an intrusion into salvation history rather than a natural or necessary aspect of creation), but misses distinguishing the age to come as a divine accomplishment rather than the eventual outworking of the life of the church. Rather than fitting the biblical drama into the constraints of the Shakespearean five-act dramatic structure, it seems wiser to be directed by the structure of the biblical narrative itself.

the movement of promise and fulfilment of biblical theology, with the gospel as hermeneutical key.[20]

Volf has hailed a return to the theological reading of the Scriptures among biblical scholars and a sustained engagement with the Scriptures by systematic theologians as "the most significant theological development in the last two decades."[21] Acknowledging that the Bible can and has been misused, even badly misused, over the centuries, Volf concludes that "the value of rediscovering the theological reading of the Bible will ultimately depend on how well it is read. But still, its being read well depends on its being read in the first place."[22] The same is true of Bible engagement within youth ministry.

Indwelling the text

Having noticed what is there is to be noticed in the Bible, DYM leaves space for an imaginative indwelling of the text. The dialogical spaces at the center of youth ministry invite young people to take the time to ruminate on the biblical text.

The image of ruminating on a text holds together the cognitive and meditative aspects of imaginative indwelling. This image is drawn from the digestive practice of ruminants, such as sheep and cattle, that digest cellulose by an initial softening of plant material in the first chamber of the stomach, followed by regurgitating the pre-digested material (the cud) to be chewed a second time, before it can be further digested in the other parts of the stomach.[23] Indwelling texts involves the work of conceptualizing meaning, allowing the text to "soften" in the mind, followed by a "re-chewing" on the text, as it is allowed to sit in the imagination. This two-part process recognizes that a text needs to be interpreted, but it is the text itself that controls the interpretation.

Ruminating on a text implies a work of abstraction involved in interpreting a text, without undermining the authority of the text itself. Interpreting literary imagery involves a movement along a spectrum, "extending from the pregnant image, full of implicit or potential application, to the developed concept, in which the underlying analogy has been articulated and delimited."[24] The theological task follows a similar progression, from the person of Christ,

20. Goldsworthy, *Christ-Centered Biblical Theology*, 25.
21. Volf, *Captive to the Word*, 14.
22. Volf, *Captive to the Word*, 15.
23. Ruminate derives from the Latin *ruminare*, to chew again.
24. Green, *Imagining God*, 70.

to the text of Scripture, to the identification of specific doctrines, and then to the construction of theological systems. Yet, "the progression . . . is not a progress, for authority remains anchored 'on the left,' to which the theologian, like every believer must continually return, lest conceptual language become dry, empty and 'abstract' in the rightly pejorative sense."[25]

For example, a biblical image such as Psalm 18:2, "YHWH is my rock and my fortress," needs first to be conceptualized by the imaginative work of connecting the image of a rock with the ideas of strength and security, and of a fortress as a place of refuge and security. The work of conceptualization needs to be guided by the text. So, imagining a rock as an irritating piece of gravel stuck in your shoe, or a fortress as a place of punishment and constraint, displays an imaginative work, but one that has not been restrained by the text. The image of Psalm 18:2 could be conceptualized as "YHWH keeps his people safe from harm." Yet, this piece of divine discourse is carried by a metaphor and not by a declarative statement. The discourse carried by the metaphor requires us to return to the image, to picture a rock of safety, to imagine how we might feel if we were safely ensconced in a fortress as a battle rages around us.

What is true of engaging metaphor applies also to narratives. A narrative will make various theological claims,[26] but any narrative is always larger than the theological claims it makes. Having "conceptualized" a narrative, the second stage of ruminating on the passage involves the imaginative journey of entering the story, picturing God and the world from within the story, and re-examining our own setting from the perspective of the story.

DYM will seek to do the same with all the different kinds of texts in Scripture: to interpret what these texts are offering as ways of making sense of the world, and to ruminate on those texts. DYM leaves time and space for young people to imagine what it would be like to be the sort of people who are shaped by obeying these laws, by singing these songs, reciting these prayers, reflecting on these proverbs, trusting in these promises, locating oneself in these genealogies, receiving these letters, and sharing these visions. And by so doing, to imagine what their own world and life would be like if they were to do the same.

This kind of imaginative indwelling of the text will also help open the door to belief. Hart argues that in order to understand something, we will be helped if we are able to imagine what is being proposed. Rendering something "meaningful" is a necessary precursor to belief and commitment, and this is the work of the imagination:

---

25. Green, *Imagining God*, 71.
26. Forbes and Harrower, *Raised from Obscurity*, 9–16.

> An important part of what imagination does in human life . . . is to present to us "meaningful" or "imaginable" states of affairs or worlds for our indwelling and consideration. This it does . . . without as yet any moral commitment to questions of truth or falsity; it is concerned simply with a certain sort of coherence. But, by showing us "how things would be if" certain things were true, imagination breathes life into concepts in a way which not only makes them easier to grasp (they remain otherwise wraith-like and transparent), but actually has a degree of persuasive force which disarms scepticism and makes "belief in" possible. Only once the imagination is taken captive, we might say, can we really be much bothered to expend intellectual energy on understanding or moral effort in acting.[27]

A dialogical youth ministry that engages their imaginations enables young people to consider Christian faith in such a way that is more likely to promote transformation than cognitive engagement alone. Imagination opens a window for cognition to look through, and from which intentional action can proceed.

Embodying the Text

The third process of imaginative BE in DYM is embodying the text. Under this heading I have gathered three activities: experimenting with the text as an aspect of noticing and indwelling what the text offers, practicing the text as a means of experiencing and promoting what the text offers, and proposing new (or renewed) action on the basis of new meanings constructed in response to the text.

Experimenting

Experimenting is a process of embodiment that enhances the ability of young people to notice what is offered in the biblical text. This follows Greene's use of engaging young people in creating their own works of art as an aspect of aesthetic perception. Students are trained to notice what is there to be noticed in an artwork through their own participation in exploring artistic mediums for themselves.[28] Creative practices such as writing lament prayers or biblical fanfiction are able to promote empathetic awareness of the way the biblical text is constructing meaning of the world.

27. Hart, "Imagination and Responsible Reading," 319–20.
28. Greene, *LL*, 187.

Experimenting with the text is not the same as applying the text. Application carries the suggestion that an action is being pursued in response to a prior cognitive conclusion: having determined what the text means, we will then be able to apply that lesson in practice. Rather, experimenting with the text is a way of gaining understanding. Entering the drama of a biblical text through pursuing the action directed by the text "requires for a moment the willing suspension of our disbelief. In the moment of that suspension, we may risk playing the role, hearing the script, and seeing the drama of our life in a wholly new way."[29] Before facing the physical challenge of pursuing concrete action, DYM encourages young people to take the less daunting step of an imaginative journey.

Practicing

Practicing the text refers to the formative influence of the Christian community that young people experience by being involved in a Christian youth ministry. Christian awareness does not arise from rational instruction alone but will also, perhaps largely, arise from inviting young people to participate in a community life that has been shaped by the message of Christ. Not only will young people be given the opportunity to hear and engage with the Bible as the central practice of spiritual formation, they will have the opportunity to experience interacting with leaders and other young people who have made personal commitments to make sense of their lives in light of this text. Involving young people as participant-observers in Christian life and practice is a formation strategy that engages the imagination and combats the formational practices of the prevailing culture.[30]

DYM invites all young people to be involved in various practices of Bible reading, including listening to the public reading of Scripture and biblical teaching (1 Tim 4:13), personal reflection and study of biblical passages, and times of open dialogue. Each young person needs to have experience of being prayed for and opportunity to join in times of corporate prayer, to at least be alongside others as they pray even if they do not pray themselves. Young people will benefit from being invited into intergenerational relationships and cross-cultural fellowship, experiencing hospitality and the opportunity to engage generously across social barriers. Young people can be given the opportunity to be involved in acts of service that meet the practical needs of others, particularly of those who are most vulnerable.

29. Brueggemann, *Texts Under Negotiation*, 69.
30. Smith, *Desiring*; Smith, *Imagining*.

Youth ministries in the Reformed tradition will also seek to provide young people the opportunity to at least witness, if not participate in, the sacraments of baptism and the Lord's Supper. That these practices are unusual in contemporary youth culture is an argument for a more prominent place in youth ministry rather than the opposite. The "strangeness" of the rituals provides a valuable moment of defamiliarization. The sacraments are an instance of meaningful actions set within a meaningful story, giving young people opportunity for aesthetic, bodily action that engages the imagination and shapes belief and practice.

Whether they be the practices of the consumer economy or the rituals of Christian worship, the bodily practices in which we are immersed "shape our background and attune our being in the world in ways that evade conceptualization and even elude our own awareness."[31] Youth ministers therefore do not face a choice between inviting young people into a transformative Christian habitus versus leaving them in a neutral space that is free of any subconscious influence. Young people are already living a habitus that is formed through their immersion in their taken-for-granted social world. Christian youth ministry invites young people to live in an alternative habitus. Therefore, not only do youth leaders need to be intentional about the environments they are creating and curating, they also need to lead young people in reflective practices that enable them to become aware of what they are participating in.

Performing

The final aspect of embodying the text is to perform new action that will be fitting to a young person's new constructions of meaning. "Performing" includes imagining how things could be otherwise, as well as pursuing concrete plans to implement meaningful action in the world. Vanhoozer's concern for how doctrine is performed in the church draws an important link between doctrine, action, and imagination. "The vocation of the church," Vanhoozer argues, "is to render—to translate, represent, give back—the reality of the gospel in its corporate form of life."[32] The challenge of spiritual life is not simply to "know the truth," but to "render the truth of the gospel . . . in patterns of speech and action."[33] DYM encourages young people to imagine how they may live in the world as the gospel declares the world to be. In the same way that enacting the text promotes an

---

31. Smith, *Imagining*, 186.
32. Vanhoozer, *Drama*, 418.
33. Vanhoozer, *Drama*, 419.

empathetic awareness of the meaning being offered in the text, performing a new set of actions that are fitting with a new construction of meaning is able to embed what has been imagined, which in turn will strengthen the imagination and drive further action.

DYM therefore seeks to give young people opportunities to enact their developing sense of meaning and significance in the world. At one level this call to action applies broadly to any of the choices being made by young people, whether in sympathy with Christian faith or not. In place of "slacktivism"[34] that is content to click a button on social media rather than participate in traditional forms of social protest, DYM directs youth leaders to assist young people by helping to identify the choices they have made, and to challenge them to consider the practical implications of their choices. Youth leaders act as witnesses of young peoples' commitments. Adult mentors keep young people accountable to their intentions to act, as well as affirming their accomplishments back to them, and in the presence of others.

DYM also directs youth leaders to pay attention to the changing patterns of a young person's participation in Christian activities. As young people move from being outsiders to insiders, youth leaders can bear witness to the ways they are displaying growing Christian understanding and commitment. Youth leaders will be alert to how a young person's involvement in Christian practice moves from disdainful mockery, through indifferent observation, curious spectating, passive involvement, active experimentation, to building competency and becoming a committed carrier of the Christian tradition. While progressing in various degrees of Christian commitment and practice is not a requirement of active membership in the youth ministry, this does not preclude youth ministers drawing attention to Christian progress if and when it occurs. As young people make various choices to participate, or not to participate, in the faith practices of the youth ministry, DYM directs youth leaders to help young people become aware of and to articulate the changing nature of their patterns of belief and practice.

Facing Alternatives

Alongside engaging with the Bible as Christian Scripture, DYM also suggests that there is value in Christian youth ministries exposing young people to belief systems other than Christianity, as well as presenting them with alternative Christian theological traditions. Doing so recognizes that the cultural landscape within which young people make their spiritual

---

34. A portmanteau word made up of "slacker" and "activism" (Rotman et al., *From Slacktivism to Activism*).

choices is one that is made up of a large number of possible forms of belief or unbelief, and a variety of expressions of Christian faith. DYM is interested neither in hiding young people from this reality, nor in taking a defensive or hostile stance against it. DYM makes a welcome acknowledgement of alternative ways of making sense of the world in order to prepare young people to take on the challenge of Christian ministry and mission as generous citizens of a pluralistic society.

Exposing young people to honest and sympathetic presentations of alternative ways of making sense of human life is not to acquiesce to the demands of relativism, nor to invite young people to pluralistic bricolage. It is fundamentally an expression of the Christian ethic of love of one's neighbor. Youth ministries need to fight for the traditional understanding of tolerance, even if it requires finding new language to resurrect a concept that has become debased. Simply to accept all alternatives as equally valid and beyond critique, as long as they have been freely chosen, expresses indifference more than love. All-embracing tolerance is a path of least resistance, whereas the invitation to love despite disagreement (as tolerance has traditionally been understood) places far greater demands on the dialogical space.

It may be challenging for Christian leaders to present alternative beliefs authentically, and if they are not able to do so it would be better not to embark on this practice in the first place. Youth ministers would need to present young people with honest and sympathetic presentations that do not belittle or misrepresent alternate beliefs. Not only do straw-man arguments undermine the goals of DYM, such presentations will quickly appear disingenuous to young people who are likely to be in genuine relationship with people who hold such beliefs.

DYM asks youth ministers to believe in young people and to believe in God. Youth ministers believe young people to be capable of making their own spiritual choices. This does not mean leaving young people to their own devices. Adult mentors need to shoulder their responsibility to help young people to develop skills in critical thinking, empathetic engagement with others, and to guide them in understanding the various possibilities of meaning available to them. Believing in young people in this way is therefore an expression of a youth minister's belief in God's purposes in creation and redemption. DYM trusts God's creative work in giving young people the human capacity to imagine and to make meaning in the world. DYM trusts the beauty of Christ to entice young people to experience the goodness of Christian faith and practice, in the hope that they might come to accept Christian truth claims for themselves.

Dialogue

The third source of content in DYM is dialogue. Recognizing dialogue as part of the content of DYM draws attention to the way dialogue with others contributes significant resources for promoting wide-awakeness and meaning-making. Dialogue in DYM is therefore different to a traditional "discussion group." Dialogue is not just a means of engagement with content generated in other sources but is in itself a source of content that is valuable for spiritual formation. As members of the youth ministry engage together in dialogue, young people and leaders alike, their various perspectives demonstrate that alternative ways of constructing meaning are available to each member. Dialogue challenges each participant to consider their own choices as they are confronted with the choices of others. Dialogue provides content that can move young people to wide-awakeness. Dialogue can also provide resources for meaning-making. In dialogue, young people have the opportunity to pool their resources from their individual explorations of meaning. That dialogue such as this takes time is consistent with DYM's invitation to an ongoing process of meaning-making.

Given the significance of the contributions that teenagers themselves make to dialogue in DYM, adult mentors will need to help build the capacity of young people to contribute freely in dialogical spaces. Youth leaders need to be aware of their own potential to dominate conversation with young people because of the role they occupy as an older leader. Youth leaders also need to be alert to social dynamics among the young people that serve to give greater prominence to some voices and marginalize others. Leaders will exercise their power in service of those parts of the body considered "weaker" or "less honorable" (1 Cor 12:23).

Values

In order to accomplish its intended outcomes, by use of its preferred means, DYM promotes the values of love, humility, and conviction. When dialogical spaces in a local church youth ministry are characterized by self-giving love, they become an expression of Christlikeness in service of the common good. Youth ministries invite all participants, whether or not they have made personal commitments of Christian faith, to be committed to one another in pursuit of their shared goal of making sense of their lived experience. Whether or not the conclusions that each young person draws will be in agreement with others or with Christian faith, all members of the youth ministry need to be willing to affirm each other in their individual quests. The commitment to love one another would be demonstrated in a commitment to defend one another's freedom to make personal choices, to challenge one another to face inconsistencies between belief and action, to confront one another with the limitations of present choices, and to invite one another to ongoing pursuit of those things that are true, noble, right, pure, lovely, admirable, excellent or praiseworthy (Phil 4:8).

The commitment to love will be particularly expressed in the hermeneutical and dialogical virtues of humility and conviction. Humility expresses love for others by not asserting the self over the contributions that others have to make. Conviction expresses love for others by not depriving others of the contribution that each individual has to offer. Defending such values will also involve identifying and rebuking the hermeneutical and dialogical vices of pride and sloth: Pride that asserts the self over others, "neglect[ing] the voice of the other in favor of its own;" and sloth that ignores one's freedom and responsibility to pursue knowledge and contribute to the shared dialogical enterprise, breeding "indifference, inattentiveness, and inaction."[35] Love replaces pride with humility without losing conviction. Love replaces sloth with conviction, humbly offered to serve the common good.

Youth ministries marked by this kind of self-giving and other-respecting love will also be places that promote interdependence between all the different "types" of people involved in the ministry. Modelled on the intra-trinitarian relations, various members of the youth ministry will be distinct but not separate. There will be certain members who are identified as leaders, and others who are not; some who are adults, others who are teenagers. The distinctions cannot and ought not be disregarded since there are significant roles and unique contributions that each has to make. But the distinctions need not produce separation, since it is in the intersubjective relationships between and across difference that promote wide-awakeness and transformative learning. The same unity-in-distinction will apply in relation to other dimensions of human diversity such as gender or culture. Many of the distinctions will not be binary categories but gradations on a spectrum, but the same principle applies. Young people will be present on shifting dimensions of belief and unbelief, of doubt and confidence, of inquiry and commitment. Yet all will be honored for the unique contribution they have to make to the common good and the shared aims of the ministry.

---

35. Vanhoozer, *Is there a Meaning?* 463.

Conclusion: Now is the Time to Wake from Slumber

In 1995, Maxine Greene said of the young people in the United States of America: "Our young, like us, their elders, inhabit a world of fearful moral uncertainty—a world where it appears that almost nothing can be done to reduce suffering, contain massacres, and protect human rights."[36] Her words were prescient of the landscape in which Australian young people and Christian youth ministries find themselves today. Ultimately though, such fears express the enduring challenge for human life in a creation "subject to futility" (Rom 8:20). The challenge to wide-awakeness is as real today as it was in the first century when the early Christian church was coming to grips with the implications of the life, death, and resurrection of Jesus for the way they made sense of their world. Youth ministry today faces the same challenge and is offered the same way forward in the gospel.

Just as Paul challenges his hearers in Rome to "wake from sleep" (Rom 13:11), so also DYM urges young people and youth ministers alike to be wide-awake in the world. For Maxine Greene that wide-awakeness is necessary so that young people might be able to break free from the constraining mystifications of their taken-for-granted world. For Paul, the need to be awake is grounded in eschatology—the "night" of "this present evil age" (Gal 1:4) is nearly over because the "daylight" of the new age will soon be ushered in at the coming of Christ. Bringing Greene's perspective together with Paul's, young people need to be awake to the structures of meaning that keep them from the kingdom of God. Indeed, they face a heightened urgency in that task because of the impending return of Christ.

"Night" is the time in which human beings are left with the question of determining how to make sense of our experience. Night is not a time for sight, but for faith, and is therefore the time for competing claims to meaningfulness. Paul places two alternatives before his hearers: to "put on the Lord Jesus Christ," or to "satisfy the fleshly desires" (Rom 13:14). Pedagogically these might be read as alternative frameworks of meaning, alternative ways of making sense of the world we experience. Young people are faced with the choice to make meaning according to the pattern of Christ as presented in the Bible, or to adopt some other interpretation on offer. Ephesians 5:15 expresses the alternatives as walking as wise people or as unwise. Paul suggests that wise people understand that though they live in a world marked by death and suffering, it is not a world entirely made up of death and suffering. The days are evil, but they are not bereft of goodness.

---

36. Greene, *RI*, 22.

The human experience is not only of death and suffering but also of life and joy. The challenge being offered is how to make sense of everything that makes up human experience. How can one account for the beauty of the sunrise, ice-cream, and friendship, at the same time as tsunamis, environmental decay, and domestic violence?

Many young people make the choice to escape; in the words of Ephesians 5:15, to "get drunk with wine;" from Romans 13:13, to engage in "carousing and drunkenness, sexual impurity and promiscuity, quarrelling and jealousy." Rather than make the effort to make sense of the world, it is simpler to "satisfy the fleshly desires" (Romans 13:14). Some young people seek the oblivion offered by drugs and alcohol; others give themselves over to the pursuit of pleasure and experience, still others make do with the taken-for-granted world they have inherited. Many young people brought up in the church on a diet of gospel-lite platitudes simply shut their eyes and ears to what doesn't make sense and sing another worship song.

DYM seeks to lure young people toward wisdom. Wise people make the most of evil circumstances by "redeeming the time" (Eph 5:16). There is a way that Christian leaders may approach this time, to set it free, at least to some extent, from its bondage of corruption (Rom 8:21). Paul instructs the Ephesian church to do so by coming to understand the will of the Lord (Eph 5:17). Paul instructs the Roman church to "put on the Lord Jesus Christ" (Rom 13:14). This is the goal of Christian spiritual formation: to adopt the pattern of life offered in Jesus in the Scriptures as the framework in which one might make meaning in the world. This is the path on which youth ministers invite young people to join them; to work together to make sense of life, in all its ambiguity and complexity, in company with Jesus.

So now is the hour for youth ministers to wake from sleep so that they in turn might wake young people from their sleep. Now is the hour for youth ministry to move young people to be wide-awake in the world by pursuing open dialogue about meaning with young people through an imaginative engagement with the Bible. Youth leaders have no guarantees that their efforts will amount to anything that will substantially alter the cultural landscape facing young people today. Yet they can be certain that responding to the pain and anxiety and fear in the world with quests for security, and safety, and control is more likely to perpetuate than to solve the problems they face. Instead, youth leaders look to open up spaces for people to come together, with mutual concern, to dialogue in pursuit of peace. Youth ministers invite conversations across difference, to give up quests for power and not give in to fear, to wait for the surprising freedom of the Spirit of God (John 3:9). Christian leaders of young people call one another to not give in to despair as they place their hope, not in themselves, but in God who raises the dead (2 Cor 1:9).

Bibliography

Abrams, Meyer Howard. "Orientation of Critical Theories." In *Twentieth Century Literary Theory: An Introductory Anthology*, edited by Vassilis Lambropoulos and David Neale Miller, 3–31. New York, NY: State University of New York Press, 1987.

Adam, Peter. *Speaking God's Words: A Practical Theology of Preaching*. 1993 Moore College Lectures. Leicester, UK: IVP, 1996.

Alexander, Robin. *Essays on Pedagogy*. Abingdon, UK: Routledge, 2008.

Alter, Robert. *The Art of Biblical Narrative*. New York, NY: Basic, 1981.

———. *The World of Biblical Literature*. New York, NY: BasicBooks, 1992.

American Bible Society. *The State of the Bible 2013: A Study of U.S. Adults*. New York, NY: American Bible Society, 2013. http://www.americanbible.org/uploads/content/State%20of%20the%20Bible%20Report%202013.pdf.

Anderson, Ray S. *The Shape of Practical Theology: Empowering Ministry with Theological Praxis*. Downers Grove, IL: IVP, 2001.

Arzola, Fernando. *Toward a Prophetic Youth Ministry: Theory and Praxis in Urban Context*. Downers Grove, IL: IVP Academic, 2008.

Auden, W. H., and Louis Kronenberger. *The Faber Book of Aphorisms*. London: Faber and Faber, 1989.

Augustine. *On Christian Doctrine*. Translated by J. F. Shaw. Mineola, NY: Dover, trans. 2009.

Australian Bureau of Statistics. "4326.0— National Survey of Mental Health and Wellbeing: Summary of Results, 2007." Canberra, 2008.

Avis, Paul. *God and the Creative Imagination: Metaphor, Symbol and Myth in Religion and Theology*. London, UK: Routledge, 1999.

Ayers, William. "Doing Philosophy: Maxine Greene and the Pedagogy of Possibility." In *A Light in Dark Times: Maxine Greene and the Unfinished Conversation*, edited by William Ayers and Janet L. Miller, 3–21. New York, NY: Teachers College Press, 1998.

———. "Social Imagination: A Conversation with Maxine Greene." *Qualitative Studies in Education* 8.4 (1995) 319–28.

Ayers, William, and Janet L. Miller, eds. *A Light in Dark Times: Maxine Greene and the Unfinished Conversation*. New York, NY: Teachers College Press, 1998.

Baldacchino, John. *Education Beyond Education: Self and the Imaginary in Maxine Greene's Philosophy*. New York, NY: Peter Lang, 2009.

Balthasar, Hans Urs von. "Nine Propositions on Christian Ethics." In *Principles of Christian Morality*, edited by Hans Urs von Balthasar, Pope Benedict XVI, and Heinz Schürmann, 75–104. San Francisco, CA: Ignatius, 1986.

———. *Theo-Drama: Theological Dramatic Theory, Vol. 1: Prolegomena*. San Francisco, CA: Ignatius, 1988.

Barenblat, Rachel. "Tranformative Work: Midrash and Fanfiction." *Religion and Literature* 43.2 (Summer 2011) 171–77.

Barone, Thomas. "Maxine Greene: Literary Influences." In *The Passionate Mind of Maxine Greene: "I Am . . . Not Yet,"* edited by William F. Pinar, 137–47. London, UK: Falmer, 1998.

Barth, Karl. *Church Dogmatics*. Translated by G. T. Thomson et al. Edinburgh: T. & T. Clark, 1936–77.

———. *Nein! Antwort an Emil Brunner*. Munich, Germany: Kaiser, 1934.

———. *The Word of God and the Word of Man*. Translated by Douglas Horton. London, UK: Hodder & Stoughton, 1928.

Bartholomew, Craig G., and Michael W. Goheen. *The Drama of Scripture: Finding Our Place in the Biblical Story*. Grand Rapids, MI: Baker, 2004.

Bauckham, Richard. *The Theology of the Book of Revelation*. Cambridge: CUP, 1993.

———. "Tradition in Relation to Scripture and Reason." In *Scripture, Tradition, and Reason: A Study in the Criteria of Christian Doctrine: Essays in Honour of Richard P. C. Hanson*, edited by Richard Bauckham and Benjamin Drewery, 117–45. Edinburgh, UK: T. & T. Clark, 1988.

Bauer, Michael J. *Arts Ministry: Nurturing the Creative Life of God's People*. Calvin Institute of Christian Worship Liturgical Studies, edited by John D. Witvliet Grand Rapids, MI: Eerdmans, 2013.

Bebbington, David W. *Evangelicalism in Modern Britain: A History from the 1730s to the 1930s*. London, UK: Unwin Hyman, 1989.

Beck, Robert H. "Kilpatrick's Critique of Montessori's Method and Theory." *Studies in Philosophy and Education* 1.4 (1961) 153–62.

Bellah, Robert N. et al. *Habits of the Heart: Individualism and Commitment in American Life*. Berkeley, CA: University of California Press, 1985.

Berriman, Jerome. *Godly Play: An Imaginative Approach to Religious Education*. Minneapolis, MN: Augsburg, 1991.

———. *The Spiritual Guidance of Children: Montessori, Godly Play, and the Future*. New York, NY: Morehouse, 2013.

———. *Teaching Godly Play: The Sunday Morning Handbook*. Nashville, TN: Abingdon, 1995.

Bevans, Stephen B. *Models of Contextual Theology*. 2nd ed. Maryknoll, NY: Orbis, 2002.

Bible Society. *Pass It On*. London, UK: Bible Society, 2014. http://www.biblesociety.org.uk/uploads/content/projects/Bible-Society-Report_030214_final_.pdf.

Bird, Michael F. *Evangelical Theology : A Biblical and Systematic Introduction*. Grand Rapids, MI: Zondervan, 2013.

Blenkinsopp, Adrian, ed. *The Bible According to Gen Z*. Minto, NSW: Bible Society Australia, 2013.

Bloch, Ernst. *The Principle of Hope*. 3 vols. Oxford, UK: Blackwell, 1986.
Bock, Darrell L., and Scott Cunningham. "Is Matthew Midrash?" *Bibliotheca Sacra* 144.574 (Apr–Jun 1987) 157–80.
Bonhoeffer, Dietrich. *Life Together, Prayerbook of the Bible*. Translated by Gerhard Ludwig Müller and Albrecht Schönherr. Dietrich Bonhoeffer Works, edited by Geoffrey B. Kelly. Vol. 5. Minneapolis, MN: Fortress, 1996. Dietrich Bonhoeffer Werke Bande 5.
Botton, Alain de, and John Armstrong. *Art as Therapy*. London, UK / New York, NY: Phaidon, 2013.
Bourdieu, Pierre. *The Logic of Practice*. Translated by Richard Nice. Stanford, CA: Stanford University Press, 1990. Le sens pratique.
Brain, Matthew Peter. *Engage!: How the Church Can Reconnect with Young People*. Barton, ACT: Barton Books, 2011.
Brown, David. "The Ascension and Transfigured Bodies." In *Faithful Performances: Enacting Christian Tradition*, edited by Trevor A. Hart and Steven R. Guthrie, 255–72. Aldershot, UK: Ashgate, 2007.
Brown, Sally A. "Hermeneutical Theory." In *The Wiley-Blackwell Companion to Practical Theology*, edited by Bonnie J Miller-McLemore, 112–22. Malden, MA: Wiley-Blackwell, 2012.
Browning, Don, S. *A Fundamental Practical Theology*. Minneapolis, MN: Fortress, 1991.
Brueggemann, Walter. "Bounded by Obedience and Praise: The Psalms as Canon." *JSOT* 50 (1991) 63–92.
———. *The Practice of Prophetic Imagination: Preaching an Emancipating Word*. Minneapolis, MN: Augsburg Fortress, 2012.
———. *Praying the Psalms: Engaging Scripture and the Life of the Spirit*. Eugene, OR: Cascade, 2007.
———. *The Prophetic Imagination*. 2nd ed. Minneapolis, MN: Fortress, 2001.
———. "Psalms and the Life of Faith: A Suggested Typology of Function." *JSOT* 17 (1980) 3–32.
———. *Texts under Negotiation: The Bible and Postmodern Imagination*. Philadelphia, PA: Fortress, 1993.
Buber, Martin. *I and Thou*. New York, NY: Charles Scribner's Sons, 1970.
Buttrick, David. *Homiletic : Moves and Structures*. Philadelphia, PA: Fortress, 1987.
Camus, Albert. "The Almond Trees." In *Lyrical and Critical Essays*. New York, NY: Alfred A Knopf, 1968.
Caputo, John D. *The Weakness of God: A Theology of the Event*. Bloomington IN: Indiana University Press, 2006.
Carson, D. A. *Divine Sovereignty and Human Responsibility: Biblical Perspectives in Tension*. Atlanta: John Knox, 1981.
Chickering, Arthur W., and Zelda F. Gamson. "Seven Principles for Good Practice in Undergraduate Education." *AAHE Bulletin* (March 1987) 3–7.
Coleridge, Samuel Taylor. *Biographia Literaria, or Biographical Sketches of My Literary Life and Opinions*. Princeton, NJ: Princeton University Press, 1983.
Connolly, Marie. "Practice Frameworks: Conceptual Maps to Guide Interventions in Child Welfare." *British Journal of Social Work* 37 (2007) 825–37.
Corney, Peter. "Assertive Self-Interest and Social Decay." *Essentials* Summer (2016) 16–17.

Cosby, Brian H. *Giving up Gimmicks: Reclaiming Youth Ministry from an Entertainment Culture*. Phillipsburg, NJ: P&R, 2012.

Côté, James. "Identity Studies: How Close Are We to Developing a Social Science of Identity?—an Appraisal of the Field." *Identity* 6.1 (2006) 3–25.

Coyne, Michael D., Edward J. Kameenui, and Douglas W. Carnine. *Effective Teaching Strategies That Accommodate Diverse Learners*. Upper Saddle River, NJ: Pearson, 2011.

Craddock, Fred B. *As One without Authority*. Nashville, TN: Abingdon, 1979.

Cristi, Renato. *Hegel on Freedom and Authority*. Cardiff, Wales: University of Wales Press, 2005.

Cuypers, Stefaan E. "Educating for Authenticity: The Paradox of Moral Education Revisited." In *Oxford Handbook of Philosophy of Education*, edited by Harvey Siegel, 122–44. Oxford, UK: Oxford University Press, 2009.

Damon, William. "What Is Positive Youth Development." *Annals of the American Academy of Political and Social Science* 591 (Jan 2004) 13–24.

Davies, Jon. "The Dialectic of Freedom." In *The Passionate Mind of Maxine Greene: "I Am . . . Not Yet,"* edited by William F. Pinar, 39–45. London, UK: Falmer, 1998.

Dean, Kenda Creasy. *Practicing Passion: Youth and the Quest for a Passionate Church*. Grand Rapids, MI: Eerdmans, 2004.

———. "We Will Find the Answers as We Go: A Response to Chap Clark's Youth Ministry as Practical Theology." *Journal of Youth Ministry* 7.1 (2008).

Dean, Kenda Creasy, and Ron Foster. *The Godbearing Life: The Art of Soul Tending for Youth Ministry*. Nashville, TN: Upper Room, 1998.

Debray, Régis. *The New Testament through 100 Masterpieces of Art*. London, UK: Merrell, 2004.

———. *The Old Testament through 100 Masterpieces of Art*. London, UK: Merrell, 2004.

Derecho, Abigail. "Archontic Literature: A Definition, a History, and Several Theories of Fan Fiction." In *Fan Fiction and Fan Communities in the Age of the Internet: New Essays*, edited by Karen Hellekson and Kristina Busse, 61–78. Jefferson, NC: McFarland, 2006.

Dewey, John. *Art as Experience*. New York, NY: Perigee, 1934/2005.

———. *The Public and Its Problems*. Chicago, IL: Swallow, 1954.

Donoghue, Denis. *The Arts without Mystery*. Boston, MS: Llittle, Brown and Company, 1983.

Douglass, Katherine M. "Aesthetic Learning Theory and the Faith Formation of Young Adults." *Religious Education* 108.5 (2013) 449–66.

Drury, Amanda Hontz. *Saying Is Believing : The Necessity of Testimony in Adolescent Spiritual Development*. Downers Grove, IL: IVP Academic, 2015.

Dunn, James D. G. *The Theology of Paul the Apostle*. Grand Rapids, MI: Eerdmans, 1998.

Eliot, T.S. *Murder in the Cathedral*. London, UK: Faber and Faber, 1965.

Erikson, Erik H. *Young Man Luther: A Study in Psychoanalysis and History*. New York, NY: Norton, 1962.

———. "Youth: Fidelity and Diversity." *Daedalus* 117.3 (1962/1988) 1–24.

Fee, Gordon D., and Douglas Stuart. *How to Read the Bible Book by Book: A Guided Tour*. Grand Rapids, MI: Zondervan, 2014.

Fennema, Jack. "Constructivism: A Critique from a Biblical Worldview." In *Faith-Based Education That Constructs: A Creative Dialogue between Constructivism and Faith-Based Education*, edited by HeeKap Lee, 23–36. Eugene, OR: Wipf & Stock, 2010.
Fields, Doug. *Purpose Driven Youth Ministry One Step Beyond*. Grand Rapids: Zondervan, 2009.
———. *Purpose Driven Youth Ministry: 9 Essential Foundations for Healthy Growth*. Grand Rapids, MI.: Zondervan, 1998.
Fisher, John. "The Four Domains Model: Connecting Spirituality, Health and Well-Being." *Religions*.2 (2011) 17–28.
Forbes, Greg W., and Scott D. Harrower. *Raised from Obscurity: A Narratival and Theological Study of the Characterization of Women in Luke-Acts*. Eugene, OR: Pickwick, 2015.
Foster, Charles R. "Response: Pedagogical Imagination in the Scholarship of Teaching and Learning in Theology and Religion." *Teaching Theology & Religion* 16.2 (April 2013) 125–26.
France, R. T. *Divine Government: God's Kingship in the Gospel of Mark*. Homebush West, NSW: Lancer, 1990.
Frankl, Viktor E. *Man's Search for Meaning*. Translated by Ilse Lasche. Boston, MS: Beacon, 2006.
Frei, Hans W. "Conflicts in Interpretation." *Theology Today* 49.3 (1992) 344–56.
Freire, Paulo. *Pedagogy of the Oppressed*. Translated by Myra Bergman Ramos. Harmondsworth, UK: Penguin, 1972.
Frye, Northrop. *Anatomy of Criticism*. Princeton, NJ: Princeton University Press, 1957.
Gadamer, Hans Georg. *Truth and Method*. Translated by Joel Weinsheimer and Donald G. Marshall. Rev. ed. London, UK: Bloomsbury Academic, 2013.
Gamson, Zelda F. "A Brief History of the Seven Principles for Good Practice in Undergraduate Education." *New Directions for Teaching and Learning* 47 (1991) 5–12.
Gamson, Zelda F., and S. J. Poulsen. "Inventories of Good Practice: The Next Step for the Seven Principles for Good Practice in Undergraduate Education." *AAHE Bulletin* 42.3 (1989) 7–8, 14.
Gates, Brian E. *Freedom and Authority in Religions and Religious Education*. London, UK: Bloomsbury Academic, 2016.
Geertz, Clifford. "Thick Description: Toward an Interpretive Theory of Culture." In *The Interpretation of Cultures: Selected Essays*, 3–30. New York, NY: Basic, 1973.
Gerkin, Charles V. *The Living Human Document: Re-Visioning Pastoral Counseling in a Hermeneutical Mode*. Nashville, TN: Abingdon, 1984.
Goldsworthy, Graham. *Christ-Centered Biblical Theology: Hermeneutical Foundations and Principles*. Leicester, UK: Inter-Varsity, 2013.
Gräb, Wilhelm. "Practical Theology as Theology of Religion. Schleiermacher's Understanding of Practical Theology as a Discipline." *International Journal of Practical Theology* 9.2 (December 2005) 181–96.
Graham, Elaine, Heather Walton, and Frances Ward, eds. *Theological Reflection: Methods*. London, UK: SCM, 2005.
———, eds. *Theological Reflection: Sources*. London, UK: SCM, 2007.
Green, Garrett. *Imagining God: Theology and the Religious Imagination*. Grand Rapids, MI: Eerdmans, 1989.

———. *Theology, Hermeneutics and Imagination: The Crisis of Interpretation at the End of Modernity*. Cambridge, UK: Cambridge University Press, 2000.

Greene, Maxine. "Aesthetic Literacy in General Education." In *Philosophy and Education: Eightieth Yearbook of the National Society for the Study of Education*, edited by Jonas F. Soltis, 115–41. Chicago, IL: University of Chicago, 1981.

———. "The Ambiguities of Freedom." *English Education* 33.1 (October 2000) 8–14.

———. "The Artistic and the Aesthetic in Aesthetic Education." Maxine Greene Center for Aesthetic Education and Social Imagination. https://maxinegreene.org/uploads/library/aesthetic_n_artistic_in_aesthetic_education.pdf.

———. *The Dialectic of Freedom*. New York, NY: Teachers College, 1988.

———. *Landscapes of Learning*. New York, NY: Teachers College, 1978.

———. "Qualitative Research and the Uses of Literature." *Journal of Thought* 21.3 (1986) 69–83.

———. "Real Toads in Imaginary Gardens." *Teachers College Record* 66.5 (1965) 416–25.

———. *Releasing the Imagination: Essays on Education, the Arts, and Social Change*. San Francisco, CA: Jossey-Bass, 1995.

———. "The Spaces of Aesthetic Education." *Journal of Aesthetic Education* 20.4 (Winter 1986) 56–62.

———. *Teacher as Stranger: Educational Philosophy for the Modern Age*. Belmont, CA: Wadsworth, 1973.

———. *Variations on a Blue Guitar: The Lincoln Center Institute Lectures on Aesthetic Education*. New York, NY: Teachers College Press, 2001.

Greenman, Jeffrey P. "Spiritual Formation in Theological Perspective: Classic Issues, Contemporary Challenges." In *Life in the Spirit: Spiritual Formation in Theological Perspective*, edited by George Kalantzis and Jeffrey P. Greenman, 23–35. Downers Grove, IL: IVP Academic, 2010.

Griffiths, Paul J. *Religious Reading: The Place of Reading in the Practice of Religion*. New York, NY: Oxford University Press, 1999.

Gundry, Robert H. *Matthew: A Commentary on His Literary and Theological Art*. Grand Rapids, MI: Eerdmans, 1982.

Gunton, Colin E. *The Promise of Trinitarian Theology*. 2nd ed. London, UK: T. & T. Clark, 1997.

Haemig, Mary Jane. "Practical Advice on Prayer from Martin Luther." *Word and World* 35.1 (Winter 2015) 22–30.

Hall, Christopher A. "Reading Christ into the Heart: The Theological Foundations of Lectio Divina." In *Life in the Spirit: Spiritual Formation in Theological Perspective*, edited by George Kalantzis and Jeffrey P. Greenman, 141–59. Downers Grove, IL: IVP Academic, 2010.

Hall, G. Stanley. *Adolescence; Its Psychology and Its Relations to Physiology, Anthropology, Sociology, Sex, Crime, Religion and Education*. New York, NY: Appleton, 1904.

Hart, David Bentley. *The Beauty of the Infinite: The Aesthetics of Christian Truth*. Grand Rapids, MI: Eerdmans, 2004.

———. "God or Nothingness." In *I Am the Lord Your God: Christian Reflections on the Ten Commandments*, edited by Carl E. Braaten and Christopher R. Seitz, 55–76. Grand Rapids, MI: Eerdmans, 2005.

Hart, Trevor A. "Imagination and Responsible Reading." In *Renewing Biblical Interpretation*, edited by Colin Greene, C.G. Bartholomew and Karl Moller, 307–34. Carlisle, UK: Paternoster, 2000.

———. "Imagination for the Kingdom of God? Hope, Promise and the Transformative Power of an Imagined Future." In *God Will Be All in All: The Eschatology of Jügen Moltmann*, edited by R. Bauckham, 49–76. Edinburgh, UK: T. & T. Clark, 1999.

———. "(Probably) the Greatest Story Ever Told? Reflections on Brueggemann's the Bible and Postmodern Imagination." In *Interpreting the Bible: Historical and Theological Studies in Honour of David F. Wright*, edited by A. N. S. Lane, 181–203. Leicester, UK: Apollos, 1997.

———. "Tradition, Authority, and a Christian Approach to the Bible as Scripture." In *Between Two Horizons: Spanning New Testament Studies and Systematic Theology*, edited by Joel B. Green and Max Turner, 183–204. Grand Rapids, MI/Cambridge, UK: Eerdmans, 2000.

Hauerwas, Stanley. *Vision and Virtue: Essays in Christian Ethical Reflection*. Notre Dame, IN: University of Notre Dame Press, 1981.

Hawkins, Tim. *Fruit That Will Last: How to Develop a Youth Ministry with Lasting Impact*. 10th anniversary ed. Baulkham Hills, NSW: Hawkins Ministry Resources, 2010.

Hays, Richard. B. *The Conversion of the Imagination: Paul as Interpreter of Israel's Scripture*. Grand Rapids, MI: Eerdmans, 2005.

Healy, Karen. *Social Work Theories in Context: Creating Frameworks for Practice*. Houndmills, Basingstoke, Hampshire, UK: Palgrave Macmillan, 2005.

Heitink, Gerben. *Practical Theology: History, Theory, Action Domains: Manual for Practical Theology*. Translated by Reinder Bruinsma. Grand Rapids, MI: Eerdmans, 1999.

Hellekson, Karen, and Kristina Busse. *Fan Fiction and Fan Communities in the Age of the Internet : New Essays*. Jefferson, NC: McFarland & Co., 2006.

Hiemstra, Rick. "Confidence, Conversation and Community: Bible Engagement in Canada, 2013." Toronto, Ontario: Faith Today, 2014.

Hoggarth, Pauline. *The Seed and the Soil : Engaging with the Word of God*. Langham Global Library. edited by David Smith and Joe Kapolyo Carlise, UK: Global Christian Library, 2011.

Howard, Vivian. "The Importance of Pleasure Reading in the Lives of Young Teens: Self-Identification, Self-Construction and Self-Awareness." *Journal of Librarianship and Information Science* 43.1 (03/01 2011) 46–55.

Hughes, Philip. "Bible Engagement among Australian Young People." In *The Bible According to Gen Z*, edited by Adrian Blenkinsopp. Bible Society Australia Essas, 7–25. Minto, NSW: Bible Society Australia, 2013.

Hughes, Philip, and Claire Pickering. "Bible Engagement among Young Australians: Patterns and Social Drivers." 1–53. Melbourne, VIC: Christian Research Association, 2010.

Hughes, Philip, Stephen Reid, Claire Pickering, and Peter Bentley. "Bible Engagement among Young People Part 2. Major Report." 1–64. Melbourne, VIC: Christian Research Association, 2010.

Jensen, Michael P. "'In Spirit and in Truth': Can Charles Taylor Help the Woman at the Well Find Her Authentic Self?" *Studies in Christian Ethics* 21.3 (2008): 325–41.

———. *Martyrdom and Identity: The Self on Trial*. London, UK/New York, NY: T. & T. Clark, 2010.

———. *Sydney Anglicanism: An Apology*. Eugene, OR: Wipf & Stock, 2012.

Jensen, Peter F. *The Revelation of God*. Contours of Christian Theology. edited by Gerald Bray Leicester, UK: IVP, 2002.

Johnson, Mark. *The Meaning of the Body*. Chicago, IL: University of Chicago, 2007.

Joyous202. "OC, OOC, and CC" [Online Forum]. https://www.fanfiction.net/topic /112036/63979196/OC-OOC-and-CC.

Kageler, Len. *Youth Ministry in a Multifaith Society: Forming Christian Identity among Skeptics, Syncretists and Sincere Believers of Other Faiths*. Downers Grove, IL: IVP, 2014.

Kahn, Kenneth B., Gloria Barczak, and Roberta Moss. "Perspective: Establishing an NPD Best Practices Framework." *Journal of Product Innovation Management* 23.2 (2006) 106–16.

Kaiser, Walter C. "A Principilizing Model." In *Four Views on Moving Beyond the Bible to Theology*, edited by G.T. Meadors, 19–50. Grand Rapids, MI: Zondervan, 2009.

———. *Toward an Exegetical Theology: Biblical Exegesis for Preaching and Teaching*. Grand Rapids, MI: Baker, 1981.

Kant, Immanuel. *Religion within the Limits of Reason Alone*. Translated by Theodore Meyer Greene and Hoyt H. Hudson. New York, NY. NY: Harper & Row, 1960.

Kaufman, Gordon D. *The Theological Imagination: Constructing the Concept of God*. Philadelphia, PA: Westminster, 1981.

Kegan, Robert. *The Evolving Self: Problem and Process in Human Development*. Cambridge, MA: Harvard, 1982.

Kilpatrick, William Heard. *The Montessori System Examined*. Boston, MS: Houghton Mifflin, 1914.

Kim, Hyun-Sook. "The Hermeneutical-Praxis Paradigm and Practical Theology." *Religious Education* 102.4 (Fall 2007) 419–36.

Kinkela, Katherine, and Peter Harris. "COSO Updates Practice Framework." *Internal Auditing* 28.4 (2013) 35.

Kinnaman, David. *You Lost Me: Why Young Christians Are Leaving Church . . . and Rethinking Faith*. Grand Rapids, MI: Baker, 2011.

Knowlton, Dave S. "Shifting toward a Constructivist Philosophy for Teaching Biblical Principles in K–12 Schools." *Christian Education Journal* 1.3 (2004) 116–29.

Knox, D. B. "Propositional Revelation the Only Revelation." *Reformed Theological Review* 19.1 (1960) 1–9.

Koffka, Kurt. *Principles of Gestalt Psychology*. International Library of Psychology, Philosophy and Scientific Method. London, UK: Routledge & K. Paul, 1935.

Kohl, Herbert. "Foreword." In *The Public School and the Private Vision: A Search for America in Education and Literature*, Maxine Greene. Classics in Progressive Education, xi–xiv. New York, NY: The New Press, 2007.

Köhler, W. *Gestalt Psychology: An Introduction to New Concepts in Modern Psychology*. rev. ed. New York, NY: Liveright, 1947.

Kohli, Wendy. "Philosopher of/for Freedom." In *A Light in Dark Times: Maxine Greene and the Unfinished Conversation*, edited by William Ayers and Janet L. Miller, 11–21. New York, NY: Teachers College Press, 1998.

Kuhn, Thomas S. *The Structure of Scientific Revolutions*. 3rd ed. Chicago, IL: University of Chicago Press, 1996.

Küng, Hans. *Theology for the Third Millennium : An Ecumenical View.* Translated by Peter Heinegg. New York, NY: Doubleday, 1988.

Kurtz, Paul, and Edwin H. Wilson. "Humanist Manifesto Ii." *Humanist* 33.5 (1973) 4–9.

Lacey, Simon, Randall Stilla, and K. Sathian. "Metaphorically Feeling: Comprehending Textual Metaphors Activates Somatosensory Cortex." *Brain & Language* 120 (2012) 416–21.

Lash, N. *Theology on the Way to Emmaus.* Eugene, OR: Wipf and Stock, 2005.

Levy, Sandra M. *Imagination and the Journey of Faith.* Grand Rapids, MI: Eerdmans, 2008.

Lewis, C.S. *An Experiment in Criticism.* Cambridge, UK: Cambridge University Press, 1961.

Lewis, Gordon R. "Is Propositional Revelation Essential to Evangelical Spiritual Formation?" *Journal of the Evangelical Theological Society* 46.2 (June 2003) 269–98.

Lincoln Center Institute. "Lincoln Center Institute Capacities for Imaginative Learning." https://imaginationnow.files.wordpress.com/2011/03/capacities.pdf.

Linhart, Terry. *Teaching the Next Generations: A Comprehensive Guide for Teaching Christian Formation.* Grand Rapids, MI: Baker, 2016.

Luther, Martin, and Mark D. Tranvik. *The Freedom of a Christian.* Luther Study Edition. Minneapolis, MN: Fortress, 1520/2008.

Makkreel, R.A., and F. Rodi, eds. *Dilthey Selected Works IV: Hermeneutics and the Study of History.* Princeton, NJ: Princeton University Press, 1996.

Marshall, Paul A. *A Kind of Life Imposed on Man : Vocation and Social Order from Tyndale to Locke.* Toronto, Canada; Buffalo, NY: University of Toronto Press, 1996.

Marx, Karl, and Friedrich Engels. *Capital: A Critique of Political Economy. Volume Iii the Process of Capitalist Production as a Whole.* New York, NY: International, 1894.

Mason, Michael. "The Spirituality of Young Australians." In *Religion and Youth*, edited by Sylvia Collins-Mayo and Pink Dandelion, 55–62. Farnham, UK: Ashgate, 2010.

Mason, Michael, Andrew Singleton, and Ruth Webber. *The Spirit of Generation Y: Young Peoples' Spirituality in a Changing Australia.* Melbourne, VIC: John Garratt, 2007.

McFague, Sallie. *Metaphorical Theology : Models of God in Religious Language.* Philadelphia, PA: Fortress, 1982.

McGrath, Alister. "An Enhanced Vision of Rationality: C. S. Lewis on the Reasonableness of Christian Faith." *Theology* 116.6 (November/December 2013) 410–17.

McKoy, Brandon K. *Youth Ministry from the Outside In: How Relationships and Stories Shape Identity.* Downers Grove, IL: IVP, 2013.

Medcalf, Stephen. "Eliot, David Jones, and Auden." In *The Oxford Handbook of English Literature and Theology*, edited by Andrew W. Hass, David Jasper and Elisabeth Jay, 523–42. Oxford: OUP, 2007.

Melucci, A. "The Process of Collective Identity." In *Social Movements and Culture*, edited by H. Johnson and B. Klandermas, 41–63. Minneapolis, MN: University of Minnesota Press, 1995.

Merleau-Ponty, Maurice. *Phenomenology of Perception.* Translated by Colin Smith. London, UK: Routledge & Kegan Paul, 1962. Phénoménologie de la Perception.

Middleton, J. Richard. "A New Heaven and a New Earth: The Case for a Holistic Reading of the Biblical Story of Redemption." *Journal for Christian Theological Research* 11 (2006) 73–97.

Milbank, John. *Theology and Social Theory: Beyond Secular Reason.* Second ed. Malden, MA: Blackwell, 2006.
Miller, Janet L., and Carole Saltz. "'Condemned to Make Meaning.'" *TC Today: The Magazine of Teachers College, Columbia University*, 2014, 32–35.
Mitchell, Keith. "Truth, Traditional Teaching, and Constructivism." In *Foundations of Education: A Christian Vision*, edited by Matthew Etherington, 86–92. Eugene, OR: Wipf & Stock, 2014.
Moltmann, Jürgen. *The Coming of God: Christian Eschatology.* Translated by Margaret Kohl. London, UK: SCM, 1996.
Moo, Douglas J. "Matthew and Midrash: An Evaluation of Robert H Gundry's Approach." *Journal of the Evangelical Theological Society* 26.1 (1983) 31–39.
Moore, Marianne. "Moore's Notes to *Observations*." In *Modernism: An Anthology*, edited by Lawrence Rainey, 661–65. Malden, MA: Blackwell, 2005.
———. "Poetry." https://poets.org/poem/poetry
Moore, T. M. "Conscientization and Christian Education: The Process Pedagogy of Paulo Freire." *JETS* 31.4 (December 1988) 453–64.
Morris, Karen, and Rod Morris. *Leading Better Bible Studies : Essential Skills for Effective Small Groups.* Sydney South, NSW: Aquila, 1997.
Morris, Marla. "Existential and Phenomenological Influences on Maxine Greene." In *The Passionate Mind of Maxine Greene: "I Am . . . Not Yet,"* edited by William F. Pinar, 124–36. London, UK: Falmer, 1998.
Moser, Ken. *Changing the World through Effective Youth Ministry.* Sydney South, NSW: Aquilla, 2000.
Moulster, Gwen, Sarah Ames, and Tom Griffiths. "Implementation of a New Framework for Practice." *Learning Disability Practice* 15.7 (2012) 21.
Moulton, Richard G. *The Literary Study of the Bible: An Account of the Leading Forms of Literature Represented in the Sacred Writings, Intended for English Readers.* Boston, MS: DC Heath, 1895.
Nash, Paul. *Authority and Freedom in Education: An Introduction to the Philosophy of Education.* New York, NY: Wiley, 1966.
Nolland, John. *The Gospel of Matthew: A Commentary on the Greek Text.* New International Greek Testament Commentary. Grand Rapids, MI: Eerdmans, 2005.
Noppe-Brandon, Scott, and Madeleine F. Holzer. "Maxine Greene and Lincoln Center Institute: Setting the Context." In *Variations on a Blue Guitar: The Lincoln Center Institute Lectures on Aesthetic Education*, edited by Maxine Greene, 1–4. New York, NY: Teachers College Press, 2001.
O'Gorman, Kathleen. "Maxine Greene: A Religious Educator's Religious Educator." In *The Passionate Mind of Maxine Greene: "I Am. . . Not Yet,"* edited by William F. Pinar, 229–36. London, UK: Falmer, 1998.
Oestreicher, Mark. *Youth Ministry 3.0: A Manifesto of Where We've Been, Where We Are and Where We Need to Go.* Grand Rapids, MI: Zondervan, 2008.
Osborn, Eric F. "Realism and Revelation." *Australian Biblical Review* 8.1–4 (1960) 29–37.
Osborne, Grant R. *The Hermeneutical Spiral : A Comprehensive Introduction to Biblical Interpretation.* Downers Grove, IL: IVP, 1991.
Osmer, Richard. *Practical Theology: An Introduction.* Grand Rapids, MI: Eerdmans, 2008.

Osmer, Richard, and Ariana Salazar-Newton. "The Practice of Reading and the Formation of the Moral Imagination." *Ecclesial Practices* 1 (2014) 51–71.
Packer, J. I. *Evangelism and the Sovereignty of God*. Downers Grove, IL: IVP, 2012.
Parker, Stephen, Leslie J. Francis, and Rob Freathy, eds. *Religious Education and Freedom of Religion and Belief*. New York, NY: Peter Lang AG, 2012.
Pattison, Stephen. "Some Straw for the Bricks: A Basic Introduction to Theological Reflection." In *Theological Reflection: Sources*, edited by Elaine Graham, Heather Walton and Frances Ward, 276–84. London, UK: SCM, 1989/2007.
Pautz, Anne E. "Views across the Expanse: Maxine Greene's *Landscapes of Learning*." In *The Passionate Mind of Maxine Greene: "I Am . . . Not Yet,"* edited by William F. Pinar, 30–38. London, UK: Falmer, 1998.
Pazmiño, Robert W. "Christian Education Is More Than Formation." *Christian Education Journal* 3.7.2 (Fall 2010) 356–65.
Pembroke, Neil. *Moving toward Spiritual Maturity: Psychological, Contemplative, and Moral Challenges in Christian Living*. Binghamton, NY: Haworth Pastoral, 2007.
———. "Theological Diagnostics in Von Balthasar's Homily, 'Joy in the Midst of Anxiety.'" *Manuscript in preparation* (2016).
Penner, James, Rachel Harder, Erika Anderson, Bruno Désorcy, and Rick Hiemstra. *Hemorrhaging Faith: Why & When Canadian Young Adults Are Leaving, Staying & Returning to the Church*. Toronto, Canada: Evangelical Fellowship of Canada, 2011.
Perrin, Ruth H., and James S. Bielo. *The Bible Reading of Young Evangelicals : An Exploration of the Ordinary Hermeneutics and Faith of Generation Y*. Eugene, OR: Pickwick, 2016.
Peterson, E.H. *Eat This Book: A Conversation in the Art of Spiritual Reading*. Grand Rapids, MI: Eerdmans, 2006.
Pinar, William F., ed. *The Passionate Mind of Maxine Greene: "I Am . . . Not Yet."* London, UK: Falmer, 1998.
Piper, Stewart. "Health Promotion: A Practice Framework for Midwives." *British Journal of Midwifery* 13.5 (2005) 284–88.
Porter, Muriel. *Sydney Anglicans and the Threat to World Anglicanism: The Sydney Experiment*. Farnham, UK; Burlington, VT.: Ashgate, 2011.
Portier, William L. "Theology and Authority: Reflections on 'the Analogical Imagination.'" *Thomist* 46.4 (1982) 593–608.
Potter, Brett D. "Living in the Moment: Mission as Improvisation in Samuel Wells, Kevin Vanhoozer, and Hans Urs Von Balthasar." *Macmaster Journal of Theology and Ministry* (2013–2014) 136–64.
Powell, Kara Eckmann, and Chap Clark. *Sticky Faith: Everyday Ideas to Build Lasting Faith in Your Kids*. Grand Rapids, MI: Zondervan, 2011.
Prasad, Rashmi, and Yong Cao. "Improving Negotiation Outcomes between American and Chinese Partners: A Framework for Practice." *The journal of applied business research* 28.1 (2012) 1–8.
Purves, Andrew. *Reconstructing Practical Theology: A Christological Foundation*. Louisville, KY: Westminster John Knox, 2004.
Raiter, Michael. *Stirrings of the Soul: Evangelicals and the New Spirituality*. Kingsford, NSW: Matthias, 2003.
Rambo, Lewis R. *Understanding Religious Conversion*. New Haven, CT: Yale, 1993.

Reich, Rob. "Educational Authority and the Interests of Children." In *Oxford Handbook of Philosophy of Education*, edited by Harvey Siegel, 469–87. Oxford, UK: Oxford University Press, 2009.

Reventlow, Henning Graf. *History of Biblical Interpretation (Vol 1–4)*. Translated by Leo G. Perdue and James O. Duke. Atlanta, GA: Society of Biblical Literature, 2009–2010.

Ricoeur, Paul. "The Bible and the Imagination." Translated by D. Pellauer. In *Figuring the Sacred: Religion, Narrative, and Imagination*, edited by M.I. Wallace, 144–66. Minneapolis, MN: Augsburg Fortress, 1995.

———. *Interpretation Theory : Discourse and the Surplus of Meaning*. Fort Worth, TX: Texas Christian University Press, 1976.

———. *Oneself as Another*. University of Chicago Press, 1995.

———. "On Interpretation." In *Philosophy in France Today*, edited by Alan Montefiore, 175–97. Cambridge: Cambridge University Press, 1983.

Ringgaard Lorensen, Marlene. *Dialogical Preaching: Bakhtin, Otherness and Homiletics*. Göttingen, Germany / Bristol, CT: Vandenhoeck & Ruprecht, 2014.

Ritchhart, R., M. Church, and K. Morrison. *Making Thinking Visible: How to Promote Engagement, Understanding, and Independence for All Learners*. San Francisco, CA: Jossey Bass, 2011.

Root, Andrew. *Christopraxis: A Practical Theology of the Cross*. Minneapolis, MN: Fortress, 2014.

———. *Faith Formation in a Secular Age: Responding to the Church's Obsession with Youthfulness*. Ministry in a Secular Age. Grand Rapids, MI: Baker Academic, 2017.

———. *Taking the Cross to Youth Ministry*. A Theological Journey through Youth Ministry. Grand Rapids, MI: Zondervan, 2012.

———. *Taking Theology to Youth Ministry*. A Theological Journey through Youth Ministry. Grand Rapids, MI: Zondervan, 2012.

———. *Unpacking Scripture in Youth Ministry*. A Theological Journey through Youth Ministry. Grand Rapids, MI: Zondervan, 2012.

Rosner, Brian S. *Known by God: A Biblical Theology of Personal Identity*. Biblical Theology for Life. edited by Jonathan Lunde Grand Rapids, MI: Zondervan, 2017.

———. "'Known by God': The Meaning and Value of a Neglected Biblical Concept." *Tyndale Bulletin* 59.2 (2008) 207–30.

Rosner, Brian S., and Loyola M. McLean. "Theology and Human Flourishing: The Benefits of Being 'Known by God.'" In *Beyond Well-Being: Spirituality and Human Flourishing*, edited by Maureen Miner, Martin Dawson, and Stuart Devenish, 65–83. Charlotte, NC: Information Age Publishing, 2012.

Rotman, Dana, et al. "From Slacktivism to Activism: Participatory Culture in the Age of Social Media." In *CHI '11 Extended Abstracts on Human Factors in Computing Systems*, 819–22. Vancouver, Canada: ACM, 2011.

Ryken, Leland. "The Bible as Literature: A Brief History." In *A Complete Literary Guide to the Bible*, edited by Leland Ryken and Tremper Longman III, 49–68. Grand Rapids, MI: Zondervan, 1993.

Rynck, Patrick de. *Understanding Paintings: Bible Stories and Classical Myths in Art*. London, UK: Thames & Hudson, 2009.

Saint Ignatius of Loyola. *The Spiritual Exercises of Saint Ignatius of Loyola*. Translated by Thomas Corbishley SJ. Mineola, NY: Dover Publications, 1963.

Santos, Jason Brian. *A Community Called Taizé: A Story of Prayer, Worship and Reconciliation*. Downers Grove, IL: IVP, 2008.
Sayers, Mark. *The Road Trip That Changed the World: The Unlikely Theory That Will Change How You View Culture, the Church, and, Most Importantly, Yourself.* Chicago, IL: Moody, 2012.
Schleiermacher, Friedrich. *Christian Caring: Selections from Practical Theology.* Translated by James O. Duke. Fortress Texts in Modern Theology. Philadelphia, PA: Fortress, 1988.
Schleiermacher, Friedrich, and Terrence N. Tice. *Brief Outline of Theology as a Field of Study: Revised Translation of the 1811 and 1830 Editions.* Louisville, KY: Westminster John Knox, 2011.
Schütz, Alfred. *The Problem of Social Reality: Collected Papers I.* The Hague: Martinus Nijhoff, 1962.
Schwartz, Seth J., Koen Luyckx, and Vivian L. Vignoles. *Handbook of Identity Theory and Research.* Vol 1. New York, NY: Springer, 2011. doi:10.1007/978-1-4419-7988-9.
Searle, Alison. *The Eyes of Your Heart: Literary and Theological Trajectories of Imagining Biblically.* Milton Keynes, UK: Paternoster, 2008.
Sedwick, Jay. "Teaching for Adoptive Ministry." In *Adoptive Youth Ministry: Integrating Emerging Generations into the Family of Faith*, edited by Chap Clark. Youth, Family, and Culture, 302–15. Grand Rapids, MI: Baker Academic, 2016.
Selby, Gary S. *Not with Wisdom of Words: Nonrational Persuasion in the New Testament.* Grand Rapids, MI: Eerdmans, 2016.
Sherlock, Charles. *The Doctrine of Humanity.* Downers Grove, IL: IVP, 1997.
Shrimpton, Roger, et al. "Nutrition Capacity Development: A Practice Framework." *Public health nutrition* 17.3 (2014) 682–88.
Smart, James D. *The Strange Silence of the Bible in the Church: A Study in Hermeneutics.* Philadelpia, PA: Westminster, 1970.
Smith, David I. "Reading Practices and Christian Pedagogy: Enacting Charity with Texts." In *Teaching and Christian Practices: Reshaping Faith and Learning*, edited by David I. Smith and James K. A. Smith, 43–60. Grand Rapids, MI: Eerdmans, 2011.
Smith, James K. A. *Desiring the Kingdom: Worship, Worldview, and Cultural Formation.* Cultural Liturgies. Grand Rapids, MI: Baker, 2009.
———. *How (Not) to Be Secular: Reading Charles Taylor.* Grand Rapids, MI: Eerdmans, 2014.
———. *Imagining the Kingdom: How Worship Works.* Cultural Liturgies. Vol 2. Grand Rapids, MI: Baker, 2013.
Stanton, Graham D. "Reforming 'Practical Theology': Can a Reformed Theologian Have Their Scripture and Practice Too?" *St. Mark's Review* 224 May (2) (2013) 13–27.
Starling, David Ian. *Hermeneutics as Apprenticeship: How the Bible Shapes Our Interpretive Habits and Practices.* Grand Rapids, MI: Baker, 2016.
Stevens, R. Paul. *The Other Six Days: Vocation, Work, and Ministry in Biblical Perspective.* Grand Rapids, MI; Vancouver, Canada: W.B. Eerdmans; Regent College, 1999.
Tacey, David. "Contemporary Spirituality." In *Oxford Textbook of Spirituality in Healthcare*, edited by Mark Cobb, Christina M. Puchalski, and Bruce Rumbold, 473–79. Oxford, UK: Oxford University Press, 2012.

———. *Reenchantment: The New Australian Spirituality*. Pymble, NSW: Harper Collins, 2000.
Taylor, Charles. *The Ethics of Authenticity*. Cambridge, MA: Harvard University Press, 1991. The Malaise of Modernity, 1991 Massey Lectures.
———. "Modern Social Imaginaries." *Public Culture* 14.1 (Winter 2002) 91–124.
———. *A Secular Age*. Cambridge, MA: Belknap Press of Harvard University Press, 2007.
———. *Sources of the Self: The Making of the Modern Identity*. Cambridge, MA: Harvard University Press, 1989.
Thayer-Bacon, Barbara. "Maria Montessori, John Dewey, and William H. Kilpatrick." *Education and Culture* 28.1 (2012) 3–20.
Thiselton, Anthony C. *Hermeneutics: An Introduction*. Cambridge, UK: Eerdmans, 2009.
Thomas, Bronwen. "What Is Fanfiction and Why are People Saying Such Nice Things About It?" *StoryWorlds: A Journal of Narrative Studies* 3 (2011) 1–24.
Thompson, Mark. *A Clear and Present Word: The Clarity of Scripture*. New Studies in Biblical Theology. Edited by D. A. Carson. Vol 21. Nottingham, UK/Downers Grove, IL: Apollos/IVP, 2006.
Tillich, Paul. *Systematic Theology*. Welwyn, UK: James Nisbet, 1968.
Toman, Rolf, Rainer Warland, and Achim Bednorz, eds. *Ars Sacra: Christian Art and Architecture of the Western World from the Very Beginning up until Today*. Potsdam, Germany: H. F. Ullmann, 2015.
Toren, Benno van den, and Liz Hoare. "Evangelicals and Contextual Theology: Lessons from Missiology for Theological Reflection." *Practical Theology* 8.2 (June 2015) 77–98.
Tracy, David. *The Analogical Imagination: Christian Theology and the Culture of Pluralism*. New York, NY: Crossroad, 1981.
———. *Blessed Rage for Order: The New Pluralism in Theology*. New York, NY: Seabury, 1975.
———. "Foundations of Practical Theology." In *Practical Theology*, edited by Don Browning, 61–82. San Francisco, CA: Harper and Row, 1983.
———. *Plurality and Ambiguity: Hermeneutics, Religion, Hope*. San Francisco, CA: Harper & Row, 1987.
Tyson, Paul. "A Spectral View of Contemporary Australian Youth." *Australian eJournal of Theology* 12.1 (2008) np.
Valler, Matt. "Why Jesus Was So into Fanfiction." Paper presented at the Youthwork Summit, Tonbridge, Kent, UK, 19–20 June 2015.
Vanhoozer, Kevin J. *The Drama of Doctrine: A Canonical-Linguistic Approach to Christian Theology*. Louisville, KY: Westminster John Knox, 2005.
———. *Is There a Meaning in This Text?: The Bible, the Reader, and the Morality of Literary Knowledge*. Anniversary ed. Grand Rapids, MI: Zondervan, 1998.
Veith, Gene Edward Jr., and Matthew P. Ristuccia. *Imagination Redeemed: Glorifying God with a Neglected Part of Your Mind*. Wheaton, IL: Crossway, 2015.
Ven, Johannes. A. van der., *Practical Theology: An Empirical Approach*. Translated by Barbara Schultz. Kampen, The Netherlands: Kok Pharos, 1993.
Village, Andrew. *The Bible and Lay People: An Empirical Approach to Ordinary Hermeneutics*. Aldershot, UK: Ashgate, 2007.

———. "The Bible and Ordinary Readers." In *Exploring Ordinary Theology: Everyday Christian Believing and the Church*, edited by R. Jeff Astley and Leslie Francis. Farnham, UK: Ashgate, 2013.

Volf, Miroslav. *Captive to the Word: Engaging the Scriptures for Contemporary Theological Reflection*. Grand Rapids, MI: Eerdmans, 2010.

———. *A Public Faith: How Followers of Christ Should Serve the Common Good*. Grand Rapids, MI: Brazos, 2011.

Vroom, Hendrik M. "Religious Hermeneutics, Culture and Narratives." *Studies in Interreligious Dialogue* 4 (1994) 189–213.

Vygotsky, Lev Semenovich. *Mind in Society: The Development of Higher Psychological Processes*. Cambridge, MA: Harvard, 1978.

Wallace, James. *Imaginal Preaching: An Archetypal Perspective*. New York, NY: Paulist, 1995.

Ward, Pete. *Participation and Mediation: A Practical Theology for the Liquid Church*. London, UK: SCM, 2008.

———. "The State of Believing: A Study in Ecclesiology and Ethnography." Paper presented at the International Association for the Study of Youth Ministry International Conference, London School of Theology, London, UK, 2015.

Warfield, B. B. *The Biblical Idea of Revelation*. Leicester, UK: Theological Students Fellowship, 1978.

Warnock, Mary. *Imagination*. London, UK: Faber & Faber, 1976.

Weber, Bruce. "Maxine Greene, 96, Dies; Education Theorist Saw Arts as Essential." *New York Times*, 4 June 2014. https://www.nytimes.com/2014/06/05/nyregion/maxine-greene-teacher-and-educational-theorist-dies-at-96.html.

Webster, John. *Confessing God: Essays in Christian Dogmatics II*. London, UK/New York, NY: T. & T. Clark, 2005.

———. *Eberhard Jüngel: An Introduction to His Theology*. Cambridge, UK/New York, NY: Cambridge University Press, 1986.

Wells, Sam. *Improvisation: The Drama of Christian Ethics*. Grand Rapids, MI: Brazos, 2004.

Wertheimer, Max. "Laws of Organization in Perceptual Forms." In *A Source Book of Gestalt Psychology*, edited by Willis D. Ellis, 71–88. London, UK: Kegan Paul, Trench, Trubner & Co., 1938.

Westerfield Tucker, Karen B. "'Knee-Bowed and Body-Bent': The Connection of Scripture with Postures and Gestures." *Liturgy* 31.1 (2016) 10–18.

White, David F. *Practicing Discernment with Youth: A Transformative Youth Ministry Approach*. Cleveland, OH: Pilgrim, 2005.

Whooley, Owen. "Collective Identity." In *Blackwell Encyclopedia of Sociology*, edited by George Ritzer, 586–98. Malden, MA: Blackwell, 2007.

Wittgenstein, Ludwig. *Philosophical Investigations*. Translated by G. E. M. Anscombe. 2nd ed. New York, NY: Macmillan, 1958.

Wolters, Albert M. *Creation Regained: Biblical Basics for a Reformational Worldview*. Grand Rapids, MI: Eerdmans, 1985.

Wolterstorff, Nicholas. *Divine Discourse: Philosophical Reflections on the Claim That God Speaks*. Cambridge, UK: Cambridge University Press, 1995.

———. *Reason within the Bounds of Religion*. 2nd ed. Grand Rapids, MI: Eerdmans, 1984.

———. "A Response to Trevor Hart." In *Renewing Biblical Interpretation*, edited by Colin Greene, C. G. Bartholomew and Karl Moller, 335–41. Carlisle, UK: Paternoster, 2000.

Wolterstorff, Nicholas, Clarence W. Joldersma, and Gloria Goris Stronks. *Educating for Shalom: Essays on Christian Higher Education*. Grand Rapids, MI: Eerdmans, 2004.

Wolterstorff, Nicholas, Gloria Goris Stronks, and Clarence W. Joldersma. *Educating for Life: Reflections on Christian Teaching and Learning*. Grand Rapids, MI: Baker Academic, 2002.

Wooden, Cindy. "Through Thick and Thin: Pope Urges Youths to Read the Bible." U.S. Conference of Catholic Bishops. http://www.catholicnews.com/services/englishnews/2015/through-thick-and-thin-pope-urges-youths-to-read-the-bible.cfm.

Wright, Almeda M. "The Kids Are Alright: Re-Thinking Problem-Based Approaches to Adolescent Spirituality." *Journal of Youth and Theology* 14.1 (2015) 91–110.

Wright, N. T. *The New Testament and the People of God*. London, UK: SPCK, 1992.

Yaconelli, Mark. *Contemplative Youth Ministry: Practicing the Presence of Jesus*. Grand Rapids, MI: Zondervan, 2006.

Yount, William R. "The Role of Scripture in Christian Education, Session I: Scripture as the Structural Steel of Christian Education." *Christian Education Journal* 9 (2012) S.

Zittoun, Tania. "Difficult Secularity: Talmud as Symbolic Resource." *Outlines: Critical Practice Studies* 8.2 (2006) 17.

———. "The Role of Symbolic Resources in Human Lives." In *The Cambridge Handbook of Sociocultural Psychology*, edited by Jaan Valsiner and Alberto Rosa, 343–61. New York, NY: Cambridge University Press, 2007.

———. *Transitions: Development through Symbolic Resources*. Greenwich, CT: Information Age Pub., 2006.

www.ingramcontent.com/pod-product-compliance
Lightning Source LLC
Chambersburg PA
CBHW062018220426
43662CB00010B/1381